Enchantress, Sorceress, Madwoman

The True Story of Sarah Althea Hill:
Adventuress of Old San Francisco

Robin C. Johnson

California Venture Books

2014

Dedication

To Dot, for everything.

Acknowledgements

The following agencies provided assistance and/or materials for use in this book: The Morgan Hill Historical Society, The Bancroft Library at UC Berkeley, the California Archives, and the San Francisco History Center of the San Francisco Public Library.

I am grateful to the staffs of the Library of Congress and University of California who have made so many historical materials available online. These resources are invaluable to researchers like myself who can now access vast repositories of information from our homes or the local coffee shop.

Dr. Alex Wellerstein very graciously took the time to scan a high resolution image of a postcard from his exceptional collection of the Stockton State Hospital.

Likewise, David Turk, historian for the U. S. Marshal Service, assisted me by researching the source of an obscure photo of Sarah Althea. With his help, I was able to locate and purchase it for this book.

Numerous friends have contributed time and enthusiasm toward the completion of this project. I've been encouraged and inspired by their excitement and anticipation of the final product. Love and thanks to you all.

TABLE OF CONTENTS

Terry Plot - Stockton Rural Cemetery

FOREWORD

As the first buds of spring open on the trees, I stroll through the historic Stockton Rural Cemetery, reading names and dates, understanding that hidden behind these scant details, under every headstone, in every marble crypt, and at the base of each monument, are moving stories of human lives in all their glorious complexity.

This cemetery dates from the 1860s, and like many old cemeteries is beautiful and stately. It contains the graves of early pioneers of California's San Joaquin Valley, both famous and obscure, indistinguishable from one another in their final resting places. Some people live quietly. Others do nothing quietly. I am looking for the grave of one of the latter, one who lived perpetually in the storm…until the storm overwhelmed and crushed her.

When I first heard of Sarah Althea Hill, she captured my interest so thoroughly that the end result is this book. A local connection was the unexpected cherry on top. Some of the chapters of Sarah Althea's life were lived in my hometown of Stockton, California, including her last chapter. She lived here for several decades and is buried in this cemetery.

I know from photos what I am searching for—a tall, slender obelisk etched with the name "Terry," the marker for the family plot of Judge David Smith Terry. Though the judge himself lived a remarkable and historically significant life, this is not his story. Judge Terry has been written about by many. In most cases, those authors have made the second Mrs. Terry a side-note curiosity. Much of what has been written about her has been sensationalized or romanticized or condensed to the point of caricature.

The same treatment of Sarah Althea can be found in the life stories of other prominent figures of nineteen-century San Francisco: Stephen J. Field, Mary Ellen Pleasant and Senator William Sharon. They, too, have been written about extensively, and those biographies invariably include Sarah Althea Hill, but because she is not the main topic, the fullness of her character is rarely realized. This is not the fault of the authors. These other people were all such luminaries that the few years they were associated with Sarah must necessarily be treated in only a few chapters. Also, several of these books were published before Sarah's death, and so obviously could not tell her complete story.

In almost any book about 1880s San Francisco, you will find Sarah Althea flouncing through in her beaded hats and sealskin coat. She seems to have been a deliciously irresistible character to authors of such far-ranging subjects as architecture, Victorian brothels, and California law. But she is mere decoration for these books. In my mind, Sarah was more interesting than many of the men and women remembered by history. She deserves to be the star for a change.

I walk the entire length of the cemetery before finding that obelisk. At the northern boundary of the property, the Terry plot sits peacefully and unassumingly. If you didn't know anything about the Terrys, you wouldn't look twice at this unremarkable collection of family graves. Surrounding the obelisk are several small marble markers, all similarly stark. Here are the graves of David Terry, his first wife Cornelia, and their sons, all of whom died before them except for Clinton. Clint's stone is out in front beside his one child, also named Cornelia, the last Terry to be buried here in 1949.

And there is Sarah Althea's headstone, set a little apart from the others like an afterthought. It is so modest that I'm taken aback by it. I have been so absorbed in her fantastic story that it seems there should be some massive shrine to her life, equal in stature to the force of her turbulent personality.

But the truth is, although she was one of the most widely known women of the 1880s, she was thoroughly silenced in 1892 when she was committed to the Stockton State Hospital, then known as the Insane Asylum of California. From that time until her death on February 14, 1937, she was no longer heard from and eventually no longer thought of. By the time she died, the melodrama of her life was long over. She lived in the asylum, not far from this cemetery, for an incredible forty-five years, longer than she had lived outside it. Her friends, relatives and enemies passed out of this world before her and she was forgotten. When she died, the staff at the hospital knew of nobody to contact, no known living relative. It was through the kindness of one woman, the aforementioned Terry granddaughter Cornelia, that Sarah ended up here in the Terry plot where she belongs.

Across the arc of her headstone is her name: Sarah A. Terry. The inscription on the front reads, "Died Feb. 14, 1937. Aged 80 Yrs." That is all. No loving memory for her. The somber stone is not only terse, but wrong. Sarah Althea Hill was born March 26, 1850. She was 86, nearly 87, when she died. But those who gave her this resting place knew little about her. She had always been one to shave a few years off her age anyway, so she would certainly have approved of the error. To my knowledge, there is not a single legal document after her childhood that contains her correct age, and most written accounts of her life have it wrong. When anyone asked, she coquettishly evaded them, right up to the end. One of Sarah's last visitors, a female journalist in 1936, said she persistently tried to discover Sarah's true age, but failed, and nobody would ever know it. To their disadvantage, earlier writers did not have the easy access to census records we now have.

I never met Sarah Althea, of course. She died long before I was born. But when I came across her story by chance, I was consumed by it. She came alive for me and I became completely absorbed in my desire to find out who this woman was and how it came to be that such a vital person lived most of her life in lonely oblivion.

Was she the victim of greed or vengeance? Was she, like many unfortunate women of her era, stuck away in a hospital to rid someone of an inconvenience? Or, if she really was insane, how had it happened? I knew the tragic and bitter end of her story. But what about the rest?

There was so much more to Sarah than this modest stone marker can convey. Based on my initial exposure to her story, judging from sketchy Internet pages and hastily composed essays, I was certain that this naive woman had been a victim of corrupt men and a corrupt system, that justice had been denied her and cruel enemies had buried her alive in the insane asylum. But this is not fiction, and the simple formula of good vs. evil rarely applies in real life. After a clear-eyed look at the facts, it is obvious to me that Sarah was not a hapless victim. She was much more than that. She was a complicated, clever woman who played a leading role in her own fate.

Before the fall of 1883, Sarah was a little known young woman struggling to retain her flagging position among the San Francisco elite. But she crashed into public consciousness in grand style when she sued U. S. Senator William Sharon for divorce, claiming he had been unfaithful with at least nine women since their marriage three years previously. The news was a shocker, not because William Sharon slept around (everybody knew that), but because of the claim that the randy old roué was married. He was thought to be a widower. But here was a beautiful young woman waving a document that represented a secret contract marriage. Even that might not have made front page news for long if Senator William Sharon hadn't been one of the richest men in America and the woman hadn't been such a gorgeous and sassy firecracker. So began a colossal fight in state, federal and Supreme Courts that lasted over eight years.

The story of Sarah Althea Hill and the havoc she wrecked in Victorian-era California is remarkable and fascinating, as much today as it was when she lived it. At the time, it was a real-life melodrama that riveted the attention of the public and created a national scandal. Today, not many people have ever heard of Sarah. No movie has been made of her story, though it has everything required for high drama: romance, sex, violence, voodoo, betrayal, jealousy, murder and madness.

As I have been able to piece it together from newspaper articles, court records, vital records and other historical documents from the time period, this is the true story of a young woman who came to San Francisco during the Gilded Age, sought her fortune and turned a city on its head.

1. THE HEIRESS

"Lay aside all your knowledge of human nature, and believe that there exists in the shape of Sarah Althea Hill a newly revealed species of woman, such as we alone know of, full of quick feelings and passions scarcely controllable; whose impulses sweep her like a torrent; who knows no reason and acts only by instinct...."[1]

This portrayal of Sarah Althea Hill was made by "General" W. H. L. Barnes, the attorney who defended Senator William Sharon against her divorce suit. Although Barnes was fond of hyperbole, his description in this case was fairly accurate. Friends and foes alike would agree that Sarah Althea, "Allie" to her friends, was remarkable and singular.

She was born March 26, 1850 in Cape Girardeau, Missouri, the second child of Samuel H. Hill, a prominent attorney, and Julia Sloan, daughter of a wealthy lumber dealer. Sarah's year of birth is often mistaken, as she routinely underreported her age. The Cape Girardeau census records of 1850 (she was four months old), 1860 and 1870 are in agreement and provide excellent detail, settling the mystery of Sarah Althea's birth year conclusively. By the 1880 census, she had mastered the feminine trick of suspended animation and reported her age as twenty-seven.

Sarah's family was well-known and accomplished, the men largely going in for law and politics. She was a niece of Lieutenant-Governor Wilson Brown of Missouri and cousin of Senator R. B. Oliver.

Sarah's brother, Hiram Morgan Hill, born 1848, was named for his maternal grandfather Hiram L. Sloan and his paternal grandfather Morgan Hill, a wealthy farmer and slave owner from New Madrid, Missouri.

Their mother died in 1854. Their father, who was also ill, moved the family to New Orleans where he died of consumption, leaving a substantial inheritance for his two children when they came of age. The orphans were cared for by relatives of their mother for a few years, then they returned to Cape Girardeau where their uncle, Isaac Hunter, acted as their guardian and Sarah attended St. Vincent's College.

Sarah Althea Hill (Courtesy of the Bancroft Library)

As a young woman, she obtained a reputation not unlike the one she would later acquire in San Francisco. The following description is the one most often quoted about her early life in Missouri, but there are very few published first-hand accounts about her, and this one has the feeling of having been created in hindsight.

> The young woman developed a spirited temper, and soon reaching legal age, made her money fly. She grew up into womanhood in much her own way, and was noted for her beauty and temper. She was a schemer, above all things, and this made her unpopular among her girl companions. It was said of her, too, that, though she was a spendthrift, she worshiped money, and gave her attention mostly to those who possessed it. She is remembered by her friends here as something of a flirt, and at one time is said to have had three engagements to marry on her hands.[2]

Sarah Althea had a tendency to manufacture fiancés, so we can take that last statement with a little skepticism. But it does appear she was engaged to a young man named Will Shaw who broke the engagement over a quarrel in 1870.

Another view of young Allie was provided by Charles A. Davis, a family friend who had known her personally. "She was of the brunette type, had a clear, peachy complexion, and was graceful, modest and brilliant in conversation."[3]

Davis seemed to be alone in thinking Sarah modest, but his assessment of her conversational skills was often repeated by others. She spoke with a nervous intensity and quick wit. She could sing and play the piano, and leapt at every chance to do both. Her hair color was usually described as blond or reddish blond, and was no doubt fashionably dyed and arranged according to the latest style. Her eyes were "forget-me-not blue," as described by George Burson, an old servant of a friend. He was, like many men, smitten with her beauty and called her "Angel."

Sarah was impetuous, flirtatious, and had the look of an innocent, with full lips and a feminine, oval face that hinted at vulnerability. She was the sort of girl who would attract attention with both her looks and her behavior. And there is no doubt she was a girl who craved attention. Given her station in society, she was not expected to work, but at various times in her life she considered a career on stage as an actor, singer or lecturer. She would have been right at home there, basking in the spotlight and the adoration of an audience.

One of Sarah's most infuriating traits was her lack of regard for truth. She was a chronic liar. Sometimes she lied for no reason other than she preferred the lie to the truth. Senator Sharon once told a friend of hers that he would like Allie better if she didn't lie so much.

Courtesy of the San Francisco Public Library

Swearing to tell the truth in a courtroom made no difference to Sarah. Almost beyond himself with wonder, William Sharon's attorney General Barnes observed, "She utters falsehood after falsehood, and finally, when brought to bay, says, 'Well, now I will tell you the truth'...and then she proceeds to utter a fresh batch of falsehoods with an adroitness that might well be envied by the father of lies himself."[4]

Early in 1871, at the age of twenty, this spirited young woman traveled from her home in Missouri with her brother Hiram Morgan Hill and uncle William R. Sloan to the vibrant young town of San Francisco. She took with her a $20,000 inheritance from her parents, a sum worth a great deal at the time, certainly enough to set her up comfortably for many years, especially if carefully invested. Sarah and Morgan had other relatives already in San Francisco: their uncle, William Bryan, a pharmacist, his wife Ada, and their maternal grandmother, a widow.

The city they came to was young and rapidly developing. It had been a Mexican settlement named Yerba Buena until it was seized by the United States in 1848, a mere twenty-three years before. That was the same year gold was discovered in the foothills near Sacramento. San Francisco grew up quickly in the style of California towns at the time, overrun with tens of thousands of fortune-seekers from around the world hoping to strike it rich.

Even though Sarah and her brother arrived in San Francisco only two decades after its founding, they were relative latecomers compared to several other important characters in this story. The earlier arrivals came during the Gold Rush when fortunes could be quickly made and lives could be easily lost. It was a land of opportunity, but only for the most resourceful, hardy, and tough-minded. Among these were entrepreneur Mary Ellen Pleasant, California Supreme Court Chief Justice David Smith Terry, and U. S. Senator William Sharon, all prominent citizens who left their marks on early California and whose association late in life with Sarah Althea would have seriously negative consequences.

In 1849 when these pioneers ventured west, the state was nearly lawless. There were few women and children and there was no established society or infrastructure. But by 1875, the city's population neared 200,000, with as many as fifteen percent of those being Chinese. There were people from every part of the world with dreams of making it big, and those who did make it displayed their success with ostentation. San Francisco had rapidly become the capital of fashion, wealth, and prestige for the western half of the country.

Sarah's life was spent attending parties, drinking champagne in fine restaurants, going to the theater, the opera, going for drives in the country with well-heeled young men in their horse-drawn carriages. She went to such historic places as the Cliff House for dinner and the Union Hotel for tea. Her "work" was to keep up an active social life, and that required the gravest attention to hair styles, dresses, shoes, hats, and gloves.

During her first year in town, she was already popular and attracting attention. At an important New Year's Eve ball attended by the city's elite, including her brother, Sarah got special mention in the gossip column of the San Francisco *Chronicle*: "Miss Allie Hill enchanted her numerous admirers in a robe of rich fawn-colored silk, with train and *panier*, the whole elaborately trimmed with cherry-colored velvet. She looked stately as well as beautiful."[5]

Sarah let the men in her life, primarily her brother, manage her money without paying much attention, which was not unusual for the time. She did not even know where all of her accounts were. When she needed money, she asked her broker or banker and she got it. "I must have made profit on my stocks," she said, "for I had enough to pay my bills. I don't know whether I was doing a gaining or losing business….I always got money when I wanted it."[6]

Sarah had a fondness for exaggerating her wealth. She told people that she had invested $90,000 in the stock market and had made $30,000 off of that, and that she had $100,000 in government bonds. She had given her brother $25,000 (or $55,000, as she told one friend) for his business and her uncle had $50,000 of her money in trust for her. What was the purpose of these lies? To inflate her ego? To seem important to other people? To engender respect? She wanted desperately to be rich. That appeared to be her main goal in life, more even than to marry well, though the two desires were not mutually exclusive.

Sarah and Morgan lived with their relatives about two years before going out on their own, taking rooms in hotels, always moving together, and eventually ending up at the Baldwin Hotel at the corner of Market and Powell Streets. The Flood Building currently occupies the site.

In those days, Morgan and Sarah were very close. Though she at one time or another launched into vicious condemnation of almost everybody she knew, she never criticized her brother in public. When someone suggested he was less than perfect, she refused to discuss him. Her love and loyalty toward Morgan remained steadfast throughout the years. Sadly, he did not feel the same about her.

2. THE BROTHER

Most visitors to the Silicon Valley town of Morgan Hill, and some of its residents as well, assume it is named for a nearby landform. As Morgan Hill's biographer, Beth Wyman, so succinctly said, "Hiram Morgan Hill was a man, not a mountain."[7] He is remembered today for two reasons. One, a town was named after him because he was one of the earliest landowners, and two, he was the brother of Sarah Althea Hill. Wyman's book is a slim volume that devotes more pages to Sarah Althea and her mentor Mary Ellen Pleasant than to Morgan. He led a reserved sort of life in blunt contrast to his sister.

After arriving in San Francisco, Morgan Hill got work as a bank clerk and a model for men's clothes for the department store Bullocks and Jones. He was tall, slender, blue-eyed like his sister, and a sharp dresser.

In January, 1879, Morgan became a partner in E. H. JONES & CO., "Importers and Jobbers of Fancy Goods and Notions." According to their newspaper ad, the company sold "Yankee notions, pocket knifes, perfumery, combs, brushes, gloves, hosiery, neckties, suspenders, linen handkerchifes, all kinds of corsets, woolen goods, laces, ribbons and hats."

We don't know how much of his own money Morgan put into this company, but we do know that he invested $10,000 of his sister's money. He became a partner by virtue of the capital (his and hers) he put up, but she had no official standing in the company. He paid her $100 a month in interest from this investment for a number of years, and was still making these payments in 1884 when she made the following statement about it, subtly hinting that she might not have gotten the best deal in this arrangement: "I don't think I became a partner in the firm of Jones & Co., in which my brother is a partner, by putting that money in. I have never had a conversation with any of the other partners of the firm about the $10,000. I only get the $100 a month."[8]

Morgan Hill retired from this business early in 1885. When the company went bankrupt later that year, he was owed between $12,000 and $15,000.

Courtesy of the Morgan Hill Historical Society

In February, 1886, after the company was liquidated, creditors were given forty cents on the dollar what they were owed. Morgan Hill would have received at least $4,800. He was completely estranged from his sister by then. His sister's investment, subsumed into his own at the company's founding, presumably was lost, though he was wealthy enough by then to have easily reimbursed her for her original investment.

Like his sister, Morgan was looking to make a marriage that would set him up handsomely for life. He succeeded spectacularly with Diana Helen Murphy. She was nicknamed "The Duchess of Durango" and was the daughter of cattle tycoon Daniel Murphy. The Murphys had come to California during the Gold Rush and made a fortune selling dry goods to the miners. Martin Murphy, Diana's grandfather, purchased a large parcel of land in what is now the southern part of Silicon Valley. It was called *Rancho Ojo del Agua de la Coche* (Pig's Spring). The town of Murphys in the Sierra foothills is also named for this pioneer family.

By the time Morgan came on the scene, Daniel Murphy, Diana's father, was an extremely wealthy man. An editorial in the Los Angeles *Herald*, May 6, 1881, described the landscape of the region: "For miles the railway is aligned by the lordly domain of the Murphys, who have acquired much land and sold next to nothing, and who, in consequence, are enormously wealthy. An appreciative eye for the beautiful and useful had that fine old Irish gentleman, one of the olden time, who laid broad and deep the fortunes of the family."

But that fine old Irish gentleman had not accumulated that fortune just to squander it on inferior suitors to his daughter. Daniel Murphy was strongly opposed to Morgan, considering him beneath Diana, so the couple was married secretly on July 31, 1882. The Hills apparently had a thing for secret marriages. They also both aimed high. By this time, Daniel Murphy was reported to be the largest landowner in the entire United States.

Just two months after the marriage, Daniel Murphy lay on his deathbed. He made his daughter promise she would never marry Hiram Morgan Hill. She gave him her word and was haunted by the false promise after he died. Driven by guilt, and perhaps not enjoying wedded bliss as much as she had anticipated, she filed for divorce, but friends persuaded her to stay with Morgan. Diana inherited 4,500 acres of *Rancho Ojo del Agua de la Coche* from her father. The Hills built their country home, the Queen Anne style Villa Miramonte, on that land.

The couple had only one child, a daughter named Diane Murphy Hill, born in 1884. The marriage had been troubled from the start, and while Diane was still a child, her parents separated. Morgan Hill went to the Murphy spread in Halleck, Nevada, turning his back on high society for a life of ranching, while his wife lived as a socialite in Washington, D.C. Both of them maintained San Francisco affiliations, returning often, but separately, to the city. Diane lived with her mother, whose society standing led to Diane's marriage to Baron H. de Reinach-Werth in 1911.

There is a recent sculpture of Morgan Hill, his wife and his daughter located at Third and Depot Streets in the town of Morgan Hill. The life-size bronze sculpture is called "Waiting for the Train."

The plaque at the base of the sculpture reads as follows:

This bronze sculpture depicts one of Morgan Hill's early founding families, Hiram Morgan Hill, his wife Diana and their daughter Diane. In 1898, when the first Southern Pacific station was built, many visitors would request the train stop at "Morgan Hill's Ranch," which is how Morgan Hill got its name.

Waiting for the Train

3. THE BOYFRIENDS

Susan E. Smith sat across the desk from her attorney, the handsome Irishman, Reuben H. Lloyd, on the afternoon of May 10, 1880. Their business had barely begun when the door burst open and, in a state of barely-controlled agitation, a stylish young woman with red-gold hair flooded in. Susan Smith recognized Sarah Althea Hill, as they had met before at the Baldwin Hotel.

Miss Hill trained her intense blue eyes on Mrs. Smith. "Mr. Lloyd," she said tensely, "has refused to see me because he has no time. Won't you please give me your time and let me see him for a little while?"[9]

Somewhat confused, Mrs. Smith got up and agreed, noting that Lloyd seemed ill at ease and unhappy, frowning at Sarah Althea. Smith left them there together and went about her business, arriving home about nine o' clock that night. She found a note waiting for her from Dr. Murphy's office that read, "Dear Madame: Miss Hill is very ill at my office, having been taken sick on the street. She desires to see you as soon as possible. May 10, 1880"[10]

Though Susan Smith barely knew Sarah and was thoroughly confused by the summons, she immediately took a carriage to Dr. Murphy's office and found Sarah lying there sick. She had taken poison, she said, because Reuben Lloyd had gone back on his promise to marry her. She was distraught and wanted to destroy herself. She had called on Mrs. Smith because she had been so kind to her earlier in the day. She asked Smith to go to Lloyd and tell him how close she had come to doing herself in over him. Smith stayed with her overnight until she had recovered, then took her home to her rooms at the Baldwin the next day.

By the time this incident occurred, Sarah and Reuben Lloyd had a long history. The stormy relationship with Sarah Althea began in 1872 or 1873, and continued off and on for many years. Lloyd was fifteen years older than Sarah and a friend of her brother's. He had come to San Francisco early, around 1853, and was called one of the city's original "pioneer lawyers." He lived with his mother, and Sarah saw her as the main impediment to their marrying. She may have had a point. Lloyd never did marry and he lived with his mother until she died. He was featured many years later in the October 15, 1899 issue of the *San Francisco Call* in an article about the city's most eligible bachelors. "Mr. Lloyd's love affairs have been more than Cupid could count on twice his fingers, and although he is past his romantic age he has not been given up entirely by persistent loveliness. The only young ladies to whom he is attentive just now are his nieces, whom he chaperones vigilantly."

When asked about the poison incident later, Sarah said that she had taken too much laudanum by accident and had not been attempting to kill herself at all. She became infuriated with Susan Smith for telling the story during the Sharon divorce trial and eventually considered Smith among her many enemies.

Shortly after the suicide attempt, Sarah picked the lock on Reuben Lloyd's desk with a hairpin and stole personal letters other women had written to him. Lloyd demanded she return the letters, but she refused. He then went to the police and accompanied an officer to Sarah's room, where they searched for and took the letters back. After this, Lloyd declared he wanted nothing more to do with her. But they had split before. As late as 1884, Sarah still claimed to be in love with Lloyd. To his credit, he never spoke publicly about her, even while his name was being tossed about in the courts.

Like she did with her wealth, Sarah also exaggerated her romantic prospects. According to her stories, she had been engaged a dozen times. She would rattle off the names of half a dozen prominent men, claiming they were in love with her and wanted to marry her. Her reason for not marrying one of them? She couldn't decide which one. To Mary Shawhan, an acquaintance, "She said that she expected to have to marry one of them to drive away the rest."[11]

Sarah claimed she had "a standing offer" of marriage from Lieutenant William Emory, whom she named as her "fourth choice" for a husband behind Reuben Lloyd, William Sharon and his son Fred Sharon. Emory was one of her regular dates. He took her out often during 1880 and 1881. He went on to marry someone else and enjoy a distinguished military career that included commanding the U. S. S. Thetis, one of two ships that pushed through the icy waters of the Arctic to make a dramatic rescue of seven survivors of the Greeley expedition in the summer of 1884.

About the time of the latest split with Reuben Lloyd, Sarah also began having financial problems. In 1878 and 1879, she had made large deposits to her bank account, accumulating $16,000 through her investments. In the 1870s, the name of the money game in San Francisco was the Comstock Lode. There was a gambling fever raging through the city; everybody was investing in Nevada silver mines. For some, like

William Sharon, who was a shrewd risk-taker, the investments paid off big-time. For others, the stock market roller-coaster would leave them wiped out. That is what happened to Sarah.

By February, 1880, her bank account contained only eleven dollars. Unable to pay her bill at the Baldwin, she offered some stocks as security. Elias J. Baldwin, known as "Lucky" Baldwin for his success in the Comstock mines, saw that the stocks were worthless and declined to accept them as payment. When Sarah cried and begged for more time to pay, Baldwin granted it. "I asked her what she had done with all her money. She said she had lost some of it in stocks and had loaned her brother $25,000. She said her brother wouldn't help her, which I thought was very strange. She asked me for an accommodation on her bill, which was about $200, saying that she did not have the money. She told me that she had made about $100,000 in stocks, and that is the reason I asked her what had become of her money when she asked me to carry her stocks."[12]

Sarah's income at this time may have been limited to the $100 a month she was getting from Morgan off of her $10,000 investment in his company. Her claims of vast sums of money in banks and stocks were simply not true. She was tapped out.

In June, 1880, Sarah left the Baldwin Hotel, where she then owed $337, to find a cheaper place to live. She moved into the Galindo House, Eighth and Franklin Streets, Oakland, and rented an apartment for herself and her brother at $75 a month.

This was a low point for Sarah Althea. She had lost her best beau and all of her money, and there was nothing bright on her horizon. But Sarah was not a woman to give in to defeat. If no opportunities came knocking, she would go out and hunt them down.

4. THE MILLIONAIRE

Like so many other men in Sarah Althea's life, William Sharon was a lawyer. He was born in Ohio in 1821 and moved to California in 1849 at the beginning of the Gold Rush. His subsequent prosperity was intimately tied to that of another early West Coast entrepreneur, William Chapman Ralston. Both men came from Ohio and both were significant figures in the development of San Francisco, but Sharon rode in on the coattails of Ralston, and in many ways profited from his ruin.

William Ralston, one of the most powerful and wealthy men in California, opened the Bank of California in 1864. It was the first commercial bank in the western United States. William Sharon became manager of the branch in Virginia City, Nevada, the position that would lead to his vast success. As a bank agent, he made loans to silver mining operations and then foreclosed when the loans defaulted, as they often did, acquiring the mines for the bank. From this position of distinct advantage, Sharon acquired lucrative businesses—silver mines, a railroad—and he just kept getting richer. Everything he touched turned to gold.

William Sharon earned the nickname "King of the Comstock" after the Comstock Lode in Nevada. He sold his mining stock at the top of the market and invested in San Francisco real estate, thus avoiding the disaster that ruined many others when the bottom fell out of silver mining.

Sharon's mentor, William Ralston, well known and well liked, was a big spender and philanthropist. Evidence of his open wallet could be seen all over the city. He had built the California Theater and the Grand Hotel, large factories and grandiose homes. He had a dream to build the most magnificent hotel in the world. With the money from his banking enterprise, he had the means to do it. The project was completed in 1875 at a cost of five, perhaps six, million dollars. The Palace Hotel at New Montgomery and Market Streets was seven stories high, had 775 guest rooms and covered three acres. "Ralston had planned the Palace as a symbol of San Francisco's coming of age. It was to mark the closing of one era and the beginning of another, the end of the transition from mining camp and raw boom town to established city."[13] It was the jewel in Ralston's crown, but its construction severely undermined his financial stability.

William Sharon (Courtesy of the Library of Congress)

The Palace Hotel 1875

Nearly concurrent with the completion of the hotel, which had not yet officially opened, there was a one-day $1,400,000 run on the Bank of California and it collapsed. The day after the bank failed, Ralston deeded all of his business holdings, including his sorely indebted assets, to William Sharon. He then went for a swim in the bay and drowned. Officially he died of a stroke, but he swam out dangerously far and may not have intended to return.

The ruin of Ralston turned into the boom of Sharon, who picked up control of the bank and the elegant new hotel for pennies on the dollar and put the bank back on its feet. Sharon also ended up with Ralston's magnificent country estate, Ralston Hall in Belmont, California, paying Mrs. Ralston $50,000 for it, about half its worth. The mansion was 55,360 square feet and eighty rooms, modeled in part on the Palace of Versailles.

In 1922, the estate was purchased by the Sisters of Notre Dame de Namur, who ran a school there for decades. Ralston Hall, located about twenty miles south of San Francisco, is now on both the California and National Registers of Historic Places. The estate, referred to by Sharon and his friends simply as "Belmont," was closed indefinitely in 2012 for renovations.

The Palace Hotel, sometimes called the first American luxury hotel, opened to great fanfare two months after Ralston's death. A New York newspaper described it as the "greatest hotel ever built, in ancient or modern times….The Union and other hotels at Saratoga have long been objects of astonishment to strangers; but these are now completely put in the shade, dwarfed and rendered insignificant; and the Palace Hotel at San Francisco must be pronounced one of the wonders of modern times."[14]

One of the special features of the hotel was the main court where the guests arrived from the carriage entrance. It was 144 x 84 feet and soared upward to the top of the building, where it was covered with glass. It was surrounded by verandas outside of the rooms and decorated with fountains, tropical plants and statues.

A suite of four adjoining rooms at the Palace Hotel served as Sharon's primary residence. Belmont was used to entertain visitors and as an extension of the hotel. Hotel guests could drive out to the country and enjoy the grounds for an extra dollar a day. Sharon used the hotel as his private home and the country house as his public one.

William Sharon served as the U. S. senator from Nevada from March 4, 1875, to March 4, 1881, at which time he lost his bid for reelection. He split his time between Virginia City in Nevada, Washington D. C., and San Francisco, and kept mistresses in every port. He had at least one illegitimate child by Gertie Dietz, a woman he knew on the East Coast. With his wife Maria, who died in 1875, he had three grown children: Fred, Flora (Florence) and Clara. Fred and Flora, both unmarried, lived at Belmont. Clara had married Francis G. Newlands, a lawyer. Newlands would go on to become a U.S. Senator like his father-in-law.

One of the interesting coincidences in this story is that Sarah Althea's beloved, Reuben Lloyd, was William Sharon's lawyer in the early days and helped Sharon save the Bank of California. He became law partners with Sharon's son-in-law Frank Newlands after Newlands married Sharon's daughter. This may account for Lloyd's reluctance to come anywhere near the messy divorce case, as he had loyalties to both sides.

In June, 1884, while Sharon vs. Sharon was ongoing, a reporter described William Sharon as follows: "He is a gentleman in manner, is a keen man of business, a devoted father to his children, a prudent manager of his fortune, a warm-hearted friend and a relentless foe. His weaknesses, as events have shown, are poetry, wine and women. His ardent love of the one is shown by his frequent quotations; his love of the other by frequent potations, and his experiences with the last in a limited sense by his luckless escapade with Sarah Althea. In person, Mr. Sharon's inches and avoirdupois are at strange variance with the list of his bonds or the record of his loves. He is, to use a homely phrase, 'a runt.' But if one peeps into his hat it will be seen that it numbers 7-1/4. His legs, too, are stalwart and his frame compact. But his chief charm is his Mark Tapley-like jollity in the face of adversity that some would think even $20,000,000 could not offset."[15]

When William Sharon met Sarah Althea, he was sixty years old, a widower, and at the height of his wealth and power. If she had been aiming for the richest unmarried man in San Francisco, he would have had a bull's-eye on his heart. And it just so happened she was a pretty good shot.

5. THE ENCHANTRESS

In 1880, Sarah Althea's account balance was hovering perilously close to zero at the Bank of California where William Sharon, the bank president, had an office on the third floor. Sarah showed up there without an appointment to ask his advice about investing. Their meeting lasted fifteen minutes. William Sharon did not recall having met her before, though she had been introduced to him and his daughter Flora at the Belmont train station the previous year. He talked in general about investing, noting the young woman's striking beauty, her elegance, and her disarming smile.

A few days later, she came again to his office and they discussed investments, but the conversation became more personal. Behind the formality of their words were the stirrings of a flirtation. William Sharon was a pushover for a pretty young woman with wiles, and Sarah was most certainly such a woman. After all, she was there for investment advice when she had no money to invest.

General Barnes said it better: "She was poor, broken in finances as she was in heart, and having no more to do with stock operations in the summer of 1880 than with the domestic economy of the palace of the Emperor of China."[16]

Despite the lack of financial records to support it, Sarah would later testify that she lost $60,000 on the stock market following Sharon's disppointing investment advice. She would also claim she loaned him $7,500 of her money to play with on the market and had a dickens of a time getting it back. As we shall see, she would eventually get $7,500 out of him, but the money was payment of an entirely different type.

"Mr. Sharon talked love almost every time I went to see him," she said. "He would say that he liked the girls and asked me if the girls liked him. Asked me if I couldn't like an old man like him....He sat down on the sofa by me and began teasing me about my gentlemen acquaintances."[17]

Bank of California (corner)

On September 9, she came to his office to let him know that the Galindo Hotel had burned down and she had moved back to the Baldwin in San Francisco. It was during this visit that Sharon learned that Sarah, despite her background and bearing, was financially destitute. She told him about her outstanding bill and said she needed money. "I gave $100," he said, "and the next day $150 more. She looked sheepish when she called, but I gave her the money."[18]

She invited him to her rooms on September 11, their first non-business meeting. He accepted the invitation and they had a pleasant evening of poetry, song and mutual flirtation. He quoted "The Maid of Athens" to her and sang "Auld Lang Syne." When questioned further about what he quoted to her that evening, he said, "Just an airy mess, you know, such as any gentleman would give a lady in a social call. In the presence of ladies, if they are spritely and good-looking, a little sentiment is always inspired in a gentleman."[19]

On September 13, he invited her to dinner in his rooms, just the two of them. Drinks and conversation lasted late into the night. By now,

Senator Sharon was smitten and as randy as a tomcat. Accustomed to buying women rather than seducing them, and knowing Sarah's need for money, he offered her $250 a month to be his mistress. "She refused," he said, "and in an instant I had offered her $500 a month."[20]

He was confident that she would accept the terms, and her manner told him he would have no trouble coaxing her to his bed. "Any young woman that will visit a gentleman in his private rooms, dine with him, drink wine, and remain alone with him until a late hour is not likely to repel any further advances."[21] She made some protest that she didn't want to sleep with him that night, but after he had given her a room of her own and a half hour had passed, she came and crawled into bed with him.

For the senator, this was his normal mode of operation. He kept mistresses and paid them well. It was merely a business deal. He said that marriage was never mentioned by either of them, that she understood the arrangement and, by coming to his bed, accepted it. He later said, to prove the point that she was nothing more than a mistress, that he never gave her a single gift, not a flower or a box of candy. He gave her money; that was all.

The foregoing was essentially William Sharon's version of how he became involved with Sarah Althea Hill. Except in minor details designed to cast herself in the role of pursued rather than pursuer, Sarah's version agrees up to the actual proposal. In her version, their courtship began earlier in the year and proceeded for a longer period of time, during which the senator was relentless in his attempts to woo her.

Eventually, she said, he offered her $1,000 a month and his daughter Flora's white horse to be his mistress. She indignantly turned him down, saying she wasn't that kind of woman, and started to leave. Then he laughed, said he was just teasing, that he loved her and wanted to marry her. But, he said, the marriage would have to be secret for a while because he was up for reelection and there was a woman back East who might cause a scandal if she heard he had married. This woman was Gertie Dietz, pregnant with his child at the time.

After discussing it for some time, during which the senator read from law books to convince her that a contract marriage was legal, she agreed to a secret marriage. On August 20, she sat down in his office with a scrap of paper while he dictated the wording of their agreement. As it was a half sheet of paper, she wrote it on both the front and partway down the back.

"When the writing was finished," she said, "he came over and put his arm around me and said, 'Well, my dear, will that do?' I said, 'Why, Senator, that is not our marriage certificate, is it?' I supposed that it was only a rough draft, to be written out properly afterward. He read it over and we signed it, and then he told me to take it home and write it out nice if I liked, but that the original would do for him."[22]

The document was not rewritten, but appeared in its original cramped and scrappy state throughout the legal battles to come. It was this piece of paper that Sarah would cling to as evidence of her clandestine marriage to William Sharon. It was this piece of paper that she would sue him over, claiming he had cheated on her and deserted her. It was this piece of paper on which she would base her demands for divorce, alimony and division of community property. And it was this piece of paper that William Sharon swore he had never seen until the divorce suit went to trial. Three years after their relationship began, so much was to hinge on this one piece of paper, which read as follows:

> In the City and County of San Francisco, State of California, on the 25th day of August, A.D. 1880, I, Sarah Althea Hill, of the city and county of San Francisco, State of California, aged 27 years, do here, in the presence of Almighty God, take Senator William Sharon of the state of Nevada to be my lawful and wedded husband, and do here acknowledge and declare myself to be the wife of Senator William Sharon of the State of Nevada.
> SARAH ALTHEA HILL.
> August 25, 1880, San Francisco, Cal.
> I agree not to make known the contents of this paper or its existence for two years, unless Mr. Sharon himself sees fit to make it known.
> S. A. HILL.

> In the city and county of San Francisco, State of California, on the 25th day of August, A.D. 1880, I, Senator William Sharon, of the State of Nevada, age 60 years, do here in the presence of Almighty God take Sarah Althea Hill of the city of San Francisco, Cal., to be my lawful and wedded wife, and do here acknowledge myself to be the husband of Sarah Althea Hill.
> WILLIAM SHARON, Nevada, August 25, 1880.

After the contract was signed, the two of them went their separate ways, Sarah taking the paper with her. Three days after the date of the contract, Senator Sharon left San Francisco on business.

"It is a fact that he remained here for three days after the wedding bells had pealed," General Barnes pointed out sarcastically, "and did not go near her....An angel in heaven would have been unable to resist clasping this pure bud of a bride to his breast at once, and such a devil as they have painted my client would not have waited an hour after satisfying her conscience."[23]

Between the two stories, a few facts can be relied upon. The first time they spoke to one another was in 1880 in the Bank of California. William Sharon was immediately taken with Sarah Althea and wanted her. By some arrangement they both agreed to, he paid her $500 a month and they became lovers that September.

6. THE HONEYMOON

Once their sexual relationship began, Senator Sharon came to the Baldwin Hotel several times to see Sarah, but soon became wary of attracting attention. On September 25, he wrote her three notes, trying to arrange to meet her in the parlor of the Grand Hotel. After crossing paths and missing one another all day, he came to her room and explained that comments had been made about his trips to the Baldwin. He had been tipped off that spies were watching, hoping to catch the lovers in the act. He asked her to move to the Grand Hotel, which was next door to the Palace Hotel where his rooms were. He owned both hotels and the two were conveniently connected by a footbridge, so they could meet more discreetly.

She moved to the Grand that night with a letter of introduction to the manager, Samuel Thorn. "My Dear Sir: The bearer, Miss Hill, a particular friend of mine, and a lady of unblemished character, and of good family, may want rooms. Give her the best, and as cheap as you can, and oblige, Wm. Sharon."[24]

Sarah picked out her furniture from the West Coast Company, and Senator Sharon paid for everything without question.

Sarah's brother, who considered himself her guardian, begrudgingly also moved, taking a room on the other side of the hotel. Her relationship with Morgan became strained after the move. He was angry at her for leaving the Baldwin and disapproved of her relationship with Sharon. His reason for disapproving, she said, was that he considered Sharon, a self-made man, beneath her station. "He considered him of low origin, while the Hills were somebody by birth, and the Sharons were like thistles in a field."[25]

As every PBS fan knows, in a class-driven society, the *nouveau riche* were often considered on a lower rung than those born into the upper classes, regardless of current wealth and property. When the news of Sarah's connection with William Sharon became public, a friend of the Hill family in Cape Girardeau, Judge John L. Wilson, was surprised to hear of it, and wrote a letter to the *San Francisco Chronicle* saying,

"His millions would hardly compensate a handsome and accomplished young woman for his age and reputation, and certainly no one can have a higher family connection than she has. I had always expected that she would make a wiser and better alliance."[26]

It is likely that Morgan disapproved simply because respectable young women did not have intimate relationships with men who were not their husbands. This was the Victorian Age. A woman's blameless reputation was essential to a successful career in society. Morgan might also have reasonably worried that his sister's behavior would hurt his own reputation, as he had not yet landed his rich wife.

Despite these Missouri opinions, in San Francisco at that time, the self-made man was king. The class system that the Hills clung to was from another time and place. Most of those who had gotten rich from the mines, like William Sharon, had come from humble origins. The idea that he was not good enough for Allie Hill was absurd. He was a man whose invited guests included the most celebrated military man of the time, General Ulysses S. Grant, as well as Cornelius Vanderbilt, son of the railroad tycoon, the richest man in history up to that time. Sharon's daughter Flora married into British royalty. His friends and business associates were at the very pinnacle of power, wealth and social standing.

In October, six weeks after the date on the marriage contract, William Sharon left again for Virginia City. Sarah Althea did not seem to remember him at all. At this time, her closest friend was the stunningly beautiful, dark-eyed Julia Bornemann, a young widow, and the two of them went out together often. While Sharon was away, Sarah spent time with Alfred S. Hossack, a divorced portrait painter. "Alfred Hossack," reported a gossip columnist, "has led a life of strange adventure, which has carried him to many parts of the world, and if he wielded the pen instead of the brush we should doubtless have had from him narratives of his many experiences....He is a good looking fellow, too, and sings in the Loring Club, and all that."[27]

Sarah and Hossack had dinner with Bornemann on October 14. On October 16, Sarah and Hossack went out on a double date with Bornemann and Mr. Howland, a photographer, to the Fourteen-mile House, a roadhouse in San Bruno. They ate oysters and drank ale and returned to the city long after midnight.

William Sharon returned to San Francisco on October 15, but the two did not meet up.

General Barnes, with his usual air of mockery, remarked, "Lord, how that poor old man must have felt, sitting up, waiting for his pure bride, while she was passing her time at such a disreputable resort as the Fourteen-mile House, in company with other men."[28]

Despite the dates with Hossack, Senator Sharon and Sarah Althea were happy together in the autumn of 1880. She slept over in his rooms two or three nights a week, and often shared breakfast and dinner with him. The waiters at the Palace were under orders to serve her meals on the silver service, not the common white dishes. She took Sharon's driver and carriage out to visit her grandmother, and bought herself clothes and household goods with the generous allowance she received. When she had a small complaint about the manager of her hotel, Samuel Thorn, Sharon sent him a note ordering him to treat her better. When she complained about a waiter, he was dismissed. She must have been overjoyed with her elevated position as Senator Sharon's "sweetheart," as she termed it.

She claimed he often sang to her and wrote her love letters, which he denied. She didn't have the letters, she said, because "Sharon burnt a lot of letters he had written her, saying that they might injure a good many Washington ladies."[29] The surviving notes between them were all curiously business-like, such as arranging for Sarah to come to his room or sending her money. These were usually delivered by his servant, Ah Ki. "When we had any difficulty about anything," she said, "he would generally send me a note and usually with money in it, to put me in good humor."[30] Indeed, it always had been money that wooed her, not love sonnets.

Sarah would have been well aware of the importance of reputation and the devastating disgrace of being a paid mistress. Her attempts to avoid the appearance of impropriety were probably at the root of many of her lies. In response to growing rumors, she told people that she and the senator were engaged to be married. She got herself an engagement ring and showed it to a couple of people to convince them of her status as his fiancee. If the lovers had conducted their relationship in secret, as Sharon usually did with his mistresses, Sarah would have had no need for the lies. But they went out in public together, to the theater, for instance, as if they were courting. This behavior was one of the most persuasive arguments against William Sharon's claim that Sarah was merely his mistress.

In November, she gave a party, a "musicale," in Sharon's honor and introduced him to all her friends.

She then took him to visit other friends, the Hardenbergs. While Sharon spoke to Mr. Hardenberg, Sarah told Mrs. Hardenberg that she and the senator were engaged to be married. Next, she invited Sharon to her Uncle Bryan's house where her uncle, aunt and grandmother lived. She told Julia Bornemann, who went along, that the purpose of the meeting was for Sharon to see what sort of family she came from because they were talking about getting married.

Sarah most certainly believed that she would soon be Mrs. Sharon. Perhaps she thought she could lead her bridegroom to the altar by surrounding him with the expectation of marriage. Or perhaps she genuinely saw marriage as the logical progression of their relationship. It is also possible that the senator's pillow talk included the subject of marriage, though he adamantly denied he ever mentioned it.

Still, he allowed two different relationships to exist: the public appearance of chivalrous courtship and the private illicit love affair or, as Sarah maintained, the secret marriage. In many ways, the public relationship was in greater accord with the idea of a secret marriage than it was with a sex-for-pay arrangement.

Eventually, the senator heard that Sarah was telling people they were engaged and he confronted her. She denied ever having said it, adding, "Senator, I hope I am too much of a lady to force any man to marry me when he does not want to. But don't you intend to marry me?"

"No, never," replied the Senator. "I shall never marry again."[31]

One can almost read a genuine inquiry in Sarah's question. Was she simply naïve? Or was she just the opposite, always posing and scheming? When an acquaintance, Fanny Sampson, asked her once why a young and pretty girl should fall in love with an old man like Sharon, she said, "I'd sooner live with Senator Sharon in a garret on a crust a day than live in a palace with a millionaire."[32]

Of course, Sharon *was* a millionaire and he lived in the Palace, so the claim of devotion could be viewed as ironic.

Sarah was not deterred by Senator Sharon's assertion that he would never marry again. She was as determined as ever to be his legal wife, but, clearly, the path to the altar would be no cake walk.

7. THE BELMONT DALLIANCES

Ralston Hall at Belmont (Courtesy of the Library of Congress)

As an extension of the Palace Hotel, William Sharon's country estate at Belmont was always teeming with guests, so Sarah's visits there were not necessarily personal. But her versions of them were. On her first visit, she invited her friend Julia Bornemann to come along. "We three went down together and stayed there three days. After the first day the Senator found that Mrs. Bornemann was in our way, and told me to invite a gentleman down to keep her company. I left the selection to her, and she named Mr. Ed. Wheeler. I telegraphed an invitation to him and he came down by the morning train."[33]

Sharon denied saying Mrs. Bornemann was in the way and denied spending any private time with Sarah at Belmont.

On her second visit, Sarah said she spent much of her time with the senator and, among other topics of conversation, they discussed the upcoming wedding of his daughter Flora. Sarah was of the firm opinion that he should get a priest to officiate.

"No such occurrence ever took place," Sharon said. "I never at any time discussed my family affairs with her."[34]

Clearly, looking back on these halcyon days of love and luxury from the vantage point of a courtroom, the pair agreed on almost nothing. The significance of Sarah's presence at Belmont was that a paid mistress, by all the principles held holy in Victorian Age society, would not have been invited there, at least not by any civilized man.

William Sharon tried to give the impression that Sarah Althea was only ever at Belmont because she begged to be invited and made an intolerable pest of herself. But at least one of his notes to her says otherwise. "My Dear Miss Hill," it read, "the parties going to Belmont would have me go with them, so you come on the 4:30 train."[35] He liked her to come down, she said, to be with him and also to sing and play piano for his guests. This was corroborated by a witness who said she was his lucky charm at a Belmont poker game where he good-humoredly announced he would buy her a new hat if he won.

During the latter months of 1880, William Sharon appeared to be thoroughly enchanted by his little Allie. Far from keeping her a secret, he introduced her to his friends and proudly paraded about with her on his arm. But he seemed to draw the line when it came to family, at least in the case of his daughter Flora.

The wedding of Flora Sharon to the English baronet of Rufford, Thomas Fermor-Hesketh, was to be the social event of the season. The pairing was in keeping with the growing fad of the daughters of California's *nouveau riche* marrying minor foreign titles, often going abroad with their millions to bolster up impoverished old family estates. The ceremony was scheduled for December 23 at Belmont.

It had not occurred to William Sharon to invite Sarah to his daughter's wedding, he said, until she made a scene about it. He cited "propriety" as his reason for excluding her. Sarah was frantic to be included. She complained "that if she was not invited she would be a marked woman, being the only one in the Grand Hotel not present. She insisted on being allowed to go in order that she should be protected from criticism."[36]

He was reluctant, but relented. With a couple of thousand other guests, he decided, it couldn't hurt, so he allowed her to attend the reception with Julia Bornemann and her brother Morgan. He stopped short of allowing her at the much more intimate wedding ceremony.

Sarah's version of events was somewhat different in that she did not acknowledge that she begged for an invitation. She went to the reception, but declined to attend the wedding ceremony out of respect for Miss Flora, who didn't like her. Flora, she explained, like all of Sharon's relatives except young Fred Sharon, disapproved of the senator's betrothal to Miss Hill.

According to William Sharon, his daughter Flora never even knew Sarah existed.

Like hundreds of other women, Sarah bought a new dress (with William Sharon's money) and sent it down to Belmont ahead of her own arrival by train.

> Multitudes of vehicles awaited the arrival of the train, and for a few moments, when it reached the depot, the scene was a very animated one. Ladies and gentlemen took their places in covered buggies, hacks, coupes, barouches, express wagons, vans and jaunting cars. The guests upon reaching the mansion were met by Senator Sharon, and a numerous corps of servants escorted them to their dressing rooms. By a quarter to 8 o'clock all the guests had been received and were grouped around the floral arch in the music hall, beneath which the bridal ceremony was to be performed. Descending the stairway and encircling the colonnade, the bridal train entered the hall....When the clergyman had shaken hands with the happy couple and pronounced them man and wife, friends crowded around, and kisses and congratulations followed. The wedding march was then resumed by the band. A lively waltz followed, and dancing was begun and one hundred couples were soon in motion. The scene was a strikingly brilliant and animated one.[37]

Sarah reported that the senator was so touched by the ceremony and her loveliness that evening that he said, "Let's go under the marriage-bell and get married."[38] She declined because she didn't want to steal the focus from Flora on her special day.

At the reception, she danced with Woods Fox, which made the senator jealous. He told her he didn't want her dancing with anyone but himself or his son Fred, but when Fred began to show her too much attention, the senator got jealous of his son as well.

"I paid her no attention there," Sharon contradicted. "I think I bowed to her once and introduced my son Fred to her."[39]

Ralston Hall - First Floor Staircase

Sarah's version of the day changed over time depending on her audience. When she told William Neilson about it in 1883, she had become the mistress of the house, arranging the seating and presiding over tables. In this version she was present at the wedding ceremony, and

related entertaining details, such as, "When Hesketh stood up he was so
intoxicated that he could hardly see, and he could not find the ring,
which was finally extracted from his pocket by Miss Bessie Sedgwick.
Miss Sedgwick also put the ring on the bride's finger."[40]

Because of the way it appeared later, Sharon regretted inviting
Sarah to his daughter's wedding. He also regretted introducing her to his
son Fred, though he probably didn't know that Sarah and Fred, who was
seven years her junior, spent some time together flirting behind the
elevator. Keeping in mind Sarah's claim that she was married to William
Sharon at the time, this was an interesting way to behave with her
twenty-three year old step-son. It is likely that Sarah's claims that Fred
Sharon was in love with her, that she could marry him if she wished,
were all based on these flirtatious minutes at Belmont. Fred Sharon was
never called to testify about the nature of his relationship to Sarah,
perhaps because it would have been an embarrassment to both sides.

None of Sharon's other mistresses were ever invited to a family
event at Belmont. But his other mistresses all seemed to be much better
behaved than Sarah. None of the others threw a fit to be invited. Sharon
did admit that he treated Sarah better than the others, but he did not
explain why. Did he do it because he liked her better and respected her
more? Or did he do it to avoid conflict with her? The main difference
between Sarah and the other women, aside from her explosive
personality, was her social standing. The others were working-class girls.
Sarah was a known socialite and an educated woman. William Sharon
understood the difference. Going out with her in public appeared
perfectly natural and respectable. She was a woman who would be
worthy of walking out on his arm to the theater, whereas the others
would not. But treating her in this special way had negative
consequences: it led her on and caused a lot of confusion and speculation
among their various acquaintances.

In April, 1881, Sarah was again invited to Belmont for a large
weekend party. Her brother, uncle and grandmother were also invited.
Senator Sharon's friends the Reigarts and the Staggs were also present,
all of whom Sarah had met a few days earlier. John and Emma Reigart
were warm people who found her charming, especially since they
believed, encouraged by Sarah's comments and their own observations,
that she and William Sharon were courting. Like anyone else, they would
have had no reason to suspect that Sarah was Sharon's mistress. If that
was the nature of his relationship with her, surely he would not be
inviting her family members to Belmont and introducing her to his
friends. He said he always introduced her as "Miss Hill" with no further
explanation. Could he have imagined that that would be sufficient, that

people would not ask questions, that Sarah would not offer her own explanation to buoy herself against the rumor mill?

Sarah and the Reigarts became close during the course of the weekend, but their friendship would be severely abused later on.

Fred Burchard, a young man with a pale face decorated by a long, curling mustache, was also at Belmont that weekend. Sarah had met him four days earlier at the Palace Hotel where he came upon her "promenading" with Senator Sharon, the Staggs and the Reigarts. Burchard was introduced to all of them on that occasion and had become immediately sweet on Sarah. They had spent the bulk of their time together since. When he asked about her relationship to the senator, she told him they were just friends and any rumors to the contrary were false. Burchard's friends led Sarah to believe he was a man of means. He later explained, "As I like to stand well with the ladies, I did not contradict them."[41]

Sarah had already told the Staggs that she was engaged to William Sharon. Not surprisingly, Mrs. Stagg suggested that she was not acting properly with Burchard if that were true. She didn't think she would marry Sharon after all, Sarah explained, because he was too old. Also, she thought she would have to turn down his proposal because the financial settlement he had promised her—$200,000 and Belmont—was not enough. He would have to up his offer if he wanted to marry her.

She seemed as fond of Fred Burchard as he was of her, and they spent the weekend flirting, riding horses, and taking walks together. After a jealous spat, the two made up, kissing and professing their love for one another.

"Fred and I have made up our tiff and are going to be married,"[42] Sarah confided to Eliza Stagg the next morning. Mrs. Stagg didn't think Burchard had enough money to support her in the style she was accustomed to. She had enough money for both of them, she replied, as she had made over $90,000 in the stock market. (Ninety thousand was surely Sarah's favorite number; she whipped it out so often.)

Burchard was about to leave for Denver to take a promising job, and asked Sarah for a loan. She gave him $250 and told him that if he behaved himself while he was gone, she might marry him when he returned. Back in San Francisco, the two of them spent all their time together canoodling until Burchard left for Denver on May 7.

After he left, Sarah went out driving with her standby beau, Lieutenant Emory, then went to the race track with the Reigarts and Senator Sharon.

Fred Burchard wasn't gone long. During his layover in Los Angeles, the position in Denver was withdrawn. Upon his return to San Francisco, he and Sarah had a fight. She accused him of lying about the

Denver job. She had been asking questions during his absence, and she discovered that he had no money, no job, and no prospects. He accused her of sleeping with William Sharon. They broke up.

Burchard immediately sat down and wrote her a long and sappy love letter, partly quoted here:

> Allie: Forgive me for addressing you in this way. It is for the last time. I have written this immediately after leaving your room. If you could look into my heart and feelings, you would know this was written, not only by a friend, but a man and a gentleman that would lay down his life for you. God knows if I did not love you as I do, I could never have stood such harsh, cruel words as I have stood from you....And above all, I love you better than my life. Oh, Allie, if you only knew what I would give for your friendship. I would be your slave, servant, wait at your commands at all times, give up everything that is dear to a man's life to be near you. I have counted the hours, minutes, when I thought I could only see you again....I shall never visit you unless you wish it, and will always be at your command, either night or day, no matter for what purpose you may need me and all I ask in return is that you will think kindly of poor Fred, who will be very lonesome, and were he not a man and thought he might some day be of use to you, would end his life right here and now....[43]

It is doubtful that this letter moved Sarah much. Once she found out Fred had no money, she lost interest.

When she had earlier told Mrs. Stagg that William Sharon wanted to marry her, Mrs. Stagg had asked her if she loved him. She replied that "all talk of love was nonsense and that she had no more love in her than a piece of marble."[44] If she didn't have love in her, then it is pretty certain she did have ambition. And Fred Burchard had failed to make the grade.

8. THE TIGRESS

Early in January, 1881, William Sharon went to Washington to serve in the Senate. As soon as he was gone, Sarah told his servant Ah Ki that she had left a letter she'd written in Sharon's room and needed to get it back. Ki let her in and she proceeded to search through all of Sharon's papers, spending considerable time at it and coming away with several items she thought might be of use. She also retrieved some of her own letters that she must have considered compromising. It isn't clear why, less than four months into their relationship, she was looking for something to use against Sharon. Perhaps it was just routine for her. She had done the same thing with Reuben Lloyd. Maybe she was preemptorily protecting herself, in case things didn't go the way she wanted. Maybe she was looking for evidence to substantiate her naturally jealous tendencies. Whatever her motives, she came away with at least one spicy letter that came in handy later, from his East Coast mistress Gertie Dietz.

During the senator's absence, Sarah hung out with Julia Bornemann, Lieutenant Emory and another naval officer, Lieutenant LeFevre. In addition to Bornemann, she also confided in Sarah Millett, her neighbor at the Grand Hotel. "I could have married Mr. Sharon before he went away, if I had wanted," she told Millett. "The night before he left, he wanted me to get in a hack and go and get married to him."[45]

Despite her claim that Sharon wanted to marry her before he left, Sarah frequently voiced her frustration that the affair was not going the way she intended. Another confidante during this time was Nellie Bacon, and nearly every day Sarah complained to her that Sharon had not yet proposed marriage. She had believed in her ability to manipulate him to her purposes, but William Sharon was a cool customer. There was nothing sentimental about him, and his immunity to marriage remained iron-clad.

Sharon's intractability led to extreme frustration for Sarah, especially when he renewed his relationship with Gertie Dietz. Dietz had been in Philadelphia where she had gone through the difficult birth of

Sharon's son. Once she recovered, she came to California, bringing the baby with her.

Sarah called on Susan Smith again to do some spying for her, saying she was worried that Gertie Dietz would be able to steal Sharon from her because of the baby. She asked Smith to tell him that Dietz was "a very improper person for him to associate with."[46] Smith declined to slander someone she didn't know. Later, Sarah asked Susan Smith to befriend Dietz so she could find out information to use against her. She offered to pay; Smith declined and advised her to drop the matter and go away quietly. As if Sarah could possibly do either!

There was nothing out of character in this manipulative behavior. There were to follow many more examples of Sarah Althea in melodramatic poses, attempting to bend others, usually without success, to her will. When simply asking didn't work, she would always offer money, and it was customary for her to follow up with threats.

In early 1881, word was getting out that Sarah Althea Hill was William Sharon's mistress. Between this bad news and the appearance of the Dietz baby, Sarah's position was weakening. According to Ah Ki, her visits to the senator's suite began to decline once he returned from Washington. She sensed his waning interest and became alarmed, and must have accused him of being with another woman when he responded with this note: "My Dear Allie: Come over and comfort me. I am awful sorry to have given you any uneasiness. You ought to know I was in good company. Old friends from Washington, and so forth, and therefore why should you be so alarmed?"[47]

Sarah blamed the Dietz baby for coming between her and the old man. But there was much more to it than that.

During the time Sarah was Sharon's mistress, she dated several other men, told many people she was in love with and wanted to marry Reuben Lloyd, got unofficially engaged to Fred Burchard, and flirted with Fred Sharon at his sister's wedding, happily telling everybody, Sharon's friends included, of her exploits. All of this was going on while she was trying to ensnare William Sharon in a matrimonial net.

He meanwhile received an anonymous letter, tipping him off to her carefree life. Though he had no qualms about multiple, simultaneous mistresses for himself, the terms of their agreement apparently assumed complete loyalty on her part. After he confronted her over the anonymous letter, she fled in tears to her friend Nellie Bacon. The senator believed the letter, she said, and might back out of his promise to marry her after all.

If she was serious about marrying him, what was she doing? She seemed to do as she pleased all the time with no regard for consequences. How did she imagine Sharon wouldn't hear about her other beaus when she made no attempt to be discreet? The only thing she was furtive about was her secret sleepovers with him. But they were not furtive enough to save her reputation. After all, the huge staff at the Palace Hotel knew what was going on.

By the end of 1881, Eliza Stagg had decided that Sarah Althea was not a proper person to associate with and began to ignore her letters. "I was afraid that she had involved herself in a case that was going to make an acquaintance with her undesirable,"[48] explained Stagg.

Other women began to close their doors on Sarah. She must have felt like she was being suffocated, watching her social world shrink house by house. Social life *was* life to a woman of her station.

As Sharon became increasingly irritated with her, she responded with understandable insecurity, behaving in ways that escalated the trouble between them. Given her nature, it seems impossible that she could have behaved any differently.

During the summer of 1881, William Sharon noticed that Sarah was no longer maintaining the strict secrecy he desired in their relationship. She hung around his room, making her presence known. She was behaving as if she wanted to be recognized as his mistress, but, of course, she wanted to be recognized as something much more legitimate: his fiancée. He couldn't have known how indiscreet she was truly being, how many people she had already told that she was soon to be Mrs. William Sharon. But what he saw for himself was enough to cause him to forbid her from coming to his room at the Palace Hotel. He would come to her if he wanted to see her, he said, as he could no longer trust her discretion. At the same time, he gave orders to the staff that Miss Hill was not to be admitted to his room. Valuables had gone missing from his pockets, papers had been taken from his drawers, and he was sure she was responsible.

This was just the sort of constraint that drove Sarah crazy. She snuck around the senator's rooms, lurking and watching, even climbing in through a window. She stalked, spied and bribed her way into his spaces. On one occasion, she lied to Ah Ki, telling him Sharon had asked her to come to dinner. Ki let her in, and when Sharon saw her, he became enraged, grabbed her by the throat and said, "What are you doing here, goddamn you?" then he shook her hard and said, "You're a thief. You steal money out of my pockets. You steal my letters, papers, everything." She cried and he choked her, saying, "I don't want you here anymore."[49]

Somehow Sarah did not get the message.

One evening she snuck in and hid in the bedroom closet. Ki heard noises and found her, whereupon Sharon ordered her out of his rooms, resorting to shoving her toward the door when she did not go willingly.

In August, Sarah snuck into Sharon's bedroom and hid behind his dresser while he took another woman to bed. He must have heard her because he said to his lover that she should look around the room as there was liable to be a tigress there. Afterward, Sarah boasted about it to Sarah Millett and had a great laugh over her stunt. But in reality she was not amused. The further she slipped in Sharon's esteem, the more furiously her jealousy and anxiety raged.

On another occasion, Harriet Martin, a elderly black maid at the Palace, found her hiding behind the door of one of the rooms. Martin reported her and the bell man made her leave. Sarah returned and asked why the maid had snitched on her. "Because I don't know who you are," Martin explained. Sarah said, "Well, I am Senator Sharon's sweetheart, and he has moved off the fourth floor with a girl named Miss Dietz, who has got a baby, which she is charging on him. I know it ain't his, and I want to get in that room where he is with the baby. If you'll let me have the key, I'll give you $5."[50] Martin said no.

Sarah then followed the maid around complaining about her problems with the senator. Martin reported, "She said he was only giving her $500 a month and that wasn't enough to support her and her maid, and she wanted $700. I advised her to go and put on her best clothes, and then go to the Senator's rooms on the fourth floor and coax him nice. In that way she could get twice as much money out of him as she could by breaking into a room where he didn't want her and making trouble. She went away, and came back again dressed in black silk, and with great big flowers big as saucepans on her bosom and side. She asked me how she looked, and I said, 'perfectly beautiful,' and told her to go right down stairs and see the Senator."[51] Which is apparently what she did.

But Harriet Martin couldn't get rid of Sarah that easily. "She followed me around the hall for two days, like a little dog after its mother. I couldn't get rid of her nohow. She said she was a lady, and lived at the Grand Hotel."[52]

Sarah then offered Martin $20 if she could find someone who could give her a love charm to make Senator Sharon love her more. Sarah already had considerable experience with love charms, as she had consulted mediums and fortune tellers in the past to help her win back the heart of Reuben Lloyd.

What is interesting about Sarah and Harriet Martin is how she dogged this woman for two days while she was trying to do her work, sought her opinion and then unquestioningly took her advice. Sarah had a tremendous respect for elderly black women, seeing them as wise and powerful. These feelings no doubt originated in her childhood where black nurses would have been the closest thing she had ever had to a mother. As we will later see, her relationship with Mary Ellen "Mammy"

Pleasant would be based on these same feelings. She believed Mary Ellen had all the answers, and did whatever she told her to do. But even Harriet Martin, a stranger who swept the floors of the Palace Hotel, held the mysteries of ageless wisdom for Sarah Althea.

Sarah became completely obsessed with William Sharon's activities. Anyone who has ever felt the desperate helplessness of a lover slipping away will know something of what she was going through. But, as usual, her behavior was amplified well beyond the norm.

Sarah was incapable of restraint, secrecy clause or not. If she had had a marriage contract with William Sharon, as distraught and desperate as she was to keep him to herself, she would not have allowed him to carry on with these other women. She would have asserted her rights then and there. After all, she never hesitated to assert her rights in any other circumstance.

One day William Sharon told Ah Ki to take his baby over to show Sarah. Perhaps Sarah asked to see him, as she was fond of babies. She held the baby on her lap, then offered Ki three or four hundred dollars to steal the baby away or kill him.[53] It is hard to believe she was serious about having the baby murdered, but Ki later reported the event as a genuine offer that he had refused. The episode was also witnessed and confirmed by Sarah Millett. Here again, if Sarah Althea had been Sharon's wife, could there be any reason under the sun that he would send his illegitimate baby over for her to play with? Even assuming she was his mistress, it was a strange thing to do.

On August 24, 1881, an incident occurred that was later used by Sarah to gain sympathy and show that she had been unfairly abused by her brute of a husband. This is from a letter she wrote in September, 1883, to her friends, the Reigarts. She said that Sharon had been trying to get her to give up her marriage contract, but she refused, knowing how important that document was to her rights. "One night he, in his temper over the matter, jumped at me and choked me until I fell on the floor in a fit, and he, believing he had killed me, took me and locked me up in a little closet in his back bedroom, and left me for dead. Some hours after, I recovered, and finding myself I knew not where, other than a dark and dismal cell, I began to cry, and in my hysterics I was heard. To find that I was not dead, but alive, he so recovered from his fright that in his pleadings and delight to find that he had not committed murder, I was forgiven, and all was lovely and amiable again for some days."[54]

She told him she had lost the contract, she said, to prevent another such episode.

It is no surprise that Sharon's version of this incident was different. He said Sarah built a makeshift ladder out of furniture—a table, chair and stool stacked atop one another—to get into his suite by dropping down through the open transom window, quite an impressive physical feat. She walked back and forth, annoying him until he said, "I wish you had broken your damned neck." He tried to get her to go, but she wouldn't, so he pushed her into another room where she threw herself on the floor and pretended to have fainted. He poured a pitcher of cold water over her and told her to get up.

After the dousing with water, Sarah seemed finally to understand that the relationship was over and she should move on.

9. THE SORCERESS

With her hopes dashed and her reputation ruined in San Francisco, Sarah Althea made plans for a trip east to visit relatives in Missouri, then to go on to New York to take singing lessons and study for a stage career. Eventually she would go to Europe, she said, and maybe never come back. In September, she hired Harriet Kenyon, an elderly woman, as companion and chaperone for the trip. They were originally to leave September 11, but Sarah lingered. Kenyon came to stay with her while waiting for the trip. After packing her things in trunks and taking pictures off the walls, Sarah lived with her possessions in disarray as she continued to vacillate about her plans.

To explain her situation, she told friends that she and Senator Sharon had had a falling out and their engagement was broken. She told some of them that Sharon's relatives, especially Frank Newlands, his son-in-law, had turned him against her. She told others that the reason they had broken up was that she had found a young woman in his bed.

Harriet Kenyon reported a quiet existence in Sarah Althea's rooms. Sarah never spent the night away, not with William Sharon or anyone else. Apparently the relationship was over, though he was still paying her monthly salary. Kenyon and Sarah had their meals together in the suite, sometimes with Martha Wilson, the black seamstress who came in to work on Sarah's dresses. Sarah's social calendar was blank, her reputation ruined.

She remained in San Francisco, her heart now returning to her old love, Reuben Lloyd. She said she hated to leave town because she loved Lloyd and wanted to be near him. Her friend Mrs. Hardenberg asked her if she loved Lloyd more than Sharon. "What do I care for Sharon!" she replied. "Only his money."[55] Apparently Sarah was able to tell the truth on occasion.

She and Lloyd reunited in the fall and winter of 1881 when she asked his advice regarding her situation with William Sharon. Lloyd seemed to relax during this time and consented to have dinner with her one evening. It was Mrs. Kenyon, who always went with Sarah on her visits to Lloyd's office, who reported Sarah's joy over this occasion. "...she was so happy that Lloyd had been induced to dine with her at last, and it seemed so nice that she and Reub. had made up. She had sat on his lap and he had caressed her as he did in the old days."[56]

While Sarah was making out with Reub, William Sharon was in his sick bed. He became quite ill at the beginning of September and remained so for nearly three months. He heard that Sarah was talking to a lawyer about her rights, making him worry that if he died, she would cause trouble for his heirs. Of course, whenever Sarah asked anyone about her rights, she told them that she and Sharon had been engaged and he had called it off. Hearing that, most people told her she had some standing for a breach of promise suit.

She consulted with others as well, not on points of law, but on supernatural solutions. Though she knew Sharon no longer wanted her, she had not given up on him. She searched unceasingly for a way to trick or coerce him into marrying her. Because he was ill and might soon die, there was a certain amount of urgency involved in her plan.

Francis Massey, a black woman known to practice voodoo, was one of Sarah's frequent and long-term consultants, beginning in August or September, 1881, and continuing through to the spring of 1883. Sarah told her she wanted a charm that would induce Sharon to marry her. She would then divorce him, take his money and marry a lawyer she loved. That lawyer was Reuben Lloyd, of course.

"She...told me she was in society, and it was talked about that she was engaged to Mr. Sharon, and now it was said it was broken off, and the ladies were putting on airs over her, and she wanted to show them she could be Mrs. Sharon; and, besides, she wanted money, for she had given money to her brother and he had lost it in stocks."[57]

Massey, who clearly didn't care for Sarah, refused to help, saying she knew no charms. After being pressed, however, she did accept a pair of Sharon's socks and a shirt to put a spell on.

In court, Massey asked what must have been the question on many people's minds regarding the plaintiff's endless attempts to become Mrs. Sharon: "If she was married to him, why did she come to me and cry and ask me to charm Mr. Sharon to marry her?"[58]

The visits with Massey point out another fact about Sarah, that she was not fully committed to marrying William Sharon, despite her persistent efforts. She was still in love with Reuben Lloyd. The many times she told people she couldn't decide who to marry (Lloyd, Fred Sharon, William Sharon, Lieutenant Emory), she may have been completely sincere. Disregarding the fact that none of them may have wanted to marry her, she never was certain who would suit her best. There is evidence of this in her brief but ardent affair with Fred

Burchard. As soon as he came on the scene, she told friends that she had changed her mind about marrying Sharon. This indecision was so pervasive with her that it seems unlikely she ever had one clear plan to follow. She certainly was not the cold-blooded schemer she was later characterized to be. Her actions seemed to have always been driven by capricious emotion, not premeditated design.

Sarah wrote William Sharon several times after he got sick, begging to see him. He said he allowed it five or six times, which would account for her ability to feed him potions and get articles of his clothing to be used for charms. At some point she also got hold of a key by giving Ah Ki five dollars.

Mrs. Kenyon accompanied Sarah on all of her visits to fortune tellers and observed her cooking magic potions in a silver sugar bowl, stealing into Sharon's rooms, and sending gifts to Ah Ki and his wife as thanks for being allowed access to the senator's suite. During the two months that Kenyon acted as Sarah's companion, she observed a great deal. At some point, this must have made Sarah nervous. When she saw Kenyon reading a newspaper one morning, she got angry, saying she didn't pay her to read the paper. Kenyon decided it was time to leave. "I never want you to mention my name or recognize me," Sarah told her. "If I hear you say anything about me, I'll string you sky high."[59] Obviously, Harriet Kenyon did not heed the warning, as she later testified for the defense.

Sarah next went to see Laura Scott, a fortune-teller, seeking help in her quest to become William Sharon's wife. "He lies sick, and subjects himself to my gentle ministrations, so I can give him anything I please. I have tried another soothsayer, but am not satisfied with the charm she gave me. It made the dear old Sen sick at the stomach, and his hands twitched nervously."[60]

Laura Scott was alarmed that Sarah might be giving Sharon something dangerous, so she concocted a harmless potion of nine drops of molasses and nine pinches of sugar, dissolved in a bottle of black tea, to be administered to the senator a teaspoon at a time, three times a day. After using up that bottle, Sarah came for another.

Sarah and Sharon quarreled and he sent her away. She returned to Laura Scott and demanded a charm that would actually work. Scott responded with a pair of the senator's socks dipped in brandy, to be tied around Sarah's left leg. She was to wear this until things were square with him. Sarah emphasized that she had to marry him right away while he was sick and before his family returned, as they would prevent the marriage. "Only arrange it so that the Senator shall take me back for one night, and I'll give you $1,000 and a house," cried Sarah.[61] When Scott asked her why she wanted such a brief reunion, she explained that she wanted to get a baby and pass it off as his. It had worked for Gertie Dietz, she reasoned, so it might work for her.

None of the magic worked. The situation between Sarah and Sharon did not improve. On a few occasions when he relented and allowed her to come over, she drove him nuts, pacing the floor, raving at him, and threatening to kill herself.

On one of these occasions, she refused to leave his room and told him she would write a humiliating note about him, pin it to her dress and kill herself so all the world would know what a horrid brute he was. That night he asked Sarah Millett to sleep with Sarah, saying she was acting crazy and he was afraid she would hurt herself. Millett reported, "She was very nervous, and he told me to see if I could not quiet her. I thought there was danger of it too, for she acted very desperate and strange-like."[62]

Both Sarah Millett and William Sharon independently labelled Sarah "desperate" on that occasion. Her behavior during the latter half of 1881 thoroughly reeked of desperation.

Because of Sharon's nervousness and Sarah's increasingly irrational behavior, he was driven to resolve the situation in the only way that made sense to him—with money.

In November, he called her over and they talked all night, settling their business. She asked for $10,000 for her final settlement. He offered her $5,000, and they agreed on $7,500. "This money was paid to buy my peace," Sharon said, "and she agreed to go away peaceably and not annoy me. I took a receipt from her, put it in my pocket-book and carried it in my overcoat pocket. I never saw it again."[63] He paid her $3,000 immediately by check. He gave her a note of $1,500 that matured on August 1, 1882, and the remaining $3,000 was to be given in installments of $250 a month during 1883.[64] Thus he would continue to support her for two more years. The receipt read, "Received of William Sharon $7,500 in full satisfaction of all demands and claims upon him of every name, nature and character. S. A. Hill. San Francisco, November 7th, 1881."[65]

After this settlement, Sarah wheedled a couple more invitations to Sharon's room. "She wrote a very pitiful letter," he said, "saying that she wanted to say good-bye, and I let her come."[66]

During one of these visits, she stole the receipt from his coat pocket. Sarah knew how that piece of paper would take away her leverage. After all he had been through with her, it is surprising that Sharon did not anticipate this move. He noticed the receipt was missing on November 18. Sarah denied taking it. He asked her to sign another receipt, which she refused. He then ordered Samuel Thorn to evict her from the Grand Hotel.

Thorn wrote her on November 19. "Miss S. A. Hill — Dear Madam: As we wish to otherwise occupy room 208 on December 1st, prox., you will please select another residence, and give up possession on that date, and much obliged. Yours, S. F. Thorn."[67]

She responded by writing to Sharon, asking him to reconsider. She wrote three letters altogether, seeking the advice of Mary Ellen Pleasant, her elderly friend, as to the wording of them.

"Mammie Pleasant was old," she said, "and had the experience of lots of girls and women—had the experience of the world....I took her advice and wrote just about what she would dictate. I was much of a baby."[68]

This was the first time Sarah mentioned being advised by Mary Ellen Pleasant on her relationship with William Sharon, but she had known her for many months already. The old woman had gained her confidence and was trusted enough to be consulted during this crisis. She would later become the most influential advisor Sarah would have in her struggle against Senator Sharon.

And so she wrote for the third time:

> My dear Mr. Sharon—
> I have written you two letters and received no reply, excepting to hear that they have been read and commented upon by others than yourself. I also hear you said you were told that I said I could and would give you trouble. Be too much of a man to listen to such talk, or allow it to give you one moment's thought. I have never said such a thing, or have I had such a thought. If no woman ever makes you any trouble until I do, you will go down to your grave without the slightest care. No, Mr. Sharon, you have been kind to me....I would not harm one hair of your dear old head, or have you turn one restless night upon your pillow through any act of mine....I had hoped to always have your friendship and best will throughout life, and always have your good advice to guide me, and this unexpected outburst and uncalled for actions was undeserved. If you would only look at how absurd and ridiculous the whole thing is, you surely would act with more reason. Why should I do such a thing, and what was I to gain by doing so? Pray give me credit for some little sense. I valued your friendship more than all the world. Have I not given up everything and everybody for it? And one million of dollars would not have tempted me to have risked its loss. I feel humiliated to death that Thorn or anyone could have it to say I was ordered out of the house. I have a world of pride, and I ask you to at least

show me the respect to let Thorn have nothing more to say or do in the affair....You have placed me in a strange position, Senator, and all the pride in me rebels against speaking upon the subject. I have been looking at some very nice places, but I cannot get them until some time during the coming months, so if you still desire me to go away, make it known to me, and I will obey you.[69]

Sharon did not reply. By now, he was truly exasperated with her and possibly afraid of her. "She was desperate," he said, "and didn't want to quit me....She seemed to think she had a pretty good thing, and I think it was the money she cared for. There was no love wasted between us. I never cared for her."[70] He may not have cared for her any more, but he had cared enough for her earlier to pay her $500 a month to be with him. Even with all of the trouble that came from Sarah Althea Hill, Senator Sharon was not the least bit wary of jumping right back in the pool. He had several mistresses on his payroll between 1881 and 1884.

Sarah had been told to vacate the hotel by December 1. On December 5, while she was out, Thorn went into action. "That afternoon," Sarah said, "I went out to my grandmother's, and when I returned to my home I found every door of my room taken off, the bells out, and the carpets up; I had only my furniture and the bare floor. My maid had fled in fright, and I was left alone."[71] Sarah had no maid. Perhaps she meant Mrs. Kenyon, but she had been gone nearly two weeks already. This is the sort of lie that came to her so easily, designed to create the appearance of importance and dignity beyond what she actually possessed. In this case, the audience was John Reigart, her friend from Belmont, someone who did still have a high regard for her.

After finding her suite dismantled, she wrote an impassioned letter to Sharon, begging to be allowed to remain. Trying to avoid eviction, she hid in a bathroom while she awaited the senator's response to her plea, copied here with mistakes intact.

> My dear Mr. Sharon: I cannot see how you can have any one treat me so—I who have always been so good and kind to you—the carpet is all taken up in my Hall, the door is taken off and away—and it does seem to me terrible that it is you who would have done —I met Mr. Thorn in the Hall as I started to come over to see you—and asked him if you had order such a thing done—& he said that I must move out, that it was your wish—I told him that I had written you a note when I received his and told you if you wished me to go—to send me word— for it was not convenient to get the place I wanted until

sometime in this month. He said that you had told him to see that I went—so I said no more but came over to see you. Oh Senator, dear, Senator don't treat me so—whilst every one else is so happy for Christmas don't try to make mine miserable remember this time last year—you have always been so good—don't act so now—let me see you & talk to you—let me come in after Ki has gone if you wish—& be to me the same Senator again—don't be cross to me please don't—or may I see you if only for a few moments—be reasonable with me and don't be unjust. You know you are all I have in this world—& a year ago you asked me to come to the Grand. Don't do things now that will make talk—you know you can find no fault with me—may I see you for a few moments & let us talk reasonable about all this—I know you will—I know it is not in your nature to be so hard to me that has been so much to you—don't be unjust—Say I may see you.[72]

This was not the actual letter sent, but the original. A revised copy was made with corrections suggested by both Mary Ellen Pleasant and Reuben Lloyd, who read her letter and thought it "too affectionate and not sufficiently dignified."[73]

Sarah Millett spent the night with Sarah Althea, who slept very little and paced the floor, repeatedly calling Sharon a "brute."

He was resolute and did not answer her letter. Sarah said she called several people, her uncle, her grandmother and Mammy Pleasant, to ask what she should do. Because of the two-year secrecy clause in the contract, they told her to wait until the time was up to assert her spousal rights. Sarah said she was advised to leave the hotel quietly.

"Feeling utterly broken-hearted, completely ruined and crushed, I did so."[74] She went to stay with her grandmother, where she remained only one night. No doubt there were difficult questions being asked there, so she left the next day and went to the home of Martha Wilson, the black seamstress and friend of Mary Ellen Pleasant, where she stayed for a few days before finding her own place.

This was the end of the romantic relationship between Sarah and the senator. Sarah felt humiliated and betrayed. She had been jilted. Her reputation had been destroyed. Worst of all, the millions of dollars she had thought would be hers were now beyond her reach.

As far as Senator Sharon was concerned, the affair was settled and over, and he was glad to be done with it. "I treated her honorably," he said. "I gave her a splendid income. But she wanted more."[75] From his point of view as a businessman, treating her "honorably" meant that he had paid her what she was worth. Sarah had quite different ideas about honor, and many people agreed with her, that there was nothing at all honorable about the way she had been treated. Sharon had bought her, used her, tired of her, and discarded her. He had not compensated her in any way for the damage done to her reputation, which was irreparable.

Their entire arrangement had lasted only fifteen months, the last several of them none too friendly. If Sarah could have chalked that time up to experience and moved past it, she might have come out ahead. But Sarah Althea Hill was incapable of letting go. Besides, there was now someone in her corner with both the interest and expertise to declare this merely the end of Round One.

10. THE CAPITALIST

Without Mary Ellen Pleasant, the Sharon divorce trials could never have taken place. Even putting aside the belief of many that she devised the entire plot, her part was critical in other ways. The case was rumored to be costing both sides about $1,000 a day at a time when $1,000 a year would have been a good working-class salary. Since the trial went on for months and hatched a healthy clutch of offspring, serious funding was needed. Obviously, William Sharon could afford it. But Sarah Althea could not. Tyler and Tyler, her attorneys, were deferring their fees, hoping to get a substantial chunk of the final payoff, but the expenses were still formidable. Enter the woman who would shoulder the financial burden: Mary Ellen Pleasant.

Mary Ellen is now a controversial and legendary figure. She was an early San Francisco pioneer who made a fortune through smart investing and other means purported to be less legitimate. Known to Sarah Althea and most of San Francisco as "Mammy" Pleasant or Pleasance, she has long been regarded as one of the most mysterious persons ever to live in San Francisco. A great deal has been written about this enigmatic woman, but the truth is hard to tease out of conjecture and myth. Woven into her history are racial prejudices trending in both directions. Where one author will portray her as a philanthropist, humanitarian, and civil rights heroine, another will characterize her as a heartless and greedy manipulator, blackmailer, and murderer. There is almost nothing one can say about Mary Ellen Pleasant that will not be passionately disputed by someone else.

In 1899, an article appeared in the *San Francisco Call* sporting a headline that speaks to this woman's ambiguous image: "Mammy Pleasant: Angel or Arch Fiend in the House of Mystery." The "House of Mystery" was the city's nickname for her Octavia Street mansion.

Mary Ellen wanted to be remembered as a civil rights champion and asked that her tombstone contain the words, "She was a friend of John Brown," and so it does. But she lost control of her legacy, largely as a result of her entanglement with Sarah Althea Hill.

The first biography of Mary Ellen Pleasant was written by Helen Holdredge. It is riveting and deeply flawed. By the time *Mammy*

Pleasant was published in 1953, the facts of her life had already become blurred, romanticized and transformed into legend. The book has been used to perpetuate many unsubstantiated stories, most of them highly negative, such as her role as a voodoo queen who presided over secret snake ceremonies and engaged in ritualistic sex orgies.

Mary Ellen Pleasant, 1901 (Courtesy of the Bancroft Library)

But Holdredge does not deserve all the blame for Mary Ellen's negative image. That was established by the tabloid press during the 1880s and 1890s. Several years before the biography was published, author Evelyn Wells wrote of Mary Ellen as "the strange and sinister 'conjure woman,'" who was suspiciously central to numerous controversies. "No one in the city knew what to think of 'Mammy Pleasant,' and every one talked of her."[76]

Of more interest to the scholar than Holdredge's book are her interview notes and extensive research materials housed at the San Francisco Public Library. She had the great good fortune of interviewing people who had first-hand experience with Mary Ellen and the family she was inextricably connected to, the Bells.

There are other more scholarly works on Mary Ellen Pleasant, but they all leave many questions unanswered, and most of them rely on the same source materials collected by Helen Holdredge. There are simply few answers to be found now that the players are all gone. Mary Ellen was secretive and liked to operate in the shadows. Even her clothing, a green shawl and large poke bonnet, were designed to obscure her features. She guarded her secrets well and gave out misinformation designed to obscure the facts. Even her place of birth has become a mystery due to her conflicting accounts. She was born probably in Philadelphia about 1814 of mixed race parents. She had black hair, light skin, and hazel eyes that did not exactly match in color. She could pass for white and did so at various times in her early life. She married an abolitionist in New England and worked with him on the Underground Railroad as a young woman, ferrying Southern slaves to freedom in Canada. After her husband died, she got together with John Plaissance, a surname anglicized to Pleasance or Pleasants. Before marrying, they had a daughter who was left with another couple to raise.

Mary Ellen came to California about 1852. She became a cook and a housekeeper in boarding houses full of rowdy men. She worked hard and opened her own businesses as soon as she could, becoming the owner of several laundries and restaurants, then a proprietor of two boarding houses. She trained cooks and housekeepers and ran an unofficial employment agency. Anybody who needed a maid or a deck hand would come to her and she would find the person for the job. In this way, she positioned hundreds of workers throughout the city. Many of these laborers were former slaves she had helped who remained loyal to her. It is often said that this was Mary Ellen's chief avenue of learning the secrets of wealthy citizens, for she seemed to have something on almost everybody in the city.

Shortly before the hanging of abolitionist John Brown (1859), Mary Ellen was chosen to meet with him in Canada because of her former abolitionist work. She was to give him money that had been raised throughout the city from both black and white supporters. She traveled to Canada and turned over the money. After Brown's death, she returned to San Francisco.

After the Civil War, Mary Ellen no longer had any need to pass as white. In 1866, she sued the Omnibus Railroad Company for $5,000 for ejecting her from a car reserved for white people. She dropped the suit when the company, encouraged by her legal action, changed their policy of excluding blacks. At the time, several other railway companies had no such exclusion policy.

Mary Ellen gradually acquired more property and continued to operate businesses in San Francisco. Some said she owned several brothels, including a high-class one that admitted only the choicest clients. This was located outside of the city and was called Geneva Cottage. William Wilmore, the son of one of Mary Ellen's longtime associates, remembered the place well, as it made quite an impression on him when he was a boy. It was lavishly decorated, he said, with "velvet-covered lounges and paintings of nude women covered with drapes. All the girls in the house wore light colored thin dresses. A hairdresser came in every day to dress their hair and their faces were carefully powdered and there was red on their cheeks. The girls sat in the main room so the men could look them over and decide. Mammy had very rare wines served by a colored maid who was very pretty and well-mannered."[77] It was at Geneva Cottage that two murders were said to have taken place. After so much scandal, Mary Ellen closed the business there and occasionally used the cottage as a personal retreat.

By the time Sarah Althea Hill entered the scene, Mary Ellen was quite wealthy. During the Hill-Sharon trials, she was often asked to post bail for anybody who got arrested on the Hill side. To be accepted as surety, she had to tell her worth. On one of these occasions, "She testified that her front name was Mamie [sic], and that she resided at 1661 Octavia street. She owned property, she said, at 920 Washington street worth $16,000, and mortgaged for $2,000. She owned a house and lot on Duncan street, near Church, worth $2,000, and lots at 719 Sutter street, valued at $25,000, and mortgaged for $12,000. On Clara street was property owned by her worth $4,000, and more on Church street, worth $10,000. Besides these lots, she owned a solid block, but she did not care to locate it unless required to do so."[78] That was most likely the block on Octavia Street where she had built her mansion.

She designed the 30-room home herself and had it constructed in the 1870s, having secret corridors installed to allow her to listen to private conversations in all the rooms. She wouldn't have wanted to say she owned that block because she had set up a situation where everyone assumed it was owned by Thomas and Teresa Bell. This sort of deception was designed to prevent gossip and also to obscure Mary Ellen's financial status. She went to extraordinary lengths to hide her assets, eventually even putting the Octavia Street property in Teresa Bell's name. That turned out to be a serious error.

The House of Mystery (Courtesy of the San Francisco Public Library)

Mary Ellen also owned a ranch in Sonoma County where she built a large house that still stands. Beltane Ranch near Glen Ellen is now operated as a B & B. In the 1890 census, Mary Ellen Pleasant's occupation was listed as "capitalist."

Many modern authors claim that Mary Ellen objected to the use of the name "Mammy," finding it offensive. Clearly, she did object to the name in a broad context, but did not seem to mind it coming from an intimate. Prior to the Sharon trials, nobody called her "Mammy." That was Sarah Althea's name for her, and it was picked up by Sarah's lawyers and then by the press, and it stuck. In 1901 she told a *Call* reporter, "I don't like to be called mammy by everybody. Put that down. I am not mammy to everybody in California."[79]

Sarah Althea was criticized by William Sharon's lawyers for her "unnatural" association and friendships with black women. They were especially critical of her friendship with Mary Ellen Pleasant, insinuating that she was a madam and Sarah one of her prostitutes.

One of her lawyers, David Terry, also a Southerner, said, "There is nothing unnatural in it. We who have drawn our sustenance from black breasts, we who have gone to our colored nurses for relief from every childish affliction, we who have looked upon them as second parents, know that the friendship and respect for them continues until late in life. We know how staunch and true they are—faithful even to death. I am one who possesses this knowledge of the character of the colored 'mammies' of my youth, and the plaintiff is another."[80]

A large percentage of Sarah's witnesses were African-American. It was generally assumed in those days that the sworn testimony of non-whites was less reliable than that of whites, and that assumption was often stated outright. A trip Sarah made to Chinatown to visit Ah Ki was viewed as somewhat scandalous. Even worse were a few days she stayed with the Wilsons after being evicted from the Grand Hotel, sleeping in the same bed as Martha Wilson. Then there was Mary Ellen, her closest advisor and intimate friend who, despite being wealthy, a citizen of long standing, and a property owner, was considered an unfit companion for a respectable white woman. These connections were highlighted in court to show Sarah's depravity.

Despite an often-told story that Mary Ellen had known Sarah when she was a girl in Missouri, and had even been the girl's nurse, that was not the case. That was a story made up later by Mary Ellen to embellish and perhaps explain her friendship with Sarah. The circumstances and date of their meeting is another of the mysteries that adorns this tale. Both women testified in court that they first met at the Grand Hotel in 1880 when Mary Ellen was in her sixties. She came to the hotel selling lace, found Sarah crying, and when she heard Sarah's story, became sympathetic. Still another story says that they met several years earlier and the lace-selling story was invented to lessen the appearance of collusion in the Sharon divorce scheme. If Mary Ellen didn't know Sarah when she got involved with William Sharon, the thinking went, she obviously could not have set the whole thing up. These three opposing stories all originated with Mary Ellen.

Whether they met in 1880 or already knew one another, Mary Ellen would have recognized an opportunity ripe for the picking in the relationship between Sarah and her senator. Here was a woman on the brink of landing one of the richest bachelors in the country. Based on the problems Sarah was having with that goal, she obviously needed help.

This task would have come naturally to Mary Ellen. She had already arranged for several beautiful young white women to marry rich husbands. Her greatest success was with Teresa Percy, whom she had paired with her old friend and business partner, Thomas Bell.

It is impossible to talk about Mary Ellen Pleasant without a brief explanation of her complex relationship to the Bell family. She met Thomas Bell, a Scottish immigrant, on the ship that originally brought her to San Francisco. They established a friendship and business partnership that benefitted both of them for many years. Some people believe that the two were lovers.

Teresa Harris or Percy or Clingan, as she was variously known, was a beautiful young woman who had sunk into desperate circumstances by the time she met Mary Ellen. Mary Ellen took her off the streets, cleaned her up and created a respectable backstory for her, passing her off as a widow.

After the house on Octavia Street was built, the three of them, Mary Ellen, Thomas Bell and Teresa lived there together in a mysterious *ménage à trois*. Eventually, Thomas Bell married Teresa, but most people believe the marriage was a hoax. Thomas and Teresa Bell were husband and wife in name only and had no relationship with one another other than what was necessary to run the house.

Publically, Mary Ellen was billed as the Bells' housekeeper, even though she owned the house and clearly took orders from nobody. This arrangement worked out nicely for everyone for many, many years. Thomas Bell served as Mary Ellen's financial partner while Teresa Bell, under the phony name of Clingham, was listed as the owner of several of Mary Ellen's properties.

The Bells acquired several children, none of them born to Teresa. All six of the children she raised were brought into the home by Mary Ellen. This was another of Mary Ellen's unofficial vocations, finding homes for the babies of unwed mothers. This work, like so many of Mary Ellen's activities, has been portrayed in two opposing ways: as a philanthropic service and as a money-making scheme that preyed on desperate people.

Some of the babies Mary Ellen placed were born to her protégés, young women like Teresa Bell that she had taken under her wing. May Thompson, the mother of the first two Bell children, Fred and Marie, was one of these. May and Mary Ellen tricked Thomas Bell into thinking he was the father so he would take the children in. For many years, Teresa Bell also thought her husband had fathered Fred and Marie. When the truth came out, Thomas Bell was heartbroken and sent Fred away to military school. He wanted nothing more to do with the boy once he learned they were not related.

One by one, other babies appeared in the home: Robina, Muriel, Eustace, and Reginald. Another one died in infancy. Teresa Bell raised them as her own, and the Bells pretended to be an ordinary family. This was the huge skeleton in the Bell closet, and it might have remained closeted if not for Sarah Althea Hill.

11. AN INTERESTING CONDITION

After losing her luxury apartment in the Grand Hotel, Sarah rented a house at 822 Ellis Street. Her cousin from Missouri, Frank Rodney, came to live with her. Rodney was twenty years old and had no job or other means of support. He became Sarah's servant, paid with room and board. The working-class family living next door, William and Mary Brackett, had a seventeen year old daughter named Helen "Nellie." She and Sarah became instant friends. Nellie Brackett was to be Sarah's intimate companion for the next two years.

Being so young and impressionable, Nellie gave herself up to Sarah's cause, believing her to have been horribly wronged by the evil old millionaire William Sharon. Nellie developed an intense affection for Sarah, whom she nicknamed "Punky." Sarah's feelings were equally passionate. By the time Nellie appeared, William Sharon's treatment of Sarah must have seemed unreasonably harsh, but the naïve and kind-hearted Nellie knew nothing of what had come before except what Sarah told her, and she devotedly believed what she was told.

As she had so often told others, Sarah told Nellie's mother that she had been engaged to Senator Sharon, but the engagement was broken off. When Mrs. Brackett said he wasn't very handsome, Sarah agreed "that he was a little, dried-up, shriveled old man, and nobody would have him except for his money."[81] Yes, she was a little bitter.

After four months living next to the Bracketts, in April, 1882, Sarah moved to Leet's boarding house at 522 Van Ness Avenue. Her young consorts Nellie and Rodney marched off with her.

In June, she went to see William Sharon to begin taking payment on the $1,500 note he had given her as part of her settlement. According to him, this was the first time he had seen her since her eviction from the Grand six months earlier. She asked for $250, which he paid.

Toward the end of June, Sarah ran into William Sharon by chance on the street and informed him she was pregnant. "Whom do you suspect?" he said, then laughed, and they parted. Why would she say such a thing to him? Impulse? Or was she testing the waters to see if he would bite? For some time, she had been thinking about getting a baby to pass off as his.

This small incident later fueled a fictional story that Nellie Brackett told in court. Sarah sent her, she said, on July 1, 1882, to tell William Sharon that she was "in an interesting condition." His reply was, "Well, who does she suspect?" To which Nellie indignantly rejoined, "She does not suspect anybody; she knows it is you."[82] Sharon told Nellie to keep the news to herself and send "Mrs. Sharon" down to see him. When they next met, Sharon offered to rent a house for Sarah and her "interesting condition."

In response to Nellie's story, General Barnes said, "Remarkably enough, although Miss Hill sent Miss Brackett down to make this communication to Mr. Sharon on the first of July concerning her state, they do not either of them appear to have paid the slightest attention to it afterward. And no one knows to-day what the result of that interesting condition was."[83]

Although the Sharon defense believed Sarah's pregnancy was invented to pressure Sharon, it appears she actually *was* pregnant in the summer of 1882. As Barnes pointed out, nobody mentioned it again. Nor would they if it were true. For an unmarried woman, a pregnancy would have been a secret and a shame to be kept thoroughly under wraps. Fortunately, the fashions of the day would cooperate with such a plan. This may have been the reason Sarah moved away from the Brackett home in April of that year. She would have been six months pregnant and having a hard time concealing it. As we will see, once the baby was born, she returned to the Brackett home.

Nellie later admitted that she had never visited William Sharon to tell him he was going to be a father. But in recanting her story, she confirmed that the pregnancy was real and not part of the Sharon plot. "Oh, she got into a delicate condition through some man. There is no truth in any testimony that she was in a delicate condition through Mr. Sharon. She told me to lay it on Sharon, and I did it."[84]

The father of the baby was Reuben Lloyd. Their reunion, beginning in the fall of 1881, was witnessed by Sarah's companion at the time, Harriet Kenyon.

As usual, Sarah had trouble keeping secrets. She may have had a reason to tell William Sharon she was pregnant, but she had no reason to tell the fortune teller Francis Massey. On one of her visits to Massey for love potions in 1882, she became distraught and began to cry. She told

Massey that "two gentlemen had deceived her and she wanted one of them back in particular; that one had rendered her pregnant, but as long as his mother was living he would not marry her...."[85] She couldn't decide if she wanted a charm to make Sharon marry her or to get Lloyd's mother out of the way or both.

On a subsequent visit to Massey, she told her she wanted to get rid of her baby. When she came back three or four days later, she "said she had gone and taken some stuff and that she was better, and I tole [sic] her it was a God's sin, so it was; there now."[86]

But did Sarah really abort the baby? Maybe she was simply sorry for telling Massey about her pregnancy, so she did what she did best to undo her error: she lied. If Mary Ellen Pleasant was coaching Sarah at this time, she would have been appalled that she was confessing such secrets to fortune tellers, and would have insisted she fix it. When it came to dealing with illegitimate babies, a business in which Mary Ellen was highly experienced, the fewer people who knew about the baby, the better. At any rate, according to Mary Ellen Pleasant and Teresa Bell, that was not the end of Sarah's interesting condition.

Who better to handle Sarah's pregnancy than Mary Ellen? According to Pleasant biographer, Helen Holdredge, Sarah was secreted away at Mary Ellen's retreat, Geneva Cottage, to give birth.

Teresa Bell wrote in her diary of the third child brought into her home after Fred and Marie. This time, the baby was acquired with Thomas Bell's full knowledge and consent. It was the daughter of Sarah Althea Hill and Reuben Lloyd.

Robina May Bell was baptized July 2, 1882.[87] That puts the latest date of her conception in October, 1881, the exact time that Lloyd and Sarah reconciled and William Sharon was seriously ill and bedridden. There is no doubt Teresa Bell believed Robina was the daughter of Sarah Althea. She mentioned it in her diaries several times and told many people over the years. After Thomas Bell died and the eldest child, Fred, sued her for custody of the younger children, she gave up all pretense of being their mother and routinely told everyone that she had never had a child of her own.

As she grew older, Teresa Bell became increasing bitter about the situation she had been put into by Mary Ellen Pleasant's manipulations, resenting the old woman and all of the children. She often complained of the sham of her life to acquaintances, and of the disloyalty and ingratitude of the children that she had nurtured as her own. She disinherited all of them in her will.

The surviving children contested the will and eventually won by bringing evidence that Teresa Bell was insane when she wrote it. As part of her delusionary state, they said, she had persuaded herself that she was not the mother of her own children. But Teresa had been denying her maternity for decades, long before the accusations of alcoholism, hallucinations and bizarre behavior.

The truth can never be known for certain, but it may be that Robina Bell, described by a school chum as short and blond, was the love child of Sarah Althea Hill and Reuben Lloyd.

12. THE ADVENTURES OF PUNKY AND NELLIE

On July 31, Sarah moved from Leet's boarding house into the Brackett home, apparently uninvited and unwanted, and stayed until November. Nellie's mother related the incident to General Barnes, who described it with his usual flair:

> Miss Hill swooped down upon her about dusk, without a word of previous negotiation, without ever saying, "by your leave," without ever undertaking to make any bargain, and took possession of the front and rear parlors of Mrs. Brackett's house. There she remained, contrary to the wish and the will of Mr. and Mrs. Brackett, they loathing her and seeing with alarm the influence she was acquiring over their daughter, observing this crop of disobedience and disrespect that was growing up in that girl's bosom, watered and nurtured by the fiendish influence of this woman, whom they were as unable to shake off as a horse in a South American pond is unable to shake a leech. She remained there, carrying on her work of destruction in this girl's moral fibre, educating and training her for the career of villainy as a witness in which she has so fearfully distinguished herself, and at last she marched out of Mrs. Brackett's as she had marched in, without a word of warning, or stopping to pay the cold courtesy of a good-bye, taking away this girl from her home, and more than a week later, the mother ascertained where they had gone, and where her child was.[88]

After Nellie left home to live with Sarah, her parents and her brother tried to persuade her to come home and give up her friendship with her darling Punky. Once her mother came to Sarah's house to speak with her and Nellie refused to even see her. Morgan Hill, perhaps at the Brackett family's request, also tried to convince Nellie to leave his sister. On one occasion, after the legal proceedings had begun, Mary Brackett followed her daughter to the lawyer's office and begged her to come home. Sarah intervened and hurled obscenities at her. In spite of the tremendous effort put forth by the Brackett family, Nellie did not budge in her devotion to her friend.

In the latter half of 1882, Sarah resumed her efforts to bewitch the senator. This plan, as was pointed out by her attorneys, was not inconsistent with a secret marriage. However, when she visited mediums, fortune-tellers and astrologers, she told them her goal was to *marry* Senator Sharon. She never told them he was her estranged husband.

She went to one astrologer who advised the most gruesome of voodoo charms, which Sarah dutifully carried out. She cut the heart out of a live pigeon and stuck nine pins in it, then wore it in a silk bag around her throat. Next she consulted a woman who told her to draw three drops of blood from her arm at midnight of the full moon, then mix it with the senator's wine. Once he drank it, within three nights, he would be hers. The next consultant told her to take a single hair from the senator and put it in her bosom for three days.

Since many of the charms required access to William Sharon, his clothing, his food and drink, or his bedroom, Sarah had to find ways to overcome her banishment from his suite at the Palace Hotel.

On December 23, 1882, having had success in the past with manipulating Ah Ki, she went to his home in Chinatown to bribe him to let her into Sharon's room in his absence on the following day. Ki took the bribe.

The next day, he let Sarah and Nellie into the suite, then watched as "She take little black powder and sprinkle little bit on his chair, little bit on table, and little bit on floor. Then she go in wine closet and put little white powder in all bottles—whisky, brandy, claret, gin, port wine."[89]

Ki had second thoughts about colluding with Sarah, worried that the powder in the liquor might be dangerous. He told his boss all about it, and Sharon was understandably angry. When Sarah came to renew the charms, Ki turned her away.

While trying to put a spell on William Sharon, Sarah continued to collect her payments from him. She came to his office in July, August and September. On October 7, 1882, she got her last payment on the $1,500 note. In January, 1883, the last segment of Sharon's payoff kicked in, the $250 per month for the duration of the year.

In addition to dabbling in magic, Sarah was also preoccupied by the possible other women her ex was seeing. She spied on him and threatened any woman she suspected. In February, 1883, she went to visit Mary Shawhan, a friend until Sarah accused her of going to dinner with Sharon. Shawhan denied it and said she hadn't seen the senator for two years. But Sarah wasn't satisfied. She threatened Shawhan and warned her off. It was a mistake to tangle with Mary Shawhan, as she would later to get herself on Sharon's payroll to help him in his court battles.

About this time, William Sharon was again extremely ill and often confined to bed. Sarah wrote him a letter offering to care for him and, of course, asking for money. "You surely have not forgotten what a nice little nurse I proved myself in your last illness," she said, "…and I assure you, you will find me just as willing and agreeable now….I would like to see you anyway, it being the first of the month, and I would like to get some money."[90]

Sharon did not answer the letter.

Sarah began visiting Fanny Sampson regularly during March, 1883. She talked constantly about how she could get even with Sharon for disgracing her. Based on what she was told, Sampson believed Sarah had strong grounds for a lawsuit and recommended the attorney William Hornblower. Fanny Sampson explained to him that there was a lot of money to be made in a breach of promise suit, but if he took the case on, he'd have to front some of his own money because the client wasn't in a position to pay until she won the case. He said he was interested and Sampson introduced them. After their conversation, Hornblower decided not to take the case. "I thought, and told Mrs. Sampson so, that it was a blackmailing suit, and would not have anything to do with it."[91]

Still looking to sue for breach of promise, Sarah must not have had a marriage contract in her back pocket…yet.

On March 29, Sarah got all dolled up and went down to the Palace Hotel, taking Nellie and Rodney along. She said Senator Sharon had invited her over to celebrate her birthday. Her birthday had been on Monday, but Sharon had postponed the dinner due to business. She knocked on his door and got no answer. A waiter came by to deliver wine and told her that Mr. Sharon had gone downstairs. When she asked him to tell him she was there, he said he wasn't there to wait on "Sharon's women." While she was hanging around in the hall, a watchman named Fogarty came by, recognized her, and told her to get out of the hotel. She explained about the birthday dinner. Fogarty didn't buy it. He ordered her to go down in the servants' elevator where she belonged, then threatened to arrest her when she refused. Fogarty nearly had to toss her out bodily, but after some trouble, Sarah swept huffily out with her two devotees in her wake.

Clearly, William Sharon was serious about keeping Sarah away from his room. What isn't clear is what Sarah intended to do, but she had shown up often enough to sneak, bribe or force her way into Sharon's suite, so perhaps this was just another such occasion. She might have thought he would open his door to her on her birthday, but Fogarty did not give her the chance to find out.

Both the waiter and the watchman had sneered at Sarah and treated her insolently. They knew she was no longer in favor with their boss and they took the opportunity to lord it over her. Now she was the lowest of the low, a prostitute. To be spoken to by servants and working men as if she were their inferiors must have been excruciating to a woman like Sarah Althea.

Full of indignation, she and Nellie went to Sharon's office at the bank the next day and asked to see him. After waiting for a while, she was told that the senator had left the building after hearing she was there.

Nellie was so enraged by these incidents that she wrote William Sharon a letter, known subsequently as the "Old Sharon" letter, which read as follows:

> Old Sharon: When I first met you I felt quite honored to think I had on my list of acquaintances a United States Senator, but to-day I feel it a double disgrace to know you. If you are a specimen of the men that are honored with the titles of the country, then I must say I pity America, for a bigger coward or upstart of a gentleman never existed, in my opinion, since last Thursday night. I was present with the lady who called on you — and to think what a coward you must be. Your own conscience would not allow you to see her and politely excuse yourself, but you must send one of your Irish hirelings to do your dirty work. I just hope God will punish you with the deepest kind of sorrow and make your old heart ache and your old head bend. I am not one to wish evil to people generally, but with all my heart I wish it to you. You did her a mean, dirty trick, and tried in every way to disgrace her, a motherless, fatherless girl, because you knew she leaned on you and was alone in the world....Instead of trying to hold her up in the world, you have tried everything you can to disgrace her. I should think you would be so ashamed of yourself, you couldn't do enough to atone for the wrong you have done her. I love her, and I just hate you. It is well I am not her, or I would advertise you from one end of the world to the other. But she feels herself so much of a lady she too tamely submits to your insults. Why, you are not good enough to wipe my shoes on, much less her. If you only knew how insignificant you look to-day, although I am a poor girl and you can ride in your

carriage....I am a poor girl, but I feel myself so much better than you, you horrible, horrible man. Miss Brackett.[92]

Nellie said Sarah told her what to write; Sarah said Nellie wrote it all on her own. Either way, she was firmly in Sarah's grasp at the time. She had bought into Sarah's feelings of betrayal and exploitation. But perhaps more importantly for determining the facts of the case, the letter gives no clue that Nellie had ever been told or been shown any evidence that Sarah was married to William Sharon. Like Sarah's own letters to him from the fall of 1881 throughout 1882, her rights as a wife and his duties as a husband were never mentioned.

Why not? If she was his wife, why wasn't she screaming for him to acknowledge her as such? She explained her silence in two ways, the first being that the marriage contract had a secrecy clause and she was afraid of violating it. Even in private correspondence between the two of them, apparently. After the two-year secrecy requirement had expired, she said she was advised by people like Mammy Pleasant not to mention being his wife in her letters lest she should rile him up and cause trouble.

When faced with this explanation in one of the spin-off court cases, Judge Matthew Deady said, "To one who has seen and heard [Miss Hill] in court...the idea that old Mammie Pleasant, or anyone else, could control her tongue or pen in her intercourse with the plaintiff is simply ridiculous."[93]

In addition to being snubbed by Palace Hotel employees, Sarah was now a social outcast among her former society. She was invited to no social functions. The only visitors to her house were her relatives. She became obsessed with bewitching William Sharon into marrying her, believing that was the only way out of her desperate situation.

One of Sarah's regular fortune tellers was Jennie Wanger, whom she had been seeing since 1880 when the object of her desire and misery had been Reuben Lloyd. "I suppose I talked with her five hundred times about her chances of marrying Mr. Sharon," said Wanger. "One day she was at my house four times."

At Sarah's insistence, Wanger prescribed a graveyard charm. Sarah was to take pieces of her beloved's underwear and bury them in a newly-dug grave under the coffin between the hours of midnight and one o' clock. The result of the charm: either the man would marry her or he would die.

Although Sarah said this never happened and Mary Ellen Pleasant helped her concoct an elaborate alibi for the date, there is no doubt that on May 1, 1883, Sarah did bury a packet of the senator's clothing in a grave. There was a witness to the deed, a cemetery employee named George Gillard who observed and assisted the entire ritual.

Nellie already knew Gillard when they approached him and asked if there were any funerals scheduled, saying they wanted to bury a package to give them luck to get rich husbands. Gillard asked her what was in the package. Nellie replied, "Oh, only some rose leaves and flowers and charms."[94] He was reluctant to give his consent, but was coaxed by Sarah, who said, "You would do us a little favor like that, wouldn't you, if it would cause Nellie to many a rich husband?"

Gillard decided there was no harm in it. There were no funerals that day, but when they returned on May 1, they were in luck. Gillard led them to the open grave destined for Anson Olin.

> Then I took the ladder that the grave diggers had used and put it into the grave. The rough box in which coffins are encased was in position in the bottom of the grave, and one of the bottom boards was loose. They generally are left loose, I believe. I lifted this up and Miss Hill came down the ladder. A little earth was scooped out from under the plank and then Miss Hill took a small package—about five or six inches square—from the breast of her shawl, cloak, or whatever she had on, and put it in the excavation. Some sand was sprinkled over it then, and as she did so she murmured something to herself that I could not understand, but I supposed from her manner that it was some sort of a spell or charm.[95]

Sarah adamantly denied all of the incidents involving potions and charms. She denied believing in astrology, voodoo and all such superstitions. "Althea Hill, the accomplished, educated and comely plaintiff in the Sharon case," wrote an *Alta* reporter, "appears to be a sincere believer in charms and wonder-working, but...confesses her weakness with the utmost reluctance." The reporter goes on to say that if Sarah read the newspapers "it would be strange indeed if, after reading the hundred odd advertisements of mediums, astrologers, fortune-tellers and such, which weekly appear in one city paper or another, she did not arrive at the conclusion that if there was any folly in consulting such people, she was foolish in a pretty considerable company."[96] This was quite true. In the closing decades of the nineteenth century, astrology, fortune-telling and séances became wild new fads, especially among upper-class women. But clearly none of these ventures were entertainment to Sarah. She honestly expected to find a magic charm that would do the trick. As a Christian, she knew she was not supposed to believe in such things. Her attempts to deny her involvement with the occult were hopeless, however. There were simply too many witnesses.

Shortly after filing her lawsuit, Sarah showed up at fortune-teller Laura Scott's house with a couple of thugs and a threat that if Scott testified in court against her, she'd end up with her throat slit. Scott was not intimidated. She came on the stand and told what she knew.

Sarah's attorney, George Tyler, asked Scott on the stand if she had ever told William Sharon's fortune. "Don't think he needs any, Honey," she replied.[97]

13. A SET OF SHARPERS

According to Sarah's servant, Delia Manning, Mary Ellen Pleasant and Sarah Althea were constantly together and had several secret meetings in the spring of 1883. It was probably not a coincidence that the marriage contract appeared for the first verifiable time not long after that.

Says biographer Helen Holdredge, "On good authority Mary Ellen had herself masterminded the idea of the marriage contract between Miss Hill and Sharon...."[98] Unfortunately, that is all the information Holdredge offers on this subject and does not identify the "good authority."

Holdredge wasn't alone in this conclusion. Judge Deady, during his ruling on the second trial, said, "In my judgment, this case, and the forgeries and perjuries committed in its support, have their origin largely in the brain of this scheming, trafficking, crafty old woman."[99]

The best evidence that Mary Ellen was the originator of the marriage contract was her consultation with George W. Tyler before the suit was initiated. This occurred before Tyler was ever approached to represent Sarah, but he had served as Mary Ellen's lawyer in the past. Mary Ellen wanted to know if a marriage by private contract was legal and, if so, what it should contain. Her pretext for asking was that a lady wanted her to furnish a house and Mary Ellen wanted to be sure that the man would be legally obligated to pay, as the two had such an arrangement. Tyler answered her in writing, detailing what the contract must contain to be legal and binding. His letter seems to have been the blueprint for the document Sarah ultimately produced.

In June, 1883, Sarah again went to visit Susan Smith, the woman who had come to her aid after she had poisoned herself over Reuben Lloyd. She implored her to go to Senator Sharon and tell him that Gertie Dietz was no good and he should dump her. Smith declined again. The point of mentioning this unproductive incident is to show that as the summer of 1883 rolled in, despite the probability that the marriage contract had already been manufactured for blackmail purposes, Sarah was still trying to get Sharon back. Her only direct contact with him were the visits she made to his office to collect money, which she did in July and August. She did not mention anything to him about the preparations going on to sue him because she was still hoping to avoid court.

Up until the summer of 1883, everything Sarah had done or said in relation to William Sharon had demonstrated that she was trying to get him to marry her. Dozens of witnesses could testify to that…and did. But now a new plan was being hatched to prove that they had been secretly married all along. The legal action Sarah had been talking about up to this point was a breach of promise suit. She might have actually had some success with that. There were reputable witnesses who had seen her and Sharon together who believed they had been engaged. A promise of marriage could be a verbal agreement. No documentation was needed to prove it. And the fact that Sarah had told everyone they were engaged from the beginning might actually have helped her win the case. It would have been her word against his. Even though she had likely been lying about the engagement, her conversations and behavior over the past couple of years supported that scenario in a way that a marriage could not be supported.

Why, then, did she switch gears so dramatically? It must have been about money. The settlement for breaking a verbal engagement would have been so much less. If she could prove marriage, Sarah would be entitled to half the property Sharon had accumulated since the summer of 1880. She would also be entitled to alimony, which would have to be a substantial sum for the ex-wife of a man that rich. Perhaps Sarah reasoned through these arguments on her own. Perhaps Mary Ellen Pleasant persuaded her to go down this road. Since neither of them ever confessed the truth, we will never know how large a role Mary Ellen played.

The next move Sarah made would propel her irrevocably forward. She recruited Australian-born newspaperman William McCann Neilson to her cause. As he recalled their first meeting, he said, "Miss Hill during nearly the whole period of my visit wept most bitterly and told me of certain financial transactions with Mr. Sharon, and complained that he had got all her money away from her…and asked my advice and assistance toward recovering her just rights."[100] Neilson described a woman in a desperate and distracted state of mind. He advised her to go away for a few months, to visit friends and relatives and give herself a chance to clear her mind.

When he came to see her the next day, she showed him the marriage contract and he realized the situation had changed dramatically, that a document like that gave her a firm leg to stand on. He agreed to act as her agent in her suit against William Sharon.

Before taking any action, Neilson sought legal advice from the well-known and highly-respected attorney W. H. L. Barnes, nicknamed "General" Barnes. Neilson told him that Sharon was secretly married and the woman was about to file for divorce and alimony. There was an informal marriage contract that Sharon had signed, he said, and he had seen the document himself.

"Who is the lady; is it Allie Hill?" asked Barnes. Neilson affirmed it and Barnes said, "Good God, I knew there must be something of that sort. She is too good a girl and too well connected to give herself up to old Sharon without something of the kind."[101]

It was a mistake to mention the case to Barnes, as it turns out, because he immediately told William Sharon what was coming down. Sharon then hired Barnes to represent him.

Neilson set out to hire lawyers for Sarah, but had trouble finding any to suit her. "The lady's whims changed almost from day to day, and I then for the first time began to realize that I had a most passionate and uncontrollable person to deal with."[102] Throughout August, they bandied names about before finally settling uneasily on Tyler and Tyler. The difficulty Neilson had in taking care of business is yet more evidence that Sarah was not thoroughly committed to the suit. She had still not made up her mind, but she had found someone who had the patience to keep her fixed on a goal.

Before she officially sued Sharon, Sarah tried to intimidate him with the threat of a law suit. She sent several emissaries to say that if he gave her a quiet divorce and agreeable settlement, she would sign a quit claim on his estate. She had apparently forgotten that she had already signed such a paper.

When Mary Ellen Pleasant visited Sharon, she told him that all Sarah wanted was the restoration of her reputation. The people she used to associate with would have nothing to do with her, but if he acknowledged that they had been married, her reputation could be repaired. Sarah had not yet signed with a lawyer, Mary Ellen told him, and Neilson would stop the suit if they could find a way to settle quietly. Sharon told her that Allie Hill was a bad and dangerous woman, that her claims were complete fabrications and she would never get a dime out of him. He was under the impression that Sarah had managed to dupe the old woman into believing her story. Like many others, he did not suspect Mary Ellen of being one of her handlers.

On September 7, 1883, Sarah sent William Neilson to the Palace Hotel to ask Sharon for money, as he was still paying her the $250 a month. The senator took offense at Neilson's manner and sent him away, telling him that if Sarah wanted money, she should come ask for it herself.

That evening she came to see him, both Neilson and Cousin Rodney in tow. Sharon was angry that Neilson had returned. He called him a "blackmailing son of a bitch" and ordered him to leave. He then invited Sarah and Rodney into his suite. Sarah saw a woman in Sharon's bedroom and said she wouldn't go in with that woman there, so Sharon suggested they go into another room. He gave her $250 for that month's payment.

Describing Sarah's behavior that evening, William Sharon said, "She stormed and raved about what she called my unkind treatment, and young Rodney told her to hush. She then turned on him, and told him, 'Shut up. I'm keeping you, and you've no right to talk to me.'" She told Sharon that a jury would believe her before it would believe him, and she would make serious trouble for him. "Then she flounced out of the room, saying, 'You'll never get married while I'm alive.'"[103]

This was the last meeting between William Sharon and Sarah Althea outside a courtroom. Two days later, he went to the train station, intending to leave for New York. Instead, he was arrested on a charge of adultery.

The warrant was brought by William M. Neilson on behalf of Sarah Althea Hill. The charges included adultery with nine different women over the previous three years. In addition, Miss Hill also claimed that she had loaned him $90,000 (her favorite number, remember?), of which he had repaid only $78,000. She was suing for the remainder.

The following day, after posting $5,000 bail, Sharon took a train east. His relatives locked themselves mutely in their houses as newspapers across the country adorned their front pages with the story: "Sharon Arrested on a Charge of Adultery" and "Senator Sharon Under Arrest." Details were few, only what was provided in the warrant and a brief statement by Neilson to the press.

> Ex-Senator William Sharon was arrested Saturday afternoon on a complaint sworn to by William M. Neilson. The charge is open and notorious adultery with Miss Gertie Dietz....It is stated by Neilson that a short time since Sharon entered into a marriage contract with Miss Aggie [sic] Hill, well known in society circles of San Francisco, and that she entrusted with him the custody of $90,000 of her money, and that the marriage contract was kept a secret at the time, for the reason that Senator Sharon was desirous of first getting rid of Miss Dietz.[104]

Senator Sharon made no public comment until he was in New York, then gave a statement to the press. "I am ready to meet those charges here, in Nevada, San Francisco or anywhere. They are false, and have been sprung upon me for blackmailing purposes. Miss Hill is being used as a tool by a set of sharpers. I have nothing to conceal either in my relations to Miss Hill, or any other woman, and I am perfectly willing that the widest publicity should be given to any act of mine."[105]

Even while inviting the "widest publicity," William Sharon could not have imagined the national media frenzy that was about to overwhelm his life.

Nobody was surprised to hear that William Sharon had a multitude of lovers. Even while his wife was alive, his love affairs were often rumored, and he had established a reputation as a libertine. But the news of the secret marriage was huge. When the story first broke, nobody outside her own social circles had ever heard of Allie Hill. The press release that was reprinted hundreds of times listed her name as "Aggie." But that would soon be corrected, and the name "Sarah Althea Hill" would be on everyone's lips. People clamored to know who this woman was and where she had come from. They wanted to know everything about her. The beautiful young woman had captured the imagination of the public and she would not release it until nearly a decade had passed.

14. SUITS AND COUNTER-SUITS

On October 21, 1883, the adultery charge came up for hearing. The courtroom was packed to capacity, but the crowd was deeply disappointed when Sarah Althea did not appear. So far, nobody knew what the woman claiming senatorial matrimony looked like. In the place of the alleged Mrs. Sharon were William Neilson, acting as her agent, and George W. Tyler, her attorney. Neilson complained that Gertie Dietz had disappeared, that his witnesses had not been subpoenaed, and that he had been offered money to stop the suit and when he refused, had been threatened.

In the first of many such occasions yet to come, George Tyler could not produce the marriage contract, as his client did not want to surrender it. As nobody seemed prepared or even willing to try the case, the judge dismissed the charges on a technicality. Almost everyone went away disappointed that the scandal was over before it had begun. Apparently, they concluded, there had been nothing to it after all. It was, as Senator Sharon had said, a poorly-designed blackmail attempt that fell apart at its first test.

But spirits around the city were lifted just a few days later, on November 1, when Sarah Althea Hill sued William Sharon for divorce, alimony and division of community property.

William Neilson had told Sarah that he was sure the case would never go to court, that Sharon would be anxious to make a settlement and avoid all that, but even after the embarrassment of being arrested for adultery, Sharon stood firm. He was too angry and feeling too persecuted to let Sarah have any satisfaction. He knew that his money could buy the best lawyers, loyal witnesses, even judges if it had to, but why would he have to go that far? He was confident in his ability to win the case, vindicate himself and humiliate the woman who was trying to suck the life out of him. She had riled him up and he wanted to crush her. But he wanted to crush Neilson more, as he believed that without being pushed into it, Sarah would never have sued. That may have been true.

In a letter she wrote to Neilson after the trial began, she said, "You asked yourself and begged to begin this fight, and promised it should never come to Court. Oh, God! that I had kept my trials to myself. These scenes are killing me. Why do you stay your fight on him! Why do you not make him bend to you! I do not want to be called into a Court to be blackened by all the false testimony his money can procure."[106]

If Neilson had "begged" her to go forward, that too indicates her reluctance. At the end of her letter, she mentions yet again her fear that her reputation will be damaged. Throughout her life, she remained highly concerned about her image.

On her own, Sarah would never have been able to follow through with the suit, even if she had wanted to. She couldn't have afforded it. But Mary Ellen Pleasant could. Some people have suggested that the money came from her employer Thomas Bell. If it did, it was without his consent. He confided in a friend that he thought the whole business was an outrageous travesty. There have always been accusations that Mary Ellen embezzled a fortune from Bell. Their finances were so intimately tied together it is hard to know if "embezzlement" is the correct term. That she used money of interest to Bell has some support in the fact that she lied to the Bells about where the money came from. Teresa Bell wrote, "We did…not know she was spending money in the Sharron [sic] case, as she told us Morgan Hill was supplying every dollar, but it was a secret as he was using his wife's money and she would bounce him if she knew that. That explanation satisfied both Mr. Bell and I."[107] Obviously, they knew nothing about Morgan Hill's relationship to his sister. He was the last person who would have bankrolled her. As it was, he couldn't get far enough away from this scandal.

Why did Mary Ellen Pleasant invest so solidly in Sarah's cause, putting up her money, attending court daily, giving Sarah advice, arranging for witnesses, contriving an alibi for Sarah for the day she was burying her magic charm in Anson Olin's grave? Perhaps because Mary Ellen was already in this thing up to her neck. If she had dreamed up the secret marriage, helped Sarah create the marriage contract, and persuaded her that she could beat Sharon, she already had a big investment in the outcome. Sarah Althea was in a position to bring down a San Francisco colossus. It isn't too surprising that Mary Ellen would want a piece of that. A lot of other people did.

There was another possible reason for her interest. Mary Ellen's experience with helping unwed mothers, some of whom must have been raped, abused and otherwise taken advantage of by men, might explain why Sarah's case touched a nerve with her. Here was another young woman preyed upon by an unrepentant rich old man, then discarded like rubbish. Maybe Mary Ellen wanted to make him pay for his crimes.

Others have suggested revenge as a motive, for Mary Ellen and Thomas Bell's investments suffered badly from William Sharon's management of the Bank of California after its collapse. A lot of people lost a lot of money during that time…except William Sharon, who just got richer.

Mary Ellen had tremendous loyalty to several beautiful young white women (Teresa Percy, May Thompson, and Sarah Althea Hill) usually referred to as her protégés. Some people believe they all worked for her at one time or another as prostitutes. Whether that was true or she developed an interest in them for some other reason, Mary Ellen felt an enduring responsibility to take care of them. She called Sarah "my child," and whatever else was between them, there was most certainly affection. Whatever her motivation, Mary Ellen was in deep.

Although she had been able to orchestrate and pull off a great many intricate schemes in her life, she misjudged the Sharon case. A secret marriage dating back to the summer of 1880 when Sarah and Sharon first met was daring, but also foolhardy. Obviously, to prove it, they had to go back in time and improve upon the facts. Executing a deception as grandiose as this required dexterity, delicacy and secrecy. That just wasn't Sarah Althea. She was not capable of playing her part properly. But the other reason the plot seemed hopeless was more important. All of the schemes that Mary Ellen had masterminded in the past had played out in private. This case was supposed to have been settled privately as well, but Sharon had surprised everyone by accepting the challenge. The opposition was more formidable than anything Mary Ellen had previously faced. If she did cook up the marriage contract for her protégé, she probably never expected it to be pored over with microscopes and the country's best handwriting experts in a court of law.

It is also likely that nobody on Sarah's team was prepared for the energy, money and dedication William Sharon would bring to the battle. He was certainly as determined to keep her from his money as she was to get it, and his tactics may not have been any more honest than hers.

On October 3, William Sharon brought a counter suit in the U. S. Circuit Court, asking the "Court to decree that Sarah Althea Hill was not and never had been his wife, that she be perpetually enjoined from making such representations and that the said contract be declared a forgery and be ordered to be delivered up to be canceled and annulled."[108]

One of the strategies employed by Sharon and his heirs was to claim that he was a citizen of Nevada, not California, which allowed him to bring suit in federal rather than state courts. It was a successful strategy, as the federal courts consistently ruled in his favor.

From the first news of Sarah's intent to sue, Sharon had called it blackmail, and he had named William Neilson as the primary culprit.

On October 23, Neilson sued Sharon for slander, asking $120,000 worth in damages. The following day Neilson was attacked by two men on the street near his home. They were in their thirties and wore "respectable" clothing. They beat him badly, blows landing on his chest, abdomen and head, and appeared to be intent on beating him to death. A couple of young boys nearby yelled for the police and the two thugs ran off before they had finished their business. The attackers were not identified or caught, and there was no evidence to link them to Senator Sharon. Following this incident, Sarah hired a bodyguard for Neilson.

If William Sharon was behind the attack, an unmistakable message was being sent: tangle with me at your peril.

Despite the initial public perception that Sarah Althea Hill and her handler, William Neilson, were just a couple of shysters off the street looking for an easy payday, information began to emerge that Sharon and Miss Hill actually had a relationship of some kind. The story was not completely trumped up after all. William Sharon even admitted it. In the latter months of 1880 and through most of 1881, they had been lovers, but, he asserted, Miss Hill was his paid mistress and that was all. He had never proposed marriage, he had never signed a marriage contract; he had never even hinted at the possibility of marriage. It had been a business arrangement, pure and simple.

Simple? Nothing was simple with Sarah Althea Hill.

In early hearings, court officials faced a considerable amount of difficulty getting hold of the main piece of documentary evidence, the marriage contract. At first, they asked George Tyler for it. He tried but failed, throwing up his hands, and brought Sarah to face the judge. He gave her an ultimatum: turn over the paper or it will be excluded from being considered in the case. She turned it over.

While Sharon vs. Sharon was gearing up, William Sharon surprised Sarah with another legal action, charging her and Neilson with forgery and conspiracy. This case came up before the divorce case, so was the first chance for the public to observe Sarah Althea in court. She was ordered to appear before the Grand Jury on November 9, 1883 at 2 p.m., and to bring the marriage contract with her. That piece of paper had been locked in a safe in the courthouse where the other trial was to take place. At 1:45 p.m. on November 9, Sarah was at the courthouse waiting for the document. Unfortunately, the judge and court clerk were unable to open the safe. Sarah became frantic.

"Then commenced a most disagreeable and unnecessary scene. Miss Hill wept profusely, and between her frequent sobs exclaimed that it was a villainous conspiracy to send her to the State Prison. That she had been subpoenaed to produce that document before the Grand Jury at 2 p.m. and would be sent to jail if she did not do so. It was just what she had expected."[109]

It isn't the least surprising that Sarah assumed there was foul play. She never expected to get fair treatment from a world in which money made the rules.

A locksmith was called and he opened the safe. When the judge tried to give the paper to George Tyler, Sarah screamed out her objection and demanded that it be given to her instead.

After this incident, she wouldn't let the document out of her sight, and, surprisingly, the court allowed her to keep it. She took it home with her and slept with it under her pillow. The handwriting experts had to examine photocopies or they could look at the original only in the courtroom when court was in session, a considerably odd and laborious constraint.

Sarah's state of mind was well illustrated in a letter she wrote to William Neilson shortly before the Grand Jury indictment. It showed a woman who was depressed and distraught, who felt abandoned by everyone and who clearly regretted having set the gears in motion.

> I have not closed my eyes this night—2:30 o'clock—but who is there to care for my troubles? Are you going to let that Grand Jury indict me? No, no; surely you will not. You have brought me into this fight making me believe you would let no harm come to me, and here I am about to be arrested as a criminal. Great God! who would have ever thought I could have ever been brought into so much trouble? I have offered you more than you wanted. I have, against my will, accepted your lawyer....I have a world of scandal, and am to appear before the Grand Jury for a horrible crime. I do not deserve this; it is terrible; it is outrageous, and you should not let Mr. Sharon rest one night in his bed while he carries on this way. Oh, God! if I could only have died before this all came. Nobody comforts me or has one kind word. It's a struggle with the world, and I don't deserve it. I never wronged man or woman in all my life.[110]

To her great relief, the Grand Jury charges of forgery and conspiracy against Sarah were dropped on March 22, 1884. She had beaten the first of Sharon's retaliatory actions.

Neilson was also cleared. He stood by her, trying to guide her case, but it was a thankless job. Her behavior and temperament were so difficult that he often thought about taking himself off the case. He described her as defiant, unreasonable, uncontrollable and violent. He begged her, in conversation and in writing, to behave better and be cooperative with her counsel, and to avoid giving any ammunition to the press. When she complained of a negative portrayal in the papers, he wrote her a letter telling her it was her own fault.

> I am heartsick and sorry that the great triumph which in the end awaits us should be marred by the reflection that during the whole course of the fight, your conduct, instead of being encouraging and helpful, has been disheartening and even paralyzing to us all. If the fight is won, as I am sure it will be, no part of the credit will attach to you, unless you at once change your course. If it is lost, and I will not believe that it can be, the fault will be entirely your own. If you would give as much time and thought to quietly assisting us as you do to destroying our every effort, you would not only win in the end, but meanwhile retain your present friends, add to them every day, feel more happy in yourself, and go through a great trial in a manner that would extort from all sides the eulogium that you had proven yourself "a lady." [111]

Whether his rebuke made an impression or not, Sarah did not seem capable of controlling herself or reining in her emotions. She must have been exhausting to be around.

Toward the end of 1883, Sarah was desperately trying to line up witnesses to shore up her case. Among these was John R. Reigart of Wisconsin. He and his wife were originally quite friendly to Sarah, and they could have been excellent and credible witnesses for her. Based on what they had seen, they believed Sarah and the senator were a legitimate couple headed toward marriage. Sarah's attempted manipulation of the Reigarts is a good example of how she typically injured her own cause.

You may recall that Sarah met the Reigarts in 1881 at Belmont and became fast friends. Once the Reigarts went back to Wisconsin, there was a steady and warm correspondence between them and Sarah. In 1883, she wrote them several letters to describe how Sharon was reneging on his promise to marry her, how his horrid relatives had turned him against her, and how he had been abusive toward her. "You will have to encounter a great deal of false swearing," Reigart cautioned in a letter to Sarah, "for Sharon's dollars will buy anything, but I think you will be fully vindicated."[112] At the time of the letter, he believed everything she had told him about her relationship with Sharon, as is clear in all of his letters, such as this excerpt from May 29, 1883:

"Dear Miss Hill: Mrs. R. received your letter yesterday, and now you will have to take a few words from the head of the family....You do not want to give up the Senator at all. Stick to him and let the family howl. Your time will come. Punch him a trifle so that you can get that big house you speak of. We will come to see you for a fact. I only wish I had charge of him and his affairs. I would run the entire machine in your interest. The simple truth is that you ought to marry the genial Senator, that his days may be long. He would be a real solid comfort to you. Fast and no mistake. Name the day and we will telegraph our blessing."[113]

Other such letters were written in the same vein, encouraging Sarah to do what needed to be done to secure her proper place as Mrs. Sharon. There was nothing against the senator in this sentiment, as Reigart obviously believed Sharon would be better off married to Sarah, and the main impediment was his relatives, whose interests were driven by greed.

After the news of the secret marriage became public, the Reigarts still believed Sarah and hoped the situation would turn out well for her. In a letter dated September 22, she wrote them as "Mrs. William Sharon," saying, "You all ought to be here to take part in the fun, if it goes to Court; but I don't think he will ever dare to face me in a court-room. I wish I could tell you the people who have been to see me. They always said I was the loveliest girl in this city."[114]

Sarah must truly have been delighted with all the attention she received after the news broke. People were beating a path to her door to ask her all about it. "I have many, many friends now," she continued, "that I never knew or counted friends, but some of the best ladies of this city have come to tell me if Mr. Sharon should with his money defeat me, they will never again think ill of me, and I will be as welcome to their house and table as I was before."[115]

There is reason to doubt the claim of so many new friends when at the same time she wrote to Neilson, "Here I am, working like a slave, fretted to death for fear they will get Nellie from me....The last of the week I must give up this house. I have no friends."[116]

On September 25, Sarah again wrote the Reigarts, paving the way for the help she would ask of them. "You all have, and always will have, my heart and best love. When I first met you, I was already then most a year Mrs. Sharon. I was dying myself to confess all to you, but under a promise I could not. Mr. Sharon said enough to Mrs. Reigart on the day we went to the race-course with him for a shooting, to fully give her to understand that I was his wife, and I fully appreciate her delicacy in not further questioning my relations to him."[117] Sarah was attempting a ploy she had tried before, to plant a false memory or at least create some doubt in a person's mind about what had really happened.

She wrote again, making subtle inroads toward gaining the Reigarts as her witnesses: "I love the man—I worship him; but I will not allow my love to longer stay my hands in upholding my honor and virtue. Newlands and the others are trying hard to make great mountains out of that Burchard affair....I say God bless the man or woman who will stand in and help defend a woman's good name and honor. This matter has been trying to be negotiated quietly for three months, so we had nothing else to do but to give it to the public to decide. You all have no idea how cruelly I have suffered at this man's hands. It simply beggars description. I may telegraph you to come here; I have confidence in you."[118]

Sarah realized that her romance with Fred Burchard, witnessed by the Reigarts, would be a problem. She was no doubt hoping to persuade them to testify that the Burchard affair was nothing at all and was being blown out of proportion by the Sharon people.

"You may command this family at any time and under all circumstances," Reigart replied. "You were always kind to us; we will show you, if you give us a chance, that it was not misplaced."[119]

With all the supportive and encouraging letters of friendship passing back and forth between Sarah and the Reigarts, she must have been certain of their support in her suit. But the day came when the Reigarts, like almost everybody else, realized they were being used by this duplicitous woman.

The first hint came when Reigart read something about himself in the newspaper on October 2. Because Sarah had told him Neilson was handling her case, he wrote to Neilson. "My Dear Sir: A telegram published in the Chicago papers of yesterday in regard to the Sharon matter, says that Senator Sharon told me at the marriage of his daughter at Belmont that he had been secretly married to Miss Hill....I judged from his marked attentions to the lady that he contemplated marriage, but as to ever hinting to me that he was married, it is all a mistake. My name is evidently wrongly mixed up in the matter, and whilst I am exceedingly friendly to the lady, I would be doing you, as her attorney, a great wrong if I did not at once deny the report as to this evidence."[120]

Sarah now became bolder in her suggestions regarding the testimony she hoped the Reigarts would provide. "If I remember well," she wrote them, "Mrs. Reigart joked Mr. Sharon that day when we were going out to the Park in his carriage, the day we got out at the race track, and tried to shoot at a mark. She joked him about my buying so many shoes, and then said something about she heard we were secretly married, and he turned to her and said, 'Let me introduce you to Mrs. Sharon; is she not pretty enough?'…if she remembers it, it is great evidence."[121] Of course, Mrs. Reigart did not remember it.

When Reigart returned to San Francisco in November, he visited Sarah and examined the marriage contract. She asked him to go to Sharon on her account, perhaps making a last ditch effort to bring about an out of court settlement. Still believing that Sarah had been somehow wronged, Reigart did as she asked. He sat down with the senator and, for the first time, heard the other side of the story.

We have often heard the saying that a lie may sound like the truth until one hears the truth. Then the lie becomes immediately obvious for what it is. That is what happened to John Reigart when he arrived as a friend to both parties to try to smooth relations between them. Once he heard what Sharon had to say, his eyes were opened.

During the trial, Reigart appeared for the defense, relating what transpired during his last visit with Sarah. "She said she would give me anything in the world to testify on this stand that Senator Sharon had introduced her to me as his wife. I told her I was on record as an honest man, and could not do it. She repeated this proposition several times, and our friendly relations ceased from that time."[122]

In all such cases, Sarah would have been better off making no attempt to buy herself witnesses, as these people backfired on her one by one.

Sharon, on the other hand, was inheriting all of Sarah's witnesses for himself, due either to their integrity or their love of money. All of the fortune tellers and astrologers she had consulted were prepared to testify for him. Several of Sarah's one-time friends, such as Susan Smith, Mary Shawhan, Fanny Sampson, Sarah Millett, and Nellie Bacon would appear against her. Her erstwhile boyfriend, Fred Burchard, cropped up to make a deposition, describing the Belmont weekend where he had become unofficially engaged to her. Referring to their break-up and subsequent estrangement, he said, "She did not claim that I forced my attentions upon her when I had money, but she did when I had no money."[123] Sarah initiated criminal charges against him for perjury the next day, saying that she had never been engaged to him and he had been paid $5,000 for his lies. He was arrested, and a few days later, the charges were dismissed.

As the two parties lined up witnesses and evidence, William Sharon was supremely confident of his position. He was only marginally concerned about the divorce case and expected it to blow over without difficulty. In the following description of him in the *Daily Alta California* prior to the trial, there is a hint of irony near the end:

At one o'clock yesterday afternoon a well-groomed span of horses, attached to a handsome landau, dashed down Pine street and halted in front of the office of Judge G. W. Tyler, on the corner of Liedesdorff street. A small, elderly man, clothed in a polished silk hat, a broadcloth suit, and a self-satisfied smile emerged from its depths, and on reaching the sidewalk was recognized as William Sharon, ex-Senator from Nevada, millionaire from California, proprietor of the Palace Hotel, father-in-law of one of the English nobility, and alleged husband of Miss Sarah Althea Hill, by virtue of a civil marriage contract.[124]

Her lawyers, meanwhile, were following up on all the information she had given them, questioning witnesses and preparing their arguments. What they were discovering was causing them a great deal of anxiety.

The more Judge Tyler learned, the more misgivings he had about the case. He told William Neilson that he had been offered $150,000 to quit it and he had considered taking it. "That woman is treacherous to us," he said, "and we shall never know where we shall land. There is no truth in her, and there is more falsehood about her case than you know anything about....I have attempted to verify her statements, and they are all false."[125]

And yet they pushed onward. In January, depositions were taken in Tyler's office. In March, 1884, the trial began, and on the second day the Tylers called in another attorney to join their team, a man highly skilled in divorce law: the renowned David Smith Terry.

15. THE WHITE KNIGHT

David Smith Terry was a respected and able lawyer with a successful, well-established practice. George W. Tyler had known him for over twenty years, their association going back to Terry's home base, the Central Valley city of Stockton, where Tyler came in 1860 to practice law. When Terry joined the plaintiff's team, he was sixty-one years old. Before the trial, he was unacquainted with Sarah Althea, who was then thirty-three.

The following description of Terry was written by Colonel Joseph D. Lynch of the Los Angeles *Herald,* November 9, 1904:

> Judge Terry, like his friend Gwin, was a man of prodigious stature, although, unlike his chief, he was rawboned and rough looking. There was nothing out of the way in his dress with the exception that he wore an enormous slouch hat; and if you were asked, "What do you think of him?" you would probably have replied; "Why, this must be the veritable God of War himself." I had been all over the United States, had had a good deal of the experience of a reporter, and I thought in those early days of July, 1872, and I think now, with my added experience, that this ex-chief justice of the state of California was the fiercest looking man I ever saw. It would not have surprised me a whit to see him reach behind his neck and draw out a knife three feet long and proceed to carving somebody. His height was probably about six feet four or five inches, and the impression he made on you was that he was as big as all outdoors. Not Sam Houston, Davy Crockett or Daniel Boone had anything like the frontiersman look of ferocity, in all likelihood, as this man.

The life of David Terry is a fascinating tale that parallels the history of California from its statehood to the end of the 19th century. He did not just live through history; he made it. Details of his long, storied career will be found in any account of California history, and many resources exist to explore his life further. His contribution to California politics and law, for instance, is extensive, but is outside the sphere of our story.

David Smith Terry (Courtesy of the Bancroft Library)

David Terry was born in 1823 in Kentucky of Scotch-Irish descent. His mother, after separating from his father, moved to Texas when he was a teenager. They settled in the area that was to become Houston to be with Terry's maternal grandmother, the redoubtable Obedience Fort Smith, a tough pioneer woman who was a colorful character herself. Terry was a Texas Ranger in his youth, exhibiting courage and fearlessness in the frontier battles of the pioneer days. He dropped out of school at thirteen and later studied law and was admitted to the bar in Houston.

When news of gold in California blazed across the country, Terry led a party of Texans overland in 1849, skirmishing with Indians along the way. Like nearly everybody else coming to California at that time, he tried his hand at mining, then gave it up and opened a law practice in Stockton with fellow Texan, Duncan W. Perley.

Stockton was then one of the most important Northern California cities both politically and geographically, and Terry soon became one of its foremost citizens. Political from an early age, he ran for mayor in 1850, but was defeated. He married Cornelia Runnels, an old sweetheart from Texas, in 1852. She was from the distinguished Runnels family for which Runnels County, Texas is named.

In one of Terry's earliest cases, court was held in a corner of a saloon, as no courthouse had yet been built. "The Judge, stern and dignified, sat in his arm-chair, elevated on a dry goods box. No decision could be made, and finally some one suggested a division of the money. 'I want my fee out of this,' said counselor Terry. 'And I shall have my fee,' said lawyer Perley, putting his hand behind him as if to draw a weapon. In an instant fifty hands went down for pistols and knives."[126]

During another trial in the old days, Terry reportedly set his revolver upon the table and demanded that the jury acquit his client.

This was the character of California law when Terry's career began. The day would come when he would be called a relic of the past who could not adapt to the modern, civilized world.

The Terrys had five sons: Samuel, David, Clinton, Jefferson and Frank. Jefferson and Frank died in infancy. In 1873, son Dave, seventeen, accidentally and fatally shot himself while cleaning his pistol. In 1882, son Sam, who was a successful attorney, became a state assemblyman. He died in 1885 at the age of thirty, leaving only one surviving son, Clinton.

David Terry became a California Supreme Court judge in 1855. In 1856, he rose to the post of Chief Justice. He gained a reputation as an honest judge during a time when corruption at all levels of the legal profession was widespread, and true justice was rare in the West.

While holding that high office, one of his most notorious deeds occurred. Operating under orders from the governor, he attempted to organize a militia to forcibly disband San Francisco's Vigilance Committee, a vigilante group that had sprung up to combat a fierce crime wave. The Committee had tried and hung two men, and had stolen a shipment of arms intended for the militia. During a skirmish with Committee members on the street, Terry stabbed Sterling A. Hopkins in the neck with his Bowie knife. He was taken into custody and secluded in Fort Vigilance on Sacramento Street, the makeshift headquarters of the Vigilance Committee, nicknamed Fort Gunnybags because of the sandbag reinforcements.

Terry was held there several weeks. If Hopkins had died from his wounds, Terry would surely have been hung by the Committee. Instead, he was tried, during which powerful men came to his aid, threatening military action against Fort Gunnybags, and Terry was freed.

Judge Terry's escape from vigilante justice was cause for celebration in the towns that knew and loved him, namely Sacramento where he sat on the bench and Stockton where he had his permanent residence. After the ordeal, he sailed up the river to Sacramento where he was given a silver-plated tea service. The water pitcher was inscribed: "Honorable David S. Terry, from the ladies of San Francisco who admire his courage, honor, his patriotism, and take the highest pride in his heroic resistance to tyranny."[127] This service was donated to the de Young Museum, San Francisco, by David Terry's granddaughter, Cornelia Terry McClure, in 1920.[128]

Terry then traveled home to Stockton on August 17 to a hero's welcome, hailed for his bravery in imperiling his life to uphold law and order.

> About five o'clock a deputation went from the city in carriages and on horseback, accompanied by the band, to meet their fellow citizen. The procession entered the city, Judge Terry occupying a carriage with Judge C. M. Creanor. As they were passing through the streets the cannon thundered forth its welcome, and the St. Charles, Weber House, New York Hotel, and Court House were illuminated.

> When they reached the Weber House Judge Terry was welcomed back to Stockton by A. C. Baine in a speech delivered from the balcony of the hotel. They then returned to the parlors and received the congratulations of friends.[129]

After the mayor's speech, Terry spoke to a cheering crowd, then fireworks were shot off and the band played *Home Again*.

Terry's other famous scrape with death earned him the nickname "Terry the Terrible," and although it was as renowned as his Vigilance Committee ordeal, the aftermath was almost completely the opposite. In the 1859 California elections, Terry gave a speech denouncing the followers of Senator David C. Broderick. The main schism between these former friends was over slavery. Terry wanted to bring slavery to California. Broderick was strongly anti-slavery. He took offense at Terry's remark and responded with his own insult, saying that he had previously considered Terry the only honest man on the bench, but now he took it all back.

The end result of the disagreement was that Terry challenged Broderick to a duel and he accepted. Dueling was technically against the law, so Terry understood that the cost of dueling was his position on the Supreme Court. He did not make this decision rashly or in haste. It was well considered, but David Terry took insults seriously. Before facing Broderick, he resigned his position.

On September 13, 1859, the Broderick-Terry duel took place near present-day Daly City at the southern end of Lake Merced. A crowd of onlookers flocked to the location. One man present, who wrote a detailed account of the event, counted seventy-one men. That same observer described the two men as they neared the moment of truth.

"Mr. Terry's lips were compressed, his countenance darkly sallow, and his whole appearance betrayed that of a man without fear, as well as without religious constraint. Wan and attenuated, he stood a solid monument on the field of strife. Mr. Broderick...held earnest conversation with Mr. Haskell....The muscles of his face were strong, and his visage unrelaxed in every particular. His lips, when not conversing, were compressed, and his whole bearing was that of a man who was about to meet a great issue, and who was firmly prepared for it."[130]

The two men took their places. The pistols used were provided by Terry's camp. The triggers on these pistols were "set on so fine a hair that no man unused to firing with them could use them."[131]

"When Mr. Colton asked: 'Gentlemen, are you ready?' Mr. Terry instantly replied, 'Ready.' without moving or relaxing a muscle. Mr. Broderick, however, spent several seconds in examining the stock of his pistol, which did not seem to fit his hand."

When the call was made to fire, "Mr. Broderick's pistol went off when he had only raised it at a very slight angle and the ball struck the ground about five feet in front of him.

Terry did not raise his pistol, but brought it down from the shoulder and fired within the time.

David Broderick (Courtesy of the Library of Congress)

The ball entered Broderick's breast just below the right shoulder. There was a moment's pause. All eyes were fixed at the Senator. He turned slowly round, then gradually sank until he was caught just as he reached the ground."[132]

The wounded senator was taken to the home of Leonidas Haskell at Black Point, San Francisco, where he died of his wounds after three days.

This duel stands as second in infamy only to the Aaron Burr, Alexander Hamilton duel of 1804 in Weehawken, New Jersey. By this time, public sentiment had turned against dueling as barbaric. Terry was widely regarded as a murderer. Newspaper editorials called for him to be hanged. "The circumstances attending the duel conspired to give Terry more condemnation, and Broderick more sympathy and exculpation, than either deserved," wrote Edwin G. Waite, a clear-headed contemporary of Terry's.[133]

With the atmosphere so hot in California, Terry fled to Nevada to practice law in the mining districts of the Comstock Lode. When his murder trial came up in the summer of 1860, the judge, Jim Hardy, a close friend of Terry's, saw to it that he was acquitted. The deed was described in a political flyer from the time: "The clock in the courtroom was put forward. The court… opened long before its time in the morning. The jury were hastily empanelled. At that time, communication with San Francisco was by sail boat. The boat containing the witnesses was in sight and hurrying over. But the judge refused a continuance until they could arrive, ordered the jury to return a verdict of acquittal, in the absence of any proof, which was done, and Terry went forth free." The arrest and trial of duelists was largely a formality at that time. They were almost always acquitted.

Though cleared by the courts, Terry's reputation was irrevocably damaged. Whatever ambitions he had for a political career had died with Senator Broderick.

Terry left California a few years after the duel to join the Confederate Army and lead a brigade of Texans in the Civil War. After the defeat of the South, he went to Mexico for a time, too bitter over the war to remain in the U. S. When he finally did come back, he settled again in Stockton and resumed his law practice.

Despite his early scuffles with violence, Judge Terry's career since then had been above reproach. He had managed to keep himself out of trouble for twenty-five years…and then he met Sarah Althea Hill.

16. SHARON VS. SHARON

On March 10, 1884, the story of the private affair began to be told in a public forum and the world became privy to the details of one of the most delicious scandals of the Gilded Age. The case played out before the public in the way only the most sensational stories can. Day by day, the titillating particulars appeared in newspapers near and far. Battles over who was right were fought outside the courtroom in lecture halls, on street corners, and at family dinner tables. And the plaintiff, Sarah Althea Hill, became a huge celebrity overnight.

The case got underway before the young and relatively inexperienced Judge Jeremiah F. Sullivan in the San Francisco Superior Court. Sarah's retinue included her lawyers, George W. Tyler, his son William Tyler, Walter H. Levy, David Terry and Colonel Flournoy, as well as William Neilson, cousin Frank Rodney, Nellie Brackett, and Mary Ellen Pleasant, who always sat directly behind Sarah and frequently whispered in her ear. On the other side, William Sharon was flanked by his numerous lawyers led by General Barnes and Oliver P. Evans.

The case hinged on the proof that a marriage existed, calling in the legal principle of "marriage by contract." Sarah had to show that there had been an assumption of marriage, at least by herself. She didn't have to prove that William Sharon believed they were married. His signing of the contract was easily explained by casting him in the role of lecherous old man preying on a trusting young woman. He had tricked her into sex, the story went, with a hastily-written pseudo legal document.

The evidence brought to prove the existence of a marriage was threefold: the marriage contract (by now heavily soiled and deeply creased from folding), several notes written by William Sharon to Sarah, addressed "Dear Wife," and the testimony of witnesses who had seen and heard behavior between the two that exhibited their status as husband and wife.

The Marriage Contract

The text of the marriage contract, plaintiff's Exhibit No. 1, is included here again as a reminder:

> In the City and County of San Francisco, State of California, on the 25th day of August, A.D. 1880, I, Sarah Althea Hill, of the city and county of San Francisco, State of California, aged 27 years, do here, in the presence of Almighty God, take Senator William Sharon of the state of Nevada to be my lawful and wedded husband, and do here acknowledge and declare myself to be the wife of Senator William Sharon of the State of Nevada.
> SARAH ALTHEA HILL.
> August 25, 1880, San Francisco, Cal.
> I agree not to make known the contents of this paper or its existence for two years, unless Mr. Sharon himself sees fit to make it known.
> S. A. HILL.

> In the city and county of San Francisco, State of California, on the 25th day of August, A.D. 1880, I, Senator William Sharon, of the State of Nevada, age 60 years, do here in the presence of Almighty God take Sarah Althea Hill of the city of San Francisco, Cal., to be my lawful and wedded wife, and do here acknowledge myself to be the husband of Sarah Althea Hill.
> WILLIAM SHARON, Nevada, August 25, 1880.

Like the Sharon camp, we have already speculated that the contract was created in the spring of 1883 by Sarah Althea and/or Mary Ellen Pleasant for blackmailing purposes. To disprove that suspicion, the prosecution brought witnesses to say that they had seen the contract prior to 1883.

On the first day of the trail, after opening arguments, the first two witnesses called were the seamstress and friend of Mary Ellen, Martha Wilson, and her friend, the dressmaker Vesta Snow. Martha Wilson said that in October, 1880, Sarah visited her house and asked her to go with her to a furniture store to pick out furniture for her rooms at the Grand Hotel, furniture that William Sharon would pay for. Wilson thought the situation was improper, so Sarah showed her the marriage contract to set her mind at ease. Wilson couldn't read, but Vesta Snow happened to come by and read it to her. The next witness called was Snow and she corroborated Mrs. Wilson's testimony, saying she had indeed seen the contract in 1880 and read it aloud to her friend.

Later, under cross-examination, Martha Wilson admitted that she had perjured herself. The truth was, she had never seen the contract until recently. Vesta Snow, she said, was part of the same deception. Sarah had made the story up and coached them on what to say in court.

Photocopy of the Marriage Contract

Wilson's new story was that Sarah showed Martha and her husband the marriage contract about the time Senator Sharon was arrested, as she was preparing her case. She asked the Wilsons to say that they had seen the contract much earlier, in 1880, and offered the couple $5,000 to testify to that effect. She told them she had had the contract since 1880 and simply needed someone to verify that fact. Mrs. Wilson believed she was telling the truth, so she agreed to testify, moved by the large sum of money being offered. Her husband, however, changed his mind and backed out, whereupon Vesta Snow was procured to replace him.

Nellie Brackett, dubbed "Lieutenant Brackett" by General Barnes, was next to testify for Sarah. She was still living with Sarah as the trial commenced and was not allowed to visit her parents without being accompanied by an attorney and was not allowed to be alone with them when she did visit. She was considered a critical witness to the case and the Tylers were determined to keep her from being influenced by anybody but Sarah and themselves. Nellie's mother attempted to bring her home and away from Sarah's control, but Judge Tyler, in court, said, "This girl shall not go home; she is an important witness for me, and I cannot lose sight of her."[134] And so she remained with Sarah, carefully protected from being persuaded to tell the truth.

When Nellie came to the stand, she was described as "a very voluble young woman, and before she had talked two minutes the shorthand reporter laid down his pencil in despair and appealed to the Court for protection."[135] An acquaintance, Mrs. Stanyan, testified that Nellie had told her "she would rattle out her evidence so fast that the Court could not understand her."[136] That was apparently her not very effective strategy for avoiding a charge of perjury, for nearly everything Nellie said was a lie or a distortion.

Nellie described how she met Sarah in the spring of 1882 and told her she couldn't associate with her because she had heard she was Mr. Sharon's mistress. In her defense, Sarah had shown her the marriage contract, after which they became the dearest of friends. She later changed her story and said she saw the contract for the first time in April, 1883 just after the humiliating birthday incident at the Palace Hotel and Nellie's scathing "Old Sharon" letter. This date coincides with the time Mary Ellen and Sarah sequestered themselves in several secret meetings.

Mary Ellen Pleasant was called to the stand and added some credence to the existence of the contract when she described the visit she paid William Sharon after his arrest for adultery. He wanted nothing to do with Allie Hill, he said. He called her a "bad and dangerous" woman. She had stolen money from his pockets and important papers from his desk, and had never been true to him since the contract was signed. He could bring a dozen men to swear that she had not been true to him. The way Mary Ellen slipped in "since the contract was signed" made it seem as if that tidbit wasn't the main point of this testimony. She was indeed a clever one.

Sarah said she showed the contract to her Uncle Sloan in December, 1881, to allay his fears that her association with Senator Sharon was illicit. But Sloan never testified one way or the other.

General Barnes attempted to show how weak Sarah's case was by discrediting those around her. She had reputable men in her sphere, such as her brother Morgan, her uncles Bryan and Sloan, and yet none of them were standing with her in this suit. That threw a great deal of suspicion on the validity of her claim. Not only that, Barnes claimed, but those who did stand with her were of questionable moral principles. "If Miss Hill had had the slightest idea that she had a valid claim against William Sharon, William M. Neilson would have been the last man on earth to whom she would have applied. He was as well-known in this community probably as any other disreputable person in it. He had been here a number of years. His standing was bad and known to be bad, justly or unjustly. There was about him a bad moral atmosphere, just as there is about his physical appearance."[137]

The total absence of her family members during the many trials was never addressed by Sarah herself. Their silence was considered by most to be proof that her claims were false.

Nellie Brackett was present when Sarah's grandmother was first told Sarah was secretly married to William Sharon. "Her grandmother seemed delighted to think that she was Mrs. Sharon. She did not promise to stand by her in so many words, but gave her to understand she would. She came there again and said her daughter Ada [Bryan] did not want her to be mixed up in the matter…so there was not any one of her family that would stand by her."[138]

The first person to see the contract whose word might be trusted, despite General Barnes' characterization of him, was William Neilson. He said Sarah showed it to him in August, 1883. "I asked to see it several times," he said, "before she finally showed it to me, when she was so afraid I would make away with it that Mr. Rodney stood by my side, armed, as I have since learned, to prevent my running away with it as she held it up to the light."[139]

Other reputable businessmen said they saw it in September, 1883. Since Sarah never was one to keep confidences, especially when spilling the beans would help her, it seems likely that the paper did not exist before about April of 1883. Sarah said she showed it to many people. She told Mr. Reigart she had shown it to 30 or 40 people over the years! Yet she bribed and coerced her few witnesses to swear they had seen it in 1880 or 1881, and all of them were lying.

Over the weeks that the case was being heard, the document came under intense analysis by several handwriting experts. Henry C. Hyde was the primary expert for Sharon's side. Max Gumpel was the expert for the plaintiff. Originally, Barnes had hired Gumpel for his side, but they disagreed about his fee and also his opinion that the document was genuine, so he was dismissed and went over to the other side.

The Sharon experts made the following points:

1. The handwriting on the contract was smaller than Sarah's normal writing, and the writing toward the end was even more condensed than the rest, with words omitted, suggesting she tried to crowd in the text above Sharon's pre-existing signature.

2. Different colored inks were used in the original text and in the many changes. At least three different inks were identified and, according to Sharon's secretary Dobinson, only one of these was used in Sharon's office where the document was allegedly dictated.

3. The paper was folded in many places; some of the writing had been done before the paper was folded and some after. Notably, Sharon's signature was judged to have been written prior to the folding, suggesting it was written before some of the other text.

4. Sharon's attorneys also made several compelling points about the wording of the contract, how it only vaguely resembled something a professional man of law would dictate. General Barnes remarked that it was beneath the learning and skill of a "jack-legged lawyer."[140]

Among those who believed the signature was genuine was Charles D. Cushman, a cashier, accountant and long-time employee of Sharon's who had seen his signature hundreds of times.

William Sharon's signature was not inconclusively proven to be a forgery. The defense proposed that among the many papers Sarah had stolen from his rooms, she had obtained one with his signature that allowed her to tear the piece of paper in half, removing whatever else was there, and write the marriage contract over the existing signature. That line of reasoning fit with the crowded and condensed nature of the writing.

The "Dear Wife" Letters

The "Dear Wife" letters were five short notes written by William Sharon in 1881 that began "My Dear Wife."

1. The first of these was one Sharon wrote in answer to Sarah's complaint that she was being treated rudely at the Grand Hotel. This was written during the Senatorial race that Sharon ultimately lost.

"My Dear Wife: In reply to your kind letter, I have written Mr. Thorn and enclosed the same to you, which you can read and then send it to him in an envelope, and he will not know that you have seen it. Sorry that anything should occur to annoy you, and think this letter will command the kind courtesy you deserve. Am having a very lively and hard fight, but I think I shall be victorious in the end. With kindest considerations and so forth, I am yours as ever, Wm. Sharon."[141]

2. Undated: "My Dear Wife—Enclosed I send you by Ki the balance, $250, which I hope will make you very happy. Will call this evening for the joke. Yours, S."

3. May 5, 1881: "My Dear Wife— You had $120; then $20; and before I left, $100— In all, $240. The balance is just $260, for which find cash enclosed. I am afraid you are getting very extravagant."

4. August 29, 1881: "My Dear Wife—Enclosed find $210 to buy bell-wire and sofa. W. S."

5. October 3, 1881: "My Dear Wife—Enclosed find $550, which will pay expenses till I get better. Will then talk about your Eastern trip. Am much better today. Hope to be up in three or four days. Yours, S." This note refers to the trip Sarah planned after the ugly incident in Sharon's rooms where he dumped water over her.

"The word 'wife' here is a forgery," Sharon said after seeing the first letter. "The balance of the letter looks like my writing, or a tracing of it, but I positively declare that I never wrote the word 'wife.'"[142]

As observed later by Judge Matthew Deady, one of many judges to rule on the Sharon cases, "The 'Dear Wife' letters have nothing wifely about them, except the word 'wife' in the address."[143]

Of the many notes passed between the Palace Hotel and the Grand Hotel in 1880 and 1881, most of them were addressed to "My Dear Allie" and sometimes "My Dear Miss Hill." A handwriting expert testified that the word "wife" in the Dear Wife letters appeared to have been written over an erasure and that the handwriting of the word "wife" differed from that of the words "My dear." Like the marriage contract itself, Sharon's lawyers contended that all of the "Dear Wife" letters were fraudulent. Other than Sarah herself, there were no witnesses to refute this conclusion.

Wife or Mistress

The third type of evidence the prosecution brought was designed to show that William Sharon treated Sarah Althea differently than his mistresses, in some cases even introducing her as his wife.

Over the course of many years of litigation, it became clear that Sarah had offered money to many people to testify to that fact. We have already seen how she tried it with the Reigarts and failed. Most of her attempts did fail. But she was able to hang on to one of these witnesses.

Harry Wells came to the stand. He said that while he and H. M. True were walking on Sutter St. in the spring of 1881, they met Senator Sharon with Sarah Althea on his arm and Sharon introduced her as "Mrs. Sharon."

H. M. True was supposed to tell the same story, but he was too ill to come to court. A delegation went to Santa Cruz to take his deposition on his death bed. Much to the aggravation of Harry Wells, True did not follow the script. He said he had only met Miss Hill six weeks before and had never been introduced to her by Sharon. "My object is now to tell the truth, and if I am injured by it I must be injured by it. I don't propose now to go to the grave with a lie on my lips. Miss Hill, Wells and myself made up this story and got it into shape, and after it was arranged Judge Tyler was told all about it. The whole statement of Miss Hill, the young man and myself, was a put-up-job, and I think Judge Tyler knew all about it as well as we did. I think so from the conversation that took place in his office, where he told me there would be enough in it to make twenty men rich."[144]

One begins to wonder if there was any evidence at all for the prosecution that was not manufactured.

Sarah told of a Mr. McCartney who had often heard Sharon refer to her as his wife. Unfortunately, Mr. McCartney was dead. "Is there any one who is not dead or in Europe who ever heard you called Mrs. Sharon?"[145] attorney Evans asked in exasperation.

The one other witness alive and in California who testified that Sharon called Sarah his wife was Nellie Brackett. On or about May 31, 1882, she said, Senator Sharon invited Sarah to dinner in his suite. In need of a witness, Sarah snuck Nellie into the bedroom and behind the dresser to listen to the couple's intimate conversation and, of course, their lovemaking. She described what she overheard "without a single blush of maiden modesty, and with many a giggle, which called forth responsive roars of laughter from the spectators....What she had remembered most vividly was that the Senator, between kisses, had said to Althea: 'You are my own dear little wife, and no one knows it but us two.'"[146] In addition, she heard Sharon say, "Baby, if you had kept that document, you would have had the whip hand of the old man."[147]

Sarah couldn't have asked for anything better. In one evening, with a witness listening, Sharon admitted to both the marriage and the marriage contract.

Nellie described the night in detail and with conviction. "I suppose I stayed there till 10 or 11 o'clock. I know it was a very long time. After a little while she got up and turned the slats of the window, so that the Senator, she said, should not sleep too long in the morning. As she crossed the room, she stumbled against the bureau and pretended to hurt her foot, and in doing that she pulled the bureau out a little, so that I could get out. I waited until I heard Sharon breathing heavily, as if he was asleep, and then I crawled out carefully and went out."[148]

This incident, known as the "great bureau act," caused a sensation in court. Sharon's counsel did not shy away from pointing out what a depraved act it was that Sarah had "secreted this vestal virgin, this fresh lily, this unsunned snow, behind a bureau that she might hear and behold the mysteries of the marriage bed. What woman in whose bosom lived a lingering spark of conscience could do it?"[149]

Between the testimony of Frank Rodney, Nellie Brackett and Sarah Althea, they described a reconciliation between the two lovers in the summer of 1882 that included that interesting overnight date. The reconciliation, a total fiction created to support the statements Nellie said she overheard, was buoyed with two letters that Rodney said he delivered into the hands of William Sharon. The first of these was dated a couple of days after the great bureau act.

> My Dear Senator —I send Frank with this note so as to make sure that you get it to-night. I am afraid it will be impossible for us to go to Belmont with you on Saturday; besides, you say you want this business kept quiet for a little while, and you know, my dear "Sen," that your wish is my law. This terrible pressure is killing me. Why do you hesitate to come out and acknowledge my rights and my place by your side! Have I not suffered enough already by it all? Have I not been ignored and snubbed already by the world, by my friends and relations, and yet I have kept my secret. Oh, what a thousand deaths I have suffered in these months of separation! But I suppose I should not recall the past as to our promise now— 'twill only be a short time until you will relieve me of this burden and allow me to take my place by your side and take me forth into the world relieved of this—this terrible odious stigma.
>
> You said the other night that I was your own little wife and only we two knew it. How glad I was to hear you again tell me that! It has rung in my ears and in my heart ever since. You know, Sen, I love you. If I had not loved you, how could I have borne all I have in silence and patience. All I could do was to pray and pray to God for his protection in my trials.
>
> Why do you hesitate to call me to you day and night, and tell the world that all these years I have been your wife? Am I not more to you than Newlands and all the gang? Don't be offended because I write so; but my heart aches so. You know I

love you; you know how I love you. Nell and I have been to look at the houses you spoke of....I don't care much for the house, though it would be better than living in those flats of yours on Polk, but then we will talk about it when I see you. So good-bye.[150]

Sarah wrote the following breezy letter to Sharon, allegedly sent toward the end of summer, known as the "egg in champagne" letter:

My Dear Senator: Won't you try and find out what Springs those were you were trying to think of today, that you said Mr. Main went to, and let me know tomorrow when I see you? And don't I wish you would make up your mind and go down to them with Nellie and I, wherever they be, on Friday or Saturday. We all could have nice times out hunting and walking or driving those lovely days, in the country. The jaunt or little recreation would do you worlds of good, and us girls would take the best of care of you, and mind you in everything.... I am crazy to see Nell try and swallow an egg in champagne. I have not told her of the feat I accomplished in that line, but I am just waiting in hopes of seeing her some day go through the performance. As I told you today, I am out to Nellie's mother's for a few days. 824 Ellis Street. What a lovely evening this is, and how I wish you would surprise us two little lone birds by coming out and taking us for a moonlight drive....'Twould do you good to get out of that stupid old hotel for a little while, and we'd do our best to make you forget all your business cares and go home feeling happy. A.[151]

General Barnes was quick to brand this letter an indecent proposal. Since Sarah Althea was having no luck enticing the senator on her own, Barnes declared with outrage, she was making him a two for one offer, holding up her fresh young friend as bait. That was not the case at all, of course, because the letter was manufactured later and never seen by William Sharon, nor was it ever intended to be seen by him, but the Barnes' spin made for good copy anyway.

William Sharon swore that he did not receive either of the letters; they were never sent. All talk of a reunion was a pack of lies. He never saw Sarah in 1882 except in his office to pay her the money they had agreed on and the one time by chance on the street when she mentioned her "interesting condition." And she had certainly never been in his bed after her eviction from the Grand Hotel.

While Nellie Brackett was on the stand, she was asked if her parents objected to her testifying in the case. Tears came to her eyes as she answered. "My father and mother came to me and said, 'We have always had a good and pure name, and it is a shame for you to bring scandal on it.'"[152] They told her that if she would leave Miss Hill, they would send her on a trip to the East Coast.

The rest of the evidence showing that Sarah was Sharon's wife relied on perceptions, what others observed of his behavior toward her.

William Sharon's public behavior with Sarah was the most persuasive argument presented that she was more to him than a mistress. As Colonel Flournoy said to Sharon's attorney Evans, "You called her his prostitute—did he send his prostitute to his elegant country residence to entertain his friends? No; he would not dare to do it."[153]

Sharon admitted that he had treated Sarah differently than his other mistresses, that she was the only one he had invited to Belmont, the only one she had introduced to friends and family members, the only one whose family he had visited.

John Reigart, though he had not taken Sarah's bribe to lie for her, did support her position when he testified that, based on the way the senator treated Miss Hill, he had assumed they were engaged to be married or at least headed in that direction.

Henry Stagg, who also met Sarah as a guest at Belmont, described the relationship between Sharon and Sarah as affectionate and familiar. He and his wife also assumed there was a courtship or engagement between them, at least until Sarah announced that she had become engaged to Fred Burchard.

Ah, yes, that little detail.

17. THE WITNESS

The main witness called to prove the marriage was Sarah herself. On March 11, she came to the stand for the first time. In anticipation of that, a huge crowd flooded into the courtroom to watch. She came up, according to the *San Francisco Chronicle*, "looking as demure, innocent and sweet as the arts of the toilet could make her." The article gave a full and detailed description of the plaintiff, noting her full lips, Roman nose, quick, gray-blue eyes, nervous expression, and luxurious auburn hair with its curls and ringlets under a bonnet decorated with butterflies. "Judging by her looks," said the piece, "Sarah Althea must be nearing 40 years, though it is asserted she is much younger." She was a couple of weeks shy of thirty-four.

The plaintiff told a few facts about herself, then broke down in a fit of sobbing. "...she would not be comforted, and sobbed and sobbed just ten minutes by the Court-room pneumatic clock before she finally gulped down her great grief, and folding her handkerchief with mathematical accuracy into the space of an inch square, proceeded to tell of her first acquaintance with her 'Dear, dear Sen.'"[154]

Once Sarah's testimony began, the spectacle of the trial blossomed into its full glory. Day after day, the courtroom was packed with the curious, most of whom were there to see and hear Sarah. The newspapers reported her appearance and behavior in great detail. She was the star of the show, no doubt about it.

"Sarah Althea was handsomely attired in black," reported the *Alta* on March 14, "with a beaded horseshoe bonnet surmounting her strangely-tinted locks and a pair of canary-colored kids on her hands. These latter were continually in motion, the right generally resting in Miss Brackett's lap, where it was affectionately caressed by the terra-cotta covered digits of the latter. She was quite calm, and but for a tired look about her eyes would have seemed really pretty."[155]

Sarah was a difficult witness to trip up. She could think on her feet. When it looked like she was headed for a trap, she was able to nimbly talk her way out of it. When Oliver Evans asked her why there was a two-year secrecy clause in the marriage contract, she said the senator wanted to prevent trouble with his reelection, fearing that his Philadelphia mistress might cause a scandal. Evans pointed out that two years was extraordinary if that were the reason, since the election was only a few months away when the contract was signed. He kept pressing this point until Sarah said, without missing a beat, "Mr. Sharon said it would take two years to get rid of the woman and her child; first he wanted three years."[156] The last detail was tacked on to give the statement credibility, which it did. A lot of witnesses stumbled under cross-examination, even when they were telling nothing but the truth, but Sarah was not one of them.

She was likewise able to head off the opposition before they had a chance to contradict her. She said she was Sharon's constant nurse when he was ill in November, 1881. As such, she must have been seen in this generous labor by his doctors. But before the doctors could be put on the stand, she undermined their anticipated testimony. Of course the doctors saw her often at his bedside, she said, but they couldn't support her in court, as much as they believed in her cause. They could not possibly afford to testify against William Sharon. They would be ruined. If anyone asked, they had told her, they would say they never saw her there, never observed her tender devotion to her ailing husband.

A notable scene occurred in court on March 18 when Evans questioned Sarah about charms and potions. She adamantly denied everything he asked about. "Did you ever try to have charms worked on his clothes?" Evans asked. "I never did," Sarah confidently replied, then added, tauntingly, "Look in my face and see if I would do such a thing."[157]

Of course, Sarah was not performing for Sharon's attorneys. She was giving her show for Judge Sullivan, the public audience, and the newspaper reporters.

She denied with equal vehemence every instance of magic, including putting a parcel of Sharon's soiled underwear in the grave of Anson Olin in the Masonic Cemetery. Evans, playing the showman, called for Dr. John L. Meares, who handed over a sealed package, apparently fresh from the exhumed grave. Evans cut it open, releasing a foul odor throughout the room and revealing "a square of black cloth, a dirty bit of white linen, a gentleman's standing collar and a sock."[158]

Everybody in the courtroom strained for a glimpse while those nearest held their handkerchiefs over their noses. Excitement reigned as Evans held up one of the rank items and asked Sarah if she had buried the package in the grave. She heatedly denied it, and said, "If you are attempting to blacken me in the eyes of these people you are making a mistake which you will repent as long as you live."[159] Nobody seemed to notice this threat, but it is worth noting because it fits into a lifelong pattern of threats, a pattern that has a direct connection with one of the worst tragedies of Sarah's life still to come.

The production of the odiferous package fresh from the grave was one of the highlights of the trial. When Sharon first heard about the charm, he had demanded that it be dug up immediately. A party including General Barnes, William Sharon, and Dr. Meares went out to observe the exhumation. The deed was done quickly and callously, hauling old Anson Olin up from his resting place without so much as a bowed head. When Sharon was asked if Olin's family had been notified, he said no, that he didn't even know who was buried there. Poor Olin, disrespected again. But not by everybody. The Masonic Lodge was indignant that Olin was dug up so unceremoniously, and filed suit against Sharon.

General Barnes, when he called Nellie Brackett, said, "We ask your Honor to put this witness on the stand to obtain the facts of this interesting episode of the trial, an episode which in itself is insignificant, but which has produced a large amount of false swearing on one side or the other."[160] That was entirely true. Employees at the graveyard said Sarah and Nellie were there on May 1. Sarah herself swore she was not. Several employees of and visitors to Thomas Bell's household, all of them loyal to Mammy Pleasant, swore that Sarah was at the Bell residence during this macabre event at the graveyard. Cleverly, Mary Ellen herself did not testify to Sarah's presence at the Bell house that day because she was away all day at a May-day picnic. The one and only time Thomas Bell appeared in court during this trial was in connection with this incident. He was there to support his housekeeper, saying that she was indeed away from the house that day. As to Sarah Althea, Bell had not seen her. One of those who said she saw Sarah at the Bell house, Eleanor Weile, would figure into the story again later. Others on the staff of the Bells, like the butler Stepney, swore that Sarah was not there at all that day.

Describing May Day at the Bell mansion, Barnes had some fun with it:

> The chance visitors who came in, one after another, looked in the room and saw her; some had never seen her before, and some have never seen her since; they looked in the dining-room, looked at the clock, saw she was making baby clothing, walked away, made a mental note of the fact, and were prepared to come here on the stand, and swear to the occasion, the actual day and time of the clock; but to the master of the house and to Stepney—the two men of the house, who were about on the floors where she claims to have been—she

was as invisible as though she had worn the invisible cap carried by the prince in the fairy tale. She sat there in the dining-room, and every time Stepney came in up would go the cap and she would disappear. When Stepney went away the cap would come off, and she would appear in all her glory. They all saw her; every time this man came into the room, like the snap of a finger or the waving of the wand of a magician, she got out of the way.[161]

When Sarah's testimony was so at odds with everyone else's, she resorted to an explanation which, if it had not been called upon so often, might have carried some weight. "No doubt you can hire lots of people to come here and swear to all such dirty stuff to get me in the newspapers. Mr. Sharon has plenty of money."[162]

Sarah often seemed more concerned about her public image than anything else. She frequently mentioned how the defense was trying to "blacken" her reputation. In some ways, the entire suit was driven by the disgrace she had suffered as a result of her relationship with William Sharon. Most of what she had done, in fact, was to save or repair her reputation. She had lost her place in society, had plummeted to the bottom, and friends and family wanted nothing to do with her. Her life, in essence, had been destroyed. If Sharon had married her, she would have been vindicated. She went to extraordinary means to get him to marry her. When that failed, she tried one last desperate strategy to save herself: to invent a marriage that had never existed. If she could succeed, she would rise up again to her rightful place in society. She would be respectable again. She would be a lady, envied and admired. From our earliest glimpses into her character, we have seen that she always struggled to be admired, lying about how wealthy she was and how desirable to men. At one point she said, "They always said I was the most beautiful girl in the city." She wanted to be talked about in such terms. But her affair with William Sharon had left her in a position where just the opposite was true, where even the wait staff at the Palace Hotel felt justified in insulting her.

Sarah remained on the stand for several days, denying that she had ever flirted with Fred Sharon or Fred Burchard, denying that she had ever consulted fortune tellers or asked anyone's advice on how to get Sharon to marry her, denying everything, in fact, that would contradict her claim to have been married to him all along.

On the morning of March 24, George Tyler announced that the plaintiff's case was concluded, surprising everyone. He had brought only a few witnesses, far fewer than everyone had been led to expect. Other than the small confederacy at Sarah's side, only one witness had testified that he heard Sharon say she was his wife (Harry Wells), and he admitted he had lied. Two people testified that they had seen the marriage contract before 1883. One of them (Martha Wilson) admitted she had lied and the other stood by her word (Vesta Snow). Though Sharon's lawyers offered Snow money to recant her story, she was afraid to do so because of the danger of being jailed for perjury. It was a valid concern, as her friend Martha Wilson had been charged with perjury when she changed her testimony, and she and Harry Wells were now awaiting trial.

Innumerable witnesses for the defense were still waiting to tell how Sarah had begged them to lie for her for exorbitant sums of money. Clearly, if all of her witnesses were lying, her case was nonexistent.

After many of the perjuries were discovered, the *Los Angeles Herald* printed, "...it would appear that the fates are against Sarah Althea, whatever the merits of her case may be, and if she succeeds it will be almost a miracle, under the circumstances."[163]

18. THE DEFENSE

The day after the prosecution rested, "The Sharon-Hill case opened to almost empty benches, the withdrawal of the female star from the witness stand having acted like a block of ice on the feverish expectation of the public."[164]

It was shortly after the beginning of the defense's case that the judge ordered the courtroom closed to the public, saying the onlookers were getting out of hand. For the time being, those without business in the courtroom had to rely on the press for their daily dose of Sarah Althea.

> The twelfth day of the trial of the *cause celebre* of Hill vs. Sharon, opened yesterday morning to a select audience of the plaintiff, the nine attorneys in the case, Cousin Rodney, Mrs. Pleasance, Judge Sullivan, nine reporters, two clerks, two stenographers, two bailiffs, Captain Bell, Fred Davis, Fred Sharon and Mr. Hyde. Judge Tyler shook the raindrops from his shaggy beard as he entered, and hummed a bit of an Italian barcarole. He was in high glee over something that he had had for breakfast, and his greeting to his client was like a bit of sunshine escaping through the howling storm without. General Barnes was pale, but fearless; Mr. Evans was stern and dignified, and the Court looked tired. Miss Hill appeared smiling, and in another new hat. This time the creation was a tasty little black-beaded bonnet. The remainder of her attire was concealed by her sealskin, so that it was not possible to discover anything new in the fashion line for the benefit of feminine readers.[165]

The defense took up its case and a procession of witnesses came forward to testify that in all of Sarah's conversations with them, she had never claimed to be Sharon's wife. Which merely goes to show, said her counsel, that she kept the secrecy clause in her marriage contract.

All of the fortune-tellers and mediums Sarah had consulted were called to testify against her, including Jennie Wanger, Francis Massey and Laura Scott, whom George Tyler dubbed the "princess of nastiness" for prescribing the most unsavory of voodoo charms.

After the initial interest raised by the practitioners of the occult, the long days of elderly black women describing their dealings with Sarah Althea began to get a bit repetitive and tedious. That is, until Jennie Wanger took the stand and made everybody's eyes pop open. She jettisoned a bomb that landed squarely on Mary Ellen Pleasant and the Bell family. The comments were so shocking that the *San Francisco Call* omitted the names and replaced them with dashes. But the *Chronicle* of April 22, 1884, told it outright. Jennie Wanger was being questioned about Sarah's often discussed plan of getting a baby to pass off on William Sharon. When Wanger was asked how Sarah would get a baby, she replied, "Why, the same as other women...Mrs. Pleasance got the babies for Mrs. Bell, and Mrs. Bell pulled the wool over Tom Bell's eyes."

Mary Ellen was seated in the courtroom at the time, but she made no move to indicate that one of her greatest schemes had just been outed to the world.

Sharon's lawyers pounced on this revelation, anxious to discredit the star witness for the plaintiff, Mary Ellen Pleasant. An exhaustive discussion took place in the courtroom about the ages of the Bell children, leading to speculation that Eustace Bell might have been the child of Bertha Bornstein (or Bornson or Bonstell, depending on which newspaper you read), an unmarried maid at the Palace Hotel. Bertha had given her baby to Mammy Pleasant to place in a home. The headline in the *Chronicle* the next day was "Where is Bertha's Baby?"

In the face of objections from Tyler and company about the irrelevance of all of this baby Bell talk, General Barnes said he wanted to show how Mammy Pleasant was responsible for the "mass of perjury" arising from the Hill camp. Apparently, painting her as a black market baby dealer was his method of proving that.

When Mary Ellen was recalled to the stand and asked if Eustace Bell was Bertha Bornstein's baby, she said she had placed Bertha's baby with a family on Bush Street, not the Bells. For reasons of confidentiality, she declined to name the family. At the same time, however, she launched a rumor that the Bornstein baby had been fathered by none other than William Sharon. Mary Ellen knew how to turn lemons into lemonade.

To refute the story that Eustace Bell was adopted, a barmaid, Suzanna Parks, swore that she was in the Bell house when Eustace was born to Teresa Bell. Not long after this loyal service, Mary Ellen gave Suzanna Parks and her husband a house.[166]

It was no wonder the defense came after Mary Ellen. She was a cunning and valuable ally to the plaintiff. Judge Tyler relied heavily on her and practically called her a saint. "I have known her for twenty-five years," he said, "and do not believe that the gold of Ophir…would induce her to tell an untruth. For years she has been engaged in finding homes for the children of friendless women whose maternity was due to the debaucheries of wealthy rakes. I tell you that I would rather my soul would be behind that old black face than behind Mr. Sharon's money bags. All his ten, twenty or thirty millions, if put into his coffin, will have no effect in obtaining a passport from old St. Peter, for up beyond the pearly gates there is a great kingly Judge, whom gold cannot corrupt, and who will render justice to all."[167]

General Barnes seemed exasperated and maybe a little impressed when he summed up the role that Mary Ellen Pleasant had played for the prosecution:

> She is the best all round witness Tyler had. She is a very useful woman, in his society. I don't wonder he likes her; I don't wonder he has canonized her. He had her on the stand five times. She proved the existence of the contract in 1882; she established Mr. Sharon's admission that he owed Miss Hill money, and she actually obtained from him the admission, after he had been arrested, that this contract of marriage had been executed….She has proved the May-day alibi to the best of her ability, found a home for Bertha Bornstein's baby, and contradicted the defendant on every vital and important item of his case. A very useful woman. She has produced a glorious lot of witnesses….I don't wonder that Tyler entertains the sentiments he does towards Mrs. Pleasance. I don't know where he would have been without her.[168]

As the trial neared its conclusion, it had become clear to everyone how monumentally crucial Mary Ellen Pleasant was to the case. But the trial focused a light on her she did not relish. Whenever she was on the stand, she was calm and subdued. Unlike her protégé Sarah, she did not want attention. Working behind the scenes had proved a successful strategy for her for decades. Months earlier, on the second day of Sharon vs. Sharon, a reporter listed Sarah Althea's companions and called each one by name except "a couple of colored women," one of whom was Mary Ellen Pleasant. The reporter did not know her at the trial's inception. Her public infamy was created by Sharon vs. Sharon. As certain facts came out about her, people got interested. For one thing, the extent of her wealth became a matter of record, and obvious questions came out of that. If she was so wealthy, why was she working as the Bells' housekeeper? And how did she accumulate all of that property and money? Rumors began to fly. The ties of the case with prostitution and voodoo, a practice associated primarily with Southern black women, rubbed off on Mary Ellen. As a character in this melodrama, she attracted wild fantasies just as Sarah herself did.

Buying the Parks a house was not the only extravagance Mary Ellen engaged in during this time, and with the exorbitant cost of the ongoing trial, she was beginning to falter financially.

The press had a field day with the topic of the Bell children, inspiring questions and rumors. *The Wasp*, a satirical magazine, ran a cartoon portraying Mammy Pleasant as a baby farmer. Irreparable damage was done to both her and the Bells as a result of the relentless press. Agatha Fay, a school friend of Marie Bell, said Marie was humiliated by the publicity. "One time I found her sitting in a clothes closet crying because of the talk about her family."[169] Fay found this ironic because Marie had habitually told the other girls that the four youngest Bell children were not related to her, that they had been brought into the house by Mary Ellen Pleasant to extort money from Thomas Bell. The story was that he paid $50,000 to his wife for each baby she was expected to raise as her own.

The windows were shuttered at the Bell mansion and visitors were turned away. Teresa Bell rarely left the house and saw no one. Thomas Bell, once a popular man, began to lose his position in society. The Bell mansion on Octavia Street became known as "The House of Mystery" because of the secrets locked up there. The carefully constructed plans of Mary Ellen Pleasant, kept together for decades, were unraveling. Her most ambitious scheme, to wrestle millions away from Senator Sharon, had taken a huge toll on not only herself, but her entire odd family.

Sarah Althea, meanwhile, withstood the onslaught of the witnesses for the defense with a dizzying and baffling array of moods.

The following is from General Barnes, so is slanted toward the negative, but is similar to how others described her. Keeping in mind that this was in a courtroom where she was the plaintiff in a monumentally important case, her behavior could be said to be bizarre.

"...her ability to rise into a passion that has no equal, ungovernable in temper, imperious in will, hardly able to preserve the dignities of civilized life when Mr. Evans was cross-examining her; snatching papers from him, threatening him, behaving in such a way that your Honor could hardly restrain her...."[170]

General Barnes found her bewildering. He commented many times on her courtroom conduct with an obvious incredulity, and his attitude is understandable. Sarah was in the midst of an ordeal that wore on and on, that consumed her life and would have left most people in despair. Witness after witness testified that she was a liar and a prostitute, and one by one all of her friends turned against her or deserted her. Likewise, her family was mortified by her and completely alienated from her. Her response to these circumstances was simply not normal. Barnes went on:

> She has a sharp, incisive mind. She has rattling, brilliant powers of conversation. She has a keen eye. She has a quick, rapid, nervous motion. She is to all appearances physically perfect, and endowed with an intellect keen-edged as the finest tempered steel. But the disclosures of the case combine to prove that never was there a woman so absolutely devoid of moral sense....She has no perception of a moral distinction. She is morally irresponsible. Truth and falsehood have the same hue and appearance to her...During the progress of the trial we have seen her, now boiling with causeless rage, and then smiling and laughing like a child. She is lonely, desperate and proven guilty. But she has had no more idea of her situation than a child brought here to play and roll on this floor....[When it became] clearer than the light of day that her testimony could not, by any possibility, have been true, she sat laughing like a child, gorging herself with candy, and occupying herself in decorating the hat of one of her counsel with flowers.[171]

She behaved in and out of court like a spoiled child. But there is no rule that says a spoiled child can't also be engaging at times. After all, Judge David Terry sat in the courtroom for months observing this woman, becoming acquainted with her over the same period of time as General Barnes, and he responded quite warmly to her. He found her charming and entertaining. He told a friend she was the smartest woman he had ever known. The two of them sat side by side every day at the plaintiff's table, becoming dearer and dearer friends. When Sarah had an aside, which was often, she leant toward Terry and spoke softly, saturating him with her wit, sarcasm, concern and outrage. Each day during lunch break, the two of them walked out arm in arm to dine together. Barnes and Terry were in the company of the same woman, but they had vastly different feelings toward her.

David Terry had so far contributed little action for the court. He was being reserved for the cross-examination of the defendant yet to come.

However, on March 19, he became outraged at what he perceived to be an unwarranted attack on Sarah by General Barnes. Oliver Evans asked her if she had ever threatened to kill Senator Sharon. Her answer was clearly unexpected. "I told Mr. Barnes that if Senator Sharon succeeded in convicting me criminally when he knew I was innocent, I would, if it lay in my power, kill him and myself both."[172]

Barnes immediately protested to being named and said that Sarah had never said any such thing to him. Judge Terry leapt up and objected, saying, "His conduct is most unprofessional, and is insolent in the highest degree to the witness, whom he thus accuses of perjury. I believe the story of the witness is true, notwithstanding the denial of counsel."[173]

The audience became excited at the confrontation as Barnes addressed Terry and dismissed him with obvious scorn. He said that he and Judge Tyler, who had a great respect for courtroom decorum, were the best of friends outside the courtroom, but he had never met Judge Terry, didn't know him, and didn't care to. He also apologized for his remark to the witness, which he said came from surprise at being named. What Barnes said next got a rousing response from the audience. "Judge Terry attempted to insult me by his remarks. I appreciate the insult, but shall disregard it. I will not take it up. I will send him no challenge, for I fight no duels."[174]

There was surely nobody in the courtroom unfamiliar with Judge Terry's infamous 1859 duel with Senator Broderick. Though it had happened so long ago, the incident followed Terry throughout his life and provided fodder for easy insults. Terry was perfectly justified in his objection that day in court, though perhaps not in the anger he expressed when voicing it. He had clearly become protective of the beautiful young woman in the stand. And he was not the only one feeling that way about her.

Public opinion was largely on Sarah's side. She was the underdog, battling against the most ferocious of opponents, a powerful and wealthy man who had already taken advantage of her and ruined her reputation and was now trying to utterly destroy her. The public was with her for other reasons that come into play when people become characters in such a melodrama. She was beautiful; he was ugly. She was young; he was old. To men, she was desirable and lusty, the stuff of fantasy. To women, she was brave and bold, a heroine in a gender war. They wanted to see William Sharon punished for his life of debauchery and, obviously, for the unforgivable sin of massive wealth.

19. NELLIE'S ESCAPE

Suddenly, on March 26, Nellie Brackett, who had been present every day of the trial so far, was absent from the courtroom. On March 31, Judge Sullivan issued a subpoena for her. The press reported that she and Sarah had had an argument about "the set of her bonnet, a truly feminine war of words, followed by a hair-pulling match."[175]

Angry Nellie had gathered her belongings and marched back to her parents' house. She arrived with "her apparel torn and disarranged, and her right foot black and blue and badly sprained."[176] Her parents were so happy to snatch her back from the clutches of the perverse Sarah Althea Hill that they immediately sent her away and would tell no one where she was. Detectives, police and lawyers scoured the city and all departing ships for Nellie to no avail. By Sunday her mother had told reporters that Nellie was staying with friends in Oakland and had no desire to see Miss Hill ever again. They had argued on several occasions, the last one being over Nellie's desire to dress more fashionably and "less like a servant."[177] Mrs. Brackett had no understanding of the powerful hold Sarah had had over her daughter, but was thankful it was broken.

While Nellie and Sarah did argue over clothes at times, the reason for this final clash and the permanent split was something more serious than Mrs. Brackett was letting on. The real reason, and a much more logical one, came out later.

One of the incidents that weakened the credibility of Sarah's case all along was her visit to the graveyard. She and Nellie did this in the full sight of and with the help of a graveyard employee, but Sarah's strategy was to completely deny it had ever happened. The incident never did have much bearing on her case, but she denied every instance of dabbling in fortune telling and the black arts, finding the subject distasteful and humiliating. Mary Ellen Pleasant, in a strategically perplexing move, went to extreme lengths to concoct an alibi for Sarah for May 1. Recall that no less than five people, all loyal to Mary Ellen, corroborated the story that Sarah was at the Bell house all day long making doll clothing with the children.

It was foolhardy to invent an elaborate scheme to deny something that ultimately wouldn't have mattered. The story couldn't stand up to examination and it didn't. The fight between Nellie and Sarah was over this very incident. Nellie wanted to tell the truth about it when the defense called her to testify. She told Sarah she wouldn't lie about it and say it had never happened. They fought and Nellie finally left.

And so the fourth week of the trial began without Nellie, with Sarah hinting that she had been bought off by the other side. The prosecution claimed that Nellie's father received $3,000 from the defense.

That the women had also argued about clothes, that Nellie felt she was being dulled down too much, is not too surprising. In some ways, the courtroom was a venue for a fashion show put on by Sarah Althea. Of course she would have objected to anyone stealing any of her limelight, just as she had objected when the courtroom had been closed to the public. She wanted an audience and she wanted it all to herself.

"When the fourteenth day of the Sharon divorce suit began yesterday morning, the plaintiff sailed into Court in another new creation of the milliner's fancy, that will tend to stir up the green-eyed monster in the bosom of any feminine beholder. It was a black velvet, trimmed with half a dozen elegant canary and ecru-colored plumes, amid which nestled two or three gauzy gorgeous-hued dragon flies."[178]

To set off such a star, there had to also be a dramatic story line. There was no lack of drama during Sharon vs. Sharon. One witness for the defense, Mary Shawhan, received at least two threatening, anonymous letters prior to testifying. Both of them warned her that Sarah would take revenge if she testified.

"Mrs. Shawhan," read one letter, "Do not go on the stand unprotected. Miss Hill swears that if you testify against her you shall not leave the Court-room alive. A Friend."[179]

Mary Shawhan, you may recall, was accused by Sarah of philandering with Senator Sharon. But she was more than just a witness for the defense. She was also an agent. She was sent to work on other witnesses, like Martha Wilson and Vesta Snow, to persuade them to change their testimony. When she was recalled to the stand, Judge Tyler tried to discredit her by showing that she went to shady dives with men. Before anything could be established about her reputation, however, she reached into her pocket, alarming the court reporter, who hollered, "Don't pull that."[180] General Barnes jumped up and said, "Stop that; we want no trouble of that kind here." Judge Tyler shoved his hand into his pocket, saying, "I can take care of myself." The entire courtroom then became excited at the prospect of gunfire.

Mary Shawhan had asked that she be excused from testifying, as she was nervous about the consequences. Since she had not been excused, she came to court prepared to defend herself, packing a pistol in her pocket. However, nobody had threatened her with anything other than unwelcome questions, yet there she was with her hand on her weapon.

"The witness had her hand in her pocket, and was moving her arm restlessly; her son, a young man of 25, small and slightly built, also had his hand in his right coat pocket; Tyler, Sr. had his right hand in his hip pocket; Tyler, Jr. was dancing about his father's chair with a pistol in his hand, nearly concealed by his coat-tails and his pocket, and bailiffs, spectators, policemen and counsel were rushing in every direction. Colonel Flournoy and Walter Levy retired to the back part of the room, clearing a space around the Tylers as they did so. For a moment the excitement was intense, and there was not a person present but what expected to see bloodshed every instant. Judge Sullivan was probably the coolest man in the room, and after a moment he succeeded in obtaining something like order."[181]

After the lunch break, Judge Sullivan announced that he would disallow weapons into the courtroom, and the following morning, everyone entering was questioned or searched to insure that no firearms were brought in.

On May 1, Nellie Brackett was subpoenaed to return to court, and so she did, no longer limited by Sarah's restrictions on her appearance. The *Alta* captured the moment in resplendent detail:

> A vision surpassing fair greeted the eyes of the earliest arrivals after lunch. It was Nellie Brackett, seated in the bailiff's big chair, but so transfigured and glorified that few would recognize in her the dumpy, bundled-up, plainly attired unstriking little girl who formerly followed the plaintiff with the fidelity of a patient poodle. Her face had filled out, little dimples nestled in her rosy cheeks, and chased each other playfully about the corners of her ripe red lips, which wore a half pout and half smile as her old friends greeted her. Her three-quarter brunette hair waved in pretty bangs over her forehead, and concluded in a cunning pigtail at her taper waist. Her hat was a broad, straight-brimmed white straw, trimmed with blue satin and marguerites, and sat coquettishly on the back of her head in the most approved picnic style. The waist and polonaise of her dress fitted her lissome figure to perfection, and were of a gay-colored check that corresponded well with her wine-colored silk skirt. The *Alta* man's eyes had barely accustomed themselves to the dazzling beauty, when the plaintiff, Mammy Pleasance and Judge Terry entered. The women looked doubtfully at each other for a moment, and then

each impulsively advanced and exchanged kisses and a word or two of greeting. Then they took seats some distance apart and swapped smiles until Court opened.[182]

Nellie testified that she and Sarah had gone to the graveyard and planted the parcel with bits of Sharon's clothing in Anson Olin's grave just as others had described. When the judge asked her if she was still in the plaintiff's camp, she said, "Yes, sir. I do not like her as well, however, but still I should like to see her win. I left her because we quarreled, but I do not care to state what the quarrel was about."[183]

When William Sharon took the stand at last, he denied almost everything that Sarah and her witnesses had said, denounced all incriminating documents as forgeries, denied that he had ever used the word "wife" in any way to anyone to refer to Sarah Althea, and said that he had made her no promises other than the monthly payment of $500 and the final settlement of $7,500.

During his testimony, Sharon mentioned that he had never paid the entire $7,500, that there was $750 left on the final note for the months of October, November and December, 1883. He had stopped paying once Sarah had him arrested and brought suit. Sarah's ears pricked up at that admission. As court was adjourned, she sent Cousin Rodney to ask Sharon for the money he still owed.

"The Senator was paralyzed, and for a minute gazed at the modest youth in open-mouthed astonishment. 'What!' he cried, 'you want money from me? Get out! How dare you speak to me.' Rodney pressed his demand and elicited the response, 'No!' thundered the now angry millionaire. 'No! not a damned cent. Get away from me, will you?' Rodney fled back to his cousin and reported, whereupon she said, 'Very well, then: I'll sue him.'"[184]

It is no wonder the senator was shocked into momentary paralysis. After all that Sarah Althea had put him through, she had the gall to ask for more money? She seemed to be out of touch with reality. She didn't feel any need to uphold her end of that same bargain, but expected him to pay the total price. She followed through with her threat and sued him the next day for the $750 owed to her, with interest. This case was brought before Judge Finn as Sarah Althea Hill vs. William Sharon, and was decided in her favor. Sharon was ordered to pay the remaining $750, plus interest and court costs.

20. SUMMER BREAK

At the end of May, the court recessed for the summer. The press took this opportunity to recap. *The Wasp* put an irreverent and entertaining cartoon on their cover showing all of the principles significantly aged, with the caption, "Anno Domini 1910—and Still on Trial."

The *Daily Alta California* ran a marvelous article with illustrations of each of the main characters, including the judge, lawyers, plaintiff, defendant, and Mary Ellen Pleasant. Each illustration was "accompanied by brief dissections of their natures and characteristics, merits and demerits, as seen by the reporter who has been in attendance at the trial from its inception."[185]

The following excerpts are from the June 1, 1884 edition of the *Daily Alta California*, titled *Sharoniana* and subtitled (among others) *A Brief History of the Prominent Actors in the Great Modern Melodrama Now Closed for the Season.*

"Sarah Althea Hill or Sharon, as Judge Sullivan may determine, the plaintiff in this action, has been, up to the time when anxiety, implied disgrace and trouble made sad inroads on her beauty, a very attractive young lady. Her linguistic accomplishments are good, she possesses a remarkably fine contralto voice, and a perfect figure after the Jersey Lily mold. Borne of her former aptitude for repartee and bright flashes of wit still lingers with her, but long talking and thinking on one subject, that of her case, have somewhat dimmed her powers as an entertainer. Her face shows the ravages of constant worry even more than her manners and character. Her cheeks wear a dry, unnatural, feverish flush, and this hectic glow never leaves them, not excepting when she is in repose and away from the excitement of Court proceedings. Crow's feet and wrinkles, that ought not to decorate the face of a woman of her age, especially one whose life has been as easy as has Sarah's, are beginning to put in a plentiful appearance, and the flesh is beginning to lose the firmness of youth, and gather in creases and saggy bunches about the curves and angles of her face....Miss Hill's ultimate destination appears to be the lecture platform, the stage, or other similar fields in view of the public, where she is bound to attract at least a portion of the attention that is now being paid her by press and people....She is invariably armed with a black leather reticule, containing her "honor," as she dramatically dubbed the famous marriage contract, and her other documentary evidences. When it becomes necessary for one of the papers to go out of her possession, her eyes never leave it until it is returned to her."

"Ex-United States Senator Wm. Sharon, the defendant, is an anomaly in himself and his fitness as a mate for the woman who lays claim to his name and estate. There is a deep vein of sentiment in his composition, and his studies of the poets have not been forced by a desire to present a favorable exterior. He quotes Shakespeare, Burns, Byron, Milton and other standard authors easily and gracefully, and should occasion call for it the Scriptures furnish him an argument or illustration as readily as would the wise words of the old philosophers. He is well read in the affairs of the world, and in conversation can entertain any and all  minds....His personal attractions do not assay very highly, but they will average well with the majority of men of his age, and physical defects would be quickly forgotten should he set out to be entertaining. He is fond of nature, animate and inanimate, and is more considerate of horses and dogs than he is of human beings. He might be a good friend, and he certainly is a bad enemy. Various propositions and advices of compromise have been submitted to him in the present case, but in his frame of mind just now he would dump the Palace Hotel into the bay and convert the site into a sand lot before he would yield a penny to the woman who has caused him such an unpleasant prominence."

"David S. Terry, second in seniority to Mr. Tyler as counsel for the plaintiff, is ponderous in frame, mind and language. He is well known here, but for some years past has made his home in the San Joaquin valley, his law office being located at Stockton. He is present, it is generally conceded, for the purpose of furnishing the major portion of the law in the case, and for his argumentative powers. He occasionally does something in the latter line, but the greater portion of his time is taken up by his client. Whether on matters relevant or irrelevant to the case are the subject of their chat is unknown. Their seats are invariably side by side, and to the lady's hard-worked tongue does Mr. Terry ever lend a kindly ear. All her confidences are made to him, and all her many stage-whispered sarcasms directed at the defendant, his witnesses and counsel reach him before they do their targets. Oftener than not he escorts her to and from lunch, and it is a not infrequent sight to behold them arm-in-arm on the street, or at the theatre, each as merry and full of glee, and

oblivious to criticising spectators as a pair of freshly-betrothed lovers of more recent date of conception. Another function assigned to Mr. Terry, and only discovered by the Court attendants when the defendant took the stand, is to permit his broad back to serve as a screen behind which Sarah may hide her blushes and murmur an astonished 'Oh, my; did you ever?' when the testimony points to her being the Sen's mistress for hire instead of his wife."

"Mrs. Mary Pleasance, Sarah's dark-complexioned

backer, is faithfully portrayed [here], or at least as much of her as is ever visible when she is buried in her immense black straw hat, tied over her head in the style of a scoop bonnet. The proceedings are in the nature of a gamble as far as 'Mammy' Pleasance is concerned, for she is risking some money, with a chance of losing it, against one of winning a good deal more. She is very stylish in her manner of locomotion, riding to and from Court in a top buggy, drawn by a neat pair of bays. She occupies a chair in Court directly behind Terry and Sarah, and often her curly head is thrust between the pair as she leans forward to impart some bit of information or get off what she considers a joke. In the case of the latter, she leans back in her chair and smiles a smile that causes the observer to make an involuntary comparison with the tombstones in a graveyard on a very dark night, with a bit of red fire thrown in."

During the hiatus, William Sharon went back east to work on various political projects. One of these was the Republican National Convention in Chicago. Fresh off the witness stand, he drew much attention with ladies craning their necks just to get a glimpse of the notorious lothario. He was happy to talk about the mess he was in with Sarah, whom he termed a "hellion." It was a condescending way to speak about a mature woman who was suing him. To him, she was a flighty and irresponsible girl of little consequence. He saw his main adversary in the case as William Neilson and believed he was responsible for manufacturing the marriage contract and other documents. It never occurred to him that the conspiracy was manufactured and led by women. While David Terry was attracted to Sarah at least partly because of her intelligence, William Sharon never noticed it.

"She was an adventuress and I was a fool," he told his colleagues. "I paid her well for my folly, and she ought to have been content with that; but egged on by Neilson and Tyler, she tried to blackmail me, and now I never will let up till justice is done."[186]

Before he left Chicago, Sharon held a party with his buddies in a posh hotel suite. Of course, the subject of most interest was the lawsuit. He was cocky and good-humored about it. Amid smoke from fine cigars, he said, "Boys, it was a scrape and a bad one, but, thank God, I'm getting out of it."[187] Then they all laughed, including Sharon. He admitted that it was painful to go on the witness stand and admit to being a fool. When one of his pals suggested he might have avoided that by paying a couple of thousand dollars, he said, "I gave her $7,500 to call it square....it wasn't enough, and then she got that scoundrel Neilson from Australia to egg on her suit....But I will not be blackmailed out of a cent. I paid that woman well. I gave her a small fortune. I mean now not only to beat her blackmail suit, but I will land her in the penitentiary."[188]

Sharon had sent two detectives to Australia to get information about

Neilson. He also sent men to Cape Girardeau, Missouri, to dig up dirt on Sarah with the goal of showing "her to have been an adventuress from her twentieth year."[189] What he meant by the now defunct word "adventuress" was a female opportunist, or, more bluntly, a gold digger.

He was willing to go to any lengths, to spend any amount of money, to win the case. It was reported that he had spent $60,000 so far, which would be worth about one and half million dollars today. There were rumors that in the end General Barnes received an incredible $150,000 for his part in the suit.

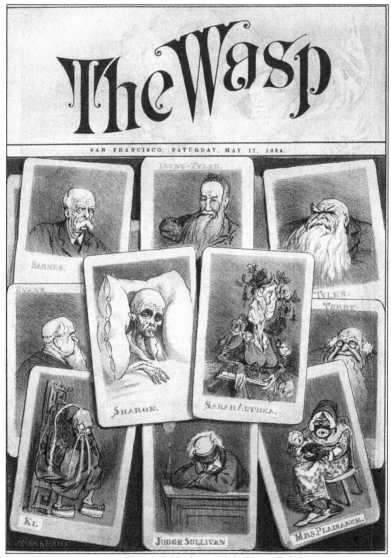

Anno Domini 1910—and Still on Trial

21. NEILSON RETREATS

What Sharon's agents discovered about Sarah's youthful exploits was never revealed, but with Neilson, they hit pay dirt. They discovered that he had been convicted of forgery in Australia and had served two years of his seven-year sentence. Sharon claimed to have ample evidence to show that Neilson was a professional blackmailer.

Shortly after this information was printed in the papers, Neilson suddenly withdrew himself from the case. He made the announcement on July 12, 1884, just before the summer break was over and the trial would resume. It was reported in the *Alta* that "he bows himself off mysteriously, announcing that he had become acquainted with certain facts that weakened, if they did not destroy his belief in the honesty of Althea's case."[190]

It is curious that Neilson, a man generally considered a shady character, should be stricken with a sudden attack of conscience. Was he concerned about what William Sharon was uncovering about his past? At any rate, the day after he quit Sarah's case, Neilson sued Sharon for $100,000 damages for slander and malicious prosecution. This case died a natural death several years later.

Neilson wrote a letter that was published in the *San Francisco Chronicle* on July 13, explaining that he was no longer on the case. He said he had left because Sarah had not treated him fairly and failed to pay his salary of $40 a week, referring to her "ingratitude and unbridled temper."[191] He also cited medical reasons, saying he had been emotionally incapacitated by the difficult position he was in, persecuted by Sharon and abused by Sarah Althea.

The *Chronicle* immediately sent a reporter to press Neilson for more details, and he was incapable of resisting the opportunity. He declared that the "Dear Wife" letters were forgeries, that he had seen the originals without the word "wife" in them in Sarah's home in June of 1883. He had seen the same letters later in Tyler's office in an altered state. He had known about the alterations in the documents for some time, but said he had struggled with how to proceed until he finally walked away. "The knowledge of the character of that evidence, together with the lady's treachery toward me, are the sole causes of my withdrawing from the case."[192]

When Neilson had first confronted Sarah about the perils of forgery, she became angry and said he wasn't brave enough, "that I was not the man she expected I was; that she expected me to stand by her right or wrong."[193] So many people disappointed Sarah with their scruples! He explained to her that in the modern world, a forged letter was impossible to pass off, that science had many ways to detect it. In response, she "burst into a flood of tears, and said, 'Oh! Neil, go and see Mr. Sharon and get this case settled on any terms, and let us go to Europe.'"[194]

The day after Sarah's confession about the letters, she sent for Neilson, having recovered her calm, and said, "If you feel badly about that thing, you had better make no trouble about it, because, just as sure as you do…I will say that you did it, and I have got all the witnesses; my word will be taken as surely as yours, and I will land you in the penitentiary."[195]

When Sarah liked someone, she did so with great passion. When Neilson was in favor, she wrote him, "Oh, I wish I was where I could see you every day—twice a day—and have you talk to me, as it always gives me so much heart."[196] But when a person was out of favor with her, he could expect her passions to run just as deeply in the opposite direction. At one time, Julia Bornemann, Nellie Bacon, Susan Smith, Sarah Millett, and Harriet Kenyon had been her intimate friends and confidantes. Now that they had testified, telling what appeared to be the truth, she had nothing but disdain for them, openly sneering at and flinging insults at them.

Once Neilson had learned that the letters were forgeries, he urged Tyler to stop the whole thing. Tyler seemed afraid of what Sarah would do if they backed out. "I am satisfied from the evidence that woman gave on the stand, that she is able to swear to anything."[197] They were worried that if they dropped her case, she would pin the forgeries on them.

Sarah was interviewed about Neilson's statements and said that he was apparently afraid of continuing or had been bought off by Sharon. At any rate, she said, his departure would have no impact on the case. "Mr. Neilson has not been of any assistance to me," she said. From the beginning Neilson had been hounding her for money and she had paid his expenses beyond what their arrangement required, such as his wife's funeral expenses and his own hospital costs.

It was clear to everyone by the time Neilson left that the case was not going well for the plaintiff. Neilson suspected she was setting him up to take the fall for the forgeries. Also, why stay if the payday wasn't coming? That Neilson sued William Sharon for his own sake showed that he was looking for a way to salvage some financial reward out of the wreck of Sarah Althea's case.

There was one other reason Neilson left when he did, one he didn't mention in his public statements. He was no longer Sarah's confidante or her constant visitor. That position had been usurped by David Terry. Neilson suggested that Terry would soon see the light himself and make a run for it. It was a reasonable assumption, but it didn't turn out to be true. Terry's wife, who was seriously ill, lived in the Terry's Stockton house while Judge Terry spent most of his time when court was in session in his San Francisco apartment, and he was spending more and more time in Sarah's company.

Judge Tyler sued the *Daily Alta California* for $50,000 for libel for publishing Neilson's statements. He did not sue the *Chronicle*, though the story had run there first. The prosecution considered the *Alta* a less friendly newspaper than the *Chronicle*. That may be because Sarah had made an effort to bribe newspaper reporters to run stories slanted in her favor and, according to Neilson, she had succeeded in pocketing a man from the *Chronicle* and the *Examiner*.[198] The *Alta*, he said, had remained out of her reach.

Suing the *Alta* was a huge misstep for Sarah Althea and company. The case brought out into the open the previously private conversations between members of the plaintiff's team, and showed that Neilson and the Tylers, and presumably Judge Terry, all knew that her case was based on forgery, fraud and perjury. They may not have known it when they originally signed on, however. Neilson described several arguments he had had with Tyler over the validity of the documents and the truthfulness of Sarah's statements as the facts began to emerge. Tyler's philosophy seemed to be "in for a penny, in for a pound."

The *Alta* brought in a renowned handwriting expert, Dr. R. U. Piper, to examine the contested documents. When the time came for Piper to look at the marriage contract and "Dear Wife" letters, Tyler refused to turn them over. To avoid their examination, the suit against the *Alta* was dropped; therefore, Sarah was ordered to pay costs, which came to about a thousand dollars.

While all of this business with Neilson's defection and the *Alta* suit was going on, Sharon vs. Sharon was drawing to a close.

In his summation, Judge Tyler said, "Either this woman (Sarah was pointed out) is Mrs. Sharon, or she is one of the most infamous blackmailers that ever lived."[199] The defense couldn't have agreed more!

In his summation, which took three days, General Barnes called Sarah "a moral idiot." He said she had no sense of right and wrong and likened her to a child of three. "Her kaleidoscope of fairy tales is something wonderful,"[200] he said. He pointed out how, when she was supposedly married to William Sharon, she talked a about how she might marry so many others: Reuben Lloyd, Fred Sharon, Dr. Bradford, Lieutenant Emory. She herself clearly knew that she was not Sharon's wife, but merely his mistress. "Why," said Barnes exuberantly, "that woman had just as much, in fact just the same idea of being the wife of Senator Sharon at that time, as she has of now being married to Judge Terry."[201] The courtroom burst into laughter. Everyone was aware by now of Terry's constant attentions to Sarah inside and outside the courtroom. Though they must have suspected a romantic relationship, they would have laughed off the idea of a marriage coming out of it, especially since Terry was already married.

On September 10, David Terry presented the closing argument for the plaintiff. Considering his growing affection for her and the fact that he had not played a large role in the courtroom drama so far, his statement was of great interest to the assembly. He argued that Sharon had dictated and signed the marriage contract as a ruse to persuade Sarah to sleep with him, that he included the secrecy clause because he always intended it as a mock contract and never intended her to be anything other than his illicit lover. She had guarded it with her life every day after it was created, proving that she believed in its validity. "If Mr. Sharon did not intend to marry this lady, but in order to overcome her scruples he signed that contract, and blundered into matrimony, he does not deserve sympathy….No one can be blamed but himself, and he must stand the consequences of the gratification of his lust."[202]

The public was with Terry in this sentiment. Even if Sharon was telling the truth, they thought, he should pay for his immoral actions. "At the conclusion of this trial," summed up Terry, "she will leave this Court-room either as an honest and virtuous woman, or as an adventuress, a blackmailer, a perjurer and a harlot."[203] Again, Sarah's attorneys had a way of making grand statements that could be read as highly ironic.

David Terry never practiced as a criminal lawyer, which he explained by saying that he did not want to defend people who were guilty of crimes. Throughout his life he had a strong reputation for honesty, integrity and incorruptibility. What he believed in his heart about Sarah's relationship with Sharon will never be known, but it is safe to say that he was offended by William Sharon's behavior and misuse of women. Sarah may have convinced him that the marriage contract was genuine or, if it wasn't, that Sharon had led her to believe he would marry her. And so he should have, if he were an honorable man. Judge Terry must have believed that William Sharon had done wrong, if not legally, then certainly morally. Terry believed in a code of honor that was disconnected from the law, as can be seen in his past and in his actions a few years into the future.

After doing his best for Sarah, Judge Terry returned to Stockton to be with his wife, whose health had deteriorated significantly. She died two and half months later on December 16.

So concluded the trial of Sharon vs. Sharon, the ultimate outcome resting with the callow Judge Sullivan, who received an 8,000 page transcript to review.

"Meanwhile," said the *Los Angeles Herald*, "the general public realizes that Sarah Althea is a rather naughty sort of a woman, but would be glad to see her get away with several millions of Sharon's hard cash.[204]

Despite the hopes of the public, those who were involved in the case, those who saw all of Sarah's witnesses scared away or discredited, those who saw first-hand all of the instances of perjury and forgery, assumed the outcome was a foregone conclusion. Sarah Althea could not possibly win.

22. MRS. SHARON

On the damp, misty morning of December 24, 1884, Judge Sullivan gave his decision in the Sharon vs. Sharon divorce case. A huge crowd was assembled. William Sharon was not in the courtroom, but Sarah was there, her appearance meticulously designed to draw all eyes.

> On the top of her head there lay a close-fitting bonnet covered with steel-blue beads, while velvet of the same color was cunningly arranged as trimming on a black silk dress, except at the wrists, where there was a pink ruffle, or something like it, coming down over well-fitting brown gloves. Over her sloping shoulders was thrown a rich cloak of black embossed velvet, trimmed with otter, a boa of the same fur running up around her neck and making a soft, warm background for her cheek, which has not yet lost its roundness. The fair hair was brushed forward on the forehead in the old well-known style, the cheeks owed much of their tint to chamois-skin with "just a little red" on it, while the eyes had yet that soft look in them which once on a time melted its way clear through the heart of William Sharon.[205]

Despite his recognition of a profound level of perjury in the case, Judge Sullivan found for the plaintiff, ruling that she was William Sharon's legal wife and would be granted a divorce on the grounds of willful desertion. He believed that the marriage contract had been signed by both parties, whatever Sharon's motives had been and whatever else Sarah had lied about. He was influenced by the fact that the senator had invited Sarah's family members to Belmont, had invited Sarah to his daughter's wedding reception, introduced her to his son, and had gone with her to be introduced to her grandmother and aunt and uncle in their home. He would not have behaved that way, the judge reasoned, if she had been merely his paid mistress, as his treatment of his other mistresses demonstrated. Sullivan focused especially on Flora's wedding, saying, "I cannot believe that this man, this father, so far forgot his duty to the memory of his deceased wife, his duty to his daughter, his duty to the friends and guests who had assembled to do honor to the occasion, as to subject them to the polluting presence of a creature who differed from the common courtesan only to the extent that her commerce was with one man. He must in his heart have regarded her as more than a mistress."[206]

Sullivan ruled that Sarah was entitled to alimony and division of community property acquired during the marriage. Community property was a huge issue in this case. William Sharon had been a man of modest means into his forties, becoming wealthy around the age of fifty. His wealth had grown exponentially as each year passed, so the value of his holdings for the years between 1880 and 1884 had likely doubled.

At the conclusion of Judge Sullivan's address, William Sharon's lawyers quickly exited the courtroom as a crowd pushed in to surround Sarah Althea with congratulations. Overwhelmed by this outpouring of good will, she broke down and sobbed quietly.

A *Chronicle* reporter complimented her on her calm demeanor throughout Sullivan's reading. "It was a great effort, though," she said, "I can assure you, but I do not believe in making scenes."[207]

"He has had the game and he now has the name of husband," observed the *Los Angeles Herald*. "He has danced and he must not grumble at having to pay the piper. The general verdict all over the State, outside of a small clique of the rich man's hangers-on, will be, 'Served him right.'"[208]

"Judge Sullivan," observed one reporter, "in rendering his decision particularly noted that no attempt had been made by the defense to impeach Sarah's morality previous to the time of her meeting with Mr. Sharon."[209] If she was the scheming, greedy succubus they made her out to be, why had they allowed her to appear as an innocent victim? It was well known that William Sharon never imagined he could lose. Wasn't there enough evidence already that Sarah and her gang of thieves had built an indefensible house of cards? Quite possibly he and his lawyers didn't think there was any need to drag the case to an even lower level of depravity by adding details of the woman's previous sexual adventures into it. At that time, a lady's most prized possession was her chastity. The issue of her prior romances was territory no gentleman would want to traverse. Unless he had to. But once Sharon lost the case, all bets were off. Judge Sullivan's remark was practically an invitation to destroy the plaintiff's moral character in the inevitable appeal.

"The verdict is a genuine surprise to the public," reported the *Sacramento Daily Union*. It was a surprise to those associated with it as well. By now, almost nobody believed that Sarah Althea Hill was an innocent, mystified young girl who had been preyed upon.

The surprise was so great that there were those who attempted to explain by saying that Judge Sullivan had a personal vendetta against Sharon, and no other judge would have made the same decision. An Englishwoman, reading clippings from the newspapers sent to her from a friend in San Francisco, was aghast that Sarah had won, that the case had been allowed to go on at all once the perjury and fraud began to surface. "It would be a lasting disgrace to San Francisco morals," she wrote her friend, "if that brazen, impecunious hussy were permitted any claim to Sharon's money....It is simply disgusting that she is not well punished by the law for her wickedness, instead of being permitted to pose as injured innocence."[210]

Sullivan's decision was only a few hours old when General Barnes said he would appeal. "I have already told [Sharon] that the case may outlast his life....I think it will outlast [the other side's] hope of getting any money out of it, if that is their object. We shall carry on this fight to the last ditch and then only we will die."[211]

George Tyler quickly filed his claim to 50% of the spoils as dictated by an agreement he had made with Sarah when he was retained. This agreement also explicitly stated that William Neilson was to act as Sarah's agent in all matters related to the suit and was to get one quarter of the proceeds. That agreement had never been amended. A few days later, Neilson stepped up to ask for his share as well. He later relinquished it, saying, "I disdain to take money fraudulently obtained....It would be a cankering worm to me as long as I live. Away with it, I want none of it!"[212] He must have seen how the situation was trending, that his quarter share of Sarah's winnings would never be realized, so he made a show of casting off the tainted booty.

"I am so happy," enthused Sarah to *The Morning Call*, "I feel just like a young kitten that has been brought into the house and set before the fire....The poor, dear old Sen. I'm sorry I beat the old man, for I love him still; he's a dear, sweet fellow."

Sarah immediately went on a shopping spree, buying Christmas gifts for her friends and servants, charging everything to Mrs. William Sharon. One wonders if she remembered poor Martha Wilson and Harry Wells, still under charges for perjury for lying on her behalf during the trial.

On Christmas Day, Sarah invited a reporter to her home to discuss her victory.

A dull, sombre, cheerless day outside. Inside, Persian rugs, Axminster carpets, lace curtains and bric-a-brac backed up by fine oil paintings and steel engravings on the walls, and a cheerful, crackling coal fire in the grate. Two pictures exactly opposite! On a richly embroidered lounge, with pillows of satin and plash, Mrs. Sarah Althea Sharon quietly perused the Christmas number of the *Alta*. A large marble-topped table, almost covered with glasses and champagne bottles, some empty and others yet to be opened, suggested the idea that the lady plaintiff in the celebrated case had received many callers before the *Alta* representative modestly presented himself before the heroine of the case of Sharon versus Sharon.[213]

Another woman in these same circumstances would have taken a deep breath and laid low for a while. But Sarah couldn't resist basking in her popularity and success. She wanted to make sure everybody knew that her legitimate place at the top of the food chain had been restored.

On New Year's Day, with a rare dusting of snow falling, the newly-minted Mrs. Sharon opened her Rincon Hill house to the city to celebrate her victory. She sent an announcement of the event to the *Chronicle*, making an open invitation to all of San Francisco. A crowd of reporters turned up along with the invited guests, altogether a couple hundred visitors. "The lady received her guests in the parlor, and was very handsomely attired in a dress of light pink silk, *en train*, and heavily trimmed with deep point lace."[214] Only one of her lawyers made an appearance, David Terry, then a widower of two weeks. Mary Ellen Pleasant was also there, reveling in triumph over what her tens of thousands of dollars had helped accomplish.

Among the guests were some who had read the notice in the *Chronicle* and invited themselves to the party. "During the day a number of persons took advantage of the season, and, armed only with pure cheek, they rang the bell and were ushered before the astonished host. She had but one recourse under the trying ordeal, which was to greet them, each and every mother's son, as personal friends, and with as little friction as possible conduct the thirsty mob to the side-board and waste good champagne and cigars upon them."[215]

Even if Sarah knew that the millions she was now entitled to would not be immediately forthcoming because of appeals, she had her honor back at least, and that was worth almost as much to her.

Among the fallout of Sharon vs. Sharon was the introduction of new legislation to make contract marriages like this one unlawful. Some laws that allowed such marriages were repealed and others amended to require "due solemnization of the marriage ceremony."

And yet more fallout: copycat litigation. "Nothing could be more natural," wrote an *Alta* reporter with tongue in cheek, "than that after reading about the Sharon litigation other young women should discover the fact, which they had not hitherto suspected, that they are the deserted wives of wealthy men, and should commence proceedings for the establishment of their claims to divorce and division of property, especially the latter."[216] One of the first of these was brought to court in New York in April, 1885 by Alice Saalfield who claimed to be the deserted contract wife of millionaire Ross B. Winans. The reporter went on to say, "Nothing is yet said about a written contract of marriage, but that will doubtless be found in good time, duly signed, folded and creased."[217]

Early in January, the lawyers were back before Judge Sullivan arguing over Sharon's total worth, the amount of property he had accumulated during the marriage, and legal fees. Sarah's side claimed Sharon's worth at fifteen million. They wanted $150,000 to cover legal costs and $10,000 a month in alimony, an amount even Sarah would find hard to spend. Sharon argued that he was worth only five million.

All of this was predictable, but of much greater interest was the bombshell about to fall on Sarah and company that would blow them completely out of the water.

23. LIEUTENANT BRACKETT: DEFECTOR

In preparation for the appeal, William Sharon's team was hard at work gathering witnesses. Their biggest prize was Nellie Brackett. In January, 1885, she gave a sworn affidavit, explaining in excruciating detail everything she knew about the case. Nellie was in a unique position as Sarah's trusted confidante to reveal facts we would otherwise never have heard. If she had known Sarah from 1880, there would be no secrets remaining in the case. Sadly for us, Nellie came on the scene after the relationship with Senator Sharon was over.

After being away from Sarah's influence for some time, Nellie wanted to set the record straight, and there is no reason to doubt her honesty, though of course Sarah claimed that Sharon's money had persuaded Nellie to betray her. It might have been Sharon's money that made her go public, but the details she gave were most certainly true. They fit in perfectly with all the other proven facts. Nellie was trying to clear her conscience, operating on the advice of her parents, and never changed her story again after this confession was put into writing.

The following are selected excerpts from that affidavit, published in its entirety on page one of the *Daily Alta California* on January 13, 1885. The events described begin in March, 1882, when Nellie and Sarah first met.

"She was very affectionate toward me, and in this way obtained complete influence and control over me. Against the wishes of my parents I went with her constantly; spent my days with her, and often slept with her while she was boarding, and lived with her most of the time while she lived in Laurel place. She obtained such control over me that I submitted to be beaten by her many times when she was in a rage about some little thing."

About the marriage contract, Nellie said, "I really never saw that paper until about the month of April, 1883, at 18 Laurel place....I do not know anything positively about its history. The plaintiff never told me how she came by it, but she often did tell me there was one secret she had not confided to me, but would do so when the case was over. I always understood that this secret was connected with the contract."

Nellie's most damaging information was about the "Dear Wife" letters. "I know all about the 'wife' letters," she said, "and assisted the plaintiff in getting them up. At first she had nothing but the contract. All of the letters were fixed up after Mr. Sharon was arrested in September, 1883....The one that is marked Plaintiff's Exhibit No. 11 was originally addressed 'My Dear Allie.' The word 'Allie' was so plain that it was easily erased with india-rubber, and she rubbed it out. She made up the word 'wife' by taking different letters from different words in some papers in Mr. Sharon's handwriting....She put the letters together, after trying a good many times, and got a good 'wife,' and then she traced it into the letter...."

Nellie went on in similar detail to describe how each of the Dear Wife letters was created. The effort that went into this process was exhaustive. "Both of us tried it. But after practicing for three or four weeks she was able to make tracings that were almost perfect....She used to practice at it until she got tired, and then she would make me try."

"We burned a good many tracings, but when there was a good one we laid it aside, and she had sometimes twenty or twenty-five on hand to select from. She got them so good that she did not know which would be best to select from....The ink bottle used in making these tracings was one she had had a good while, and when she left Laurel place she was afraid to take it with her for fear they would ask to examine the ink she had, and she threw it in the ash barrel."

Sarah's Chinese servant, Ah Sam, corroborated Nellie's story by saying that he saw her put dirt and coffee on the new documents to make them look old and yellow, and that he ironed them for her.[218]

As to the incidents of the summer of 1882 and the reconciliation with Sharon, Nellie confirmed that it was all made up. Sarah never reconciled with the senator. Nellie never went to see him to tell him Sarah was "in an interesting condition." As to hiding behind the dresser to listen to Sharon and Sarah's pillow talk, she said, "The plaintiff got up the story about the bedroom scene. It never happened." The "egg in champagne" letter was written later when they were making up evidence and was never sent to Sharon. The same was true of the other letter that Cousin Rodney said he delivered to the senator.

Nellie corroborated William Neilson's statements about the potential for passing forged documents and her threats to put the blame on him if he squealed.

She then spoke of the last violent fight that caused her to leave Sarah for good. "One morning early she got angry at me, and as she had done many times before struck me and hurt me a good deal....She threw me down and beat me cruelly, and would have hurt me much more, but Frank intervened and saved me." She then packed her things and returned to her parents.

By now, we are aware of most of the points Nellie confirmed in this affidavit, that most of the letters produced in evidence were forgeries, that Sarah bribed witnesses and threatened several others, that Sarah was physically abusive, vindictive, paranoid, jealous, tyrannical and somewhat irrational. If there was any doubt left that the evidence in the plaintiff's case was spurious, Nellie's statement would have finally removed it. However, even Nellie was unable to say whether the marriage contract was genuine or not. Sarah had told her that she didn't feel her case was strong enough based solely on that document, so she produced others to bolster it. Nellie believed that the one secret Sarah was still keeping that she was dying to tell was about the contract. If Nellie was right, it seems the secret could have been only one thing— that it too was a forgery. It was the single piece of evidence that Sarah always maintained was the real thing. Maybe it was. But Sarah was not the sort of woman to keep that secret, especially considering how distressed and desperate she was when Sharon threw her over. It seems she would have unhesitatingly shown the document to everyone who questioned her moral or social position if it had been genuine. She would have shown it around like she did the engagement ring, to enhance her cachet.

After Nellie Brackett's confession, there was speculation about the consequences for her. The other witnesses who admitted perjury, Martha Wilson and Harry Wells, had been arrested and charged. William Sharon admitted that he had become friendly with the Brackett family, and vowed to help Nellie if she needed it. The press assumed that his protection would keep her safe from prison. Sarah made a half-hearted attempt to get Nellie indicted for perjury. But the matter was quickly dropped and Nellie was never charged with a crime.

During the course of the trial, William Sharon himself made few direct statements. But on the same day as Nellie's confession was read in court, a statement by Sharon, now sixty-four, was also read. It was primarily a request that he not be made to pay anything while the case was under appeal.

> My state of health is such that I realize my life cannot be
> much further prolonged, and my bodily ailments and physical
> weakness have been greatly augmented by the shock I received

in the decision of this case. I never proposed marriage to her at any time, at any place, or in any form of words. I never executed the alleged marriage contract....I declare that I am the victim of an infamous conspiracy concocted by the plaintiff and her confederates for the purpose of extorting money....I found myself unable to bear the strain on my mind and nerves caused by the production of so much testimony against me, which I knew to be false, and by discovering in what a net of wicked and criminal conspiracy I was taken....if I am not compelled to furnish money to reward the plaintiff for her numerous crimes, her forgeries, perjuries, conspiracies and subornation of perjury...I shall ultimately be able to establish the fact that I am the victim of the most atrocious, bold and shameless attempt to extort money of which I have ever heard.[219]

In February, Judge Sullivan granted Sarah the sum of $2,500 a month alimony, back alimony of $7,500, and attorney fees of $55,000 payable on March 9. Sharon again vowed that he wouldn't pay a cent of the award.

24. THE PRISONER

It came as no surprise to anybody that George W. Tyler was soon on Sarah's bad side, especially since she didn't much care for him even before the trial. Under their agreement, he had let her bill float during the trial, at the end of which he and her other financial supporter, Mary Ellen Pleasant, would split half of the spoils. Sarah did not begrudge Mary Ellen her share, but she was having a hard time swallowing the fact that she would hand over such a fortune to the annoying old scoundrel Judge Tyler.

She began to complain publicly about him, and must certainly have been trying to think of a way to back out of their deal. "No one knows what I have had to stand from that man. Why, I have been cursed by him worse than any woman could be by a drunken husband, and his abuse has been abundant whenever the opportunity was offered him."[220]

Although Tyler remained on the case, he was demoted to second banana. From now on, David Terry was the lead, and eventually Tyler would drift out of the picture altogether.

In early 1885, there were three other cases in the courts running concurrently where Sarah was either defendant or plaintiff. In the William Sharon vs. Sarah Althea Hill case, Sharon had asked that the marriage contract be judged a forgery and declared invalid. Then there was the case where Sarah had sued the *Daily Alta California* for $50,000 damages for libel when they published Neilson's statement that he knew the "Dear Wife" letters were forgeries. Interestingly, Sarah did not sue Nellie Brackett for her even more damaging statement. It seemed that the coy, fond looks they gave each other during their public reunion in the courtroom revealed that they still loved one another in spite of everything. The third case was Sarah's attempt to harass William Neilson for all of his damaging testimony. Sarah accused him of embezzling $200 from her. On the eve of his departure for a visit to Australia, he was arrested.

Cousin Rodney had been a loyal slave to Sarah throughout the long divorce trial, repeating whatever she told him to say on the stand, running errands, taking her abuse and standing by her doggedly. But now he was in trouble. She wanted him to testify against Neilson in the embezzlement suit, but he declined. Even Cousin Rodney had apparently had enough. For his betrayal, Sarah threw him out of her house. But Rodney was out on the streets no more than two days before she took him back.

At the conclusion of the embezzlement trial, Neilson's attorney, Judge Davis Louderback, called the charges "malicious and vengeful," designed to intimidate Neilson against testifying in the *Alta* libel case. He tried to persuade the jury that Sarah's word could not be trusted. "...when a woman lost her chastity, she lost her credibility."[221]

Sarah was sitting in the courtroom at the time. "I don't wish to have my character attacked in this Court," she said.

Louderback suggested she would be more comfortable leaving the room during his argument because he was bound to speak plainly about her. When the judge agreed, Sarah started to cry. "'Trust not a woman when she cries,' Louderback sang, 'for it is her nature and she will cry when she wanteth her will.' Sarah then, with a toss of her head, dried her eyes and turned off the lachrymal fountain."[222]

Louderback went on, calling Sarah "a lewd woman" twice more before he finished. The jury went out and came back in fifteen minutes, finding Neilson not guilty.

In these few years, Sarah must have gotten to know the various courtrooms of San Francisco well. It had become her full-time occupation to go to court, and any courtroom where she was to appear was always crowded with the curious public. They were there for two reasons: to see a celebrity and to have a ringside seat for the best in courtroom drama. Sarah Althea almost never disappointed them. But if they thought the main show was over after Sharon vs. Sharon, they were wrong. That was merely the warm-up act.

Judge Lorenzo Sawyer was the judge presiding over the case of the validity of the marriage contract, and David Terry acted as Sarah's attorney. By now it was obvious to everybody that there was a blossoming romance afoot. When Sarah and Terry appeared in court together, Sarah hung on his arm and talked continuously to him. An *Alta* reporter, observing them together, said, "The Tylers were also present for a short time, but Sarah had eyes for none but the portly gentleman from Stockton...."[223] He was likewise enthralled with her. It is no great mystery as to why Terry would succumb to this charming woman. He was lonely and in mourning for his wife, who had been ill for such a long time. Sarah was vivacious and energetic, full of high spirits. She must have represented life itself to Terry.

The celebrated handwriting expert from Chicago, Dr. R. U. Piper, was on hand to examine the marriage contract. Before Sarah would allow him to touch it, she asked to see his hands. With a pen-knife, she cleaned and pared his fingernails. "At any rate," she said, "you will be able to say some day that you had your nails cleaned for you by Mrs. Sharon."[224]

When Piper said he wanted to take a small ink sample from one of the "Dear Wife" letters, Sarah had a fit. Judge Terry tried to reassure her that it was okay, but she wouldn't be calmed. "Seeing the expert was about to commence his investigations, Sarah suddenly snatched the documents from the table and hurriedly left the room and building, leaving the expert and spectators so paralyzed with astonishment that no one made an effort to check her progress until she was out of the building and scurrying away towards home."[225]

Judge Sawyer ordered her to return the documents, but on the day examination was to resume, she was a no-show. The judge threatened to charge her with contempt, but still she stayed away. After three days of waiting for her, Sawyer issued a warrant for her arrest. The U. S. marshals assigned to the case staked out her house on Larkin Street and Terry's city residence on Kearny, but Sarah eluded them. They learned from a witness that she had been at Terry's place, veiling herself coming and going, and using "a narrow exit into Morton street, used only by servants, and as a coal elevator."[226]

Judge Terry, meanwhile, left San Francisco for Stockton, as his son Sam was seriously ill. He returned on March 28 to make a court date and was surprised that Sarah Althea was still absent. He asked the court for a few more days, no doubt intending to persuade her to come back to court with the marriage contract. But Terry had a more pressing obligation. Since court was adjourned until Tuesday, he returned to Stockton to be with his son over the weekend. Samuel L. Terry, a Stockton lawyer and former state legislator, died on April 1. David Terry remained in Stockton for the rest of the week. Sarah stayed in hiding, while three different cases convened without them, with George Tyler, Walter Levy and Colonel Flournoy filling in.

After burying his son in the Stockton Rural Cemetery on Friday, Judge Terry returned to San Francisco to champion his wayward client.

One of the marshals looking for Sarah had been staking out her house from a saloon across the street. That finally paid off on Sunday, April 5, when he saw her return home. He went over and rang the bell, then stuck his foot in the door when she answered. He asked if Miss Hill lived there. "'No, she don't,' was the Antarctic reply; 'Mrs. *Sharon* lives here.'"[227] She ran into the parlor and locked herself in. Judge Terry emerged and spoke to the marshal about his orders to arrest Sarah, then said, "It is a very unpleasant matter to force a lady to go to jail on

Sunday."[228] He promised that she would be in court Monday morning. Meanwhile, she refused to come out of the parlor. Terry and the marshal agreed that if bail was put up, Sarah could avoid jail for the time being.

She was in court on Monday as promised, but did not produce the documents. Terry attempted to bring up the issue of Sharon's residency again, saying that, as he had clearly been a resident of San Francisco for many years, this court had no jurisdiction in the case. The judge was merely annoyed. After over two weeks waiting for Sarah to show up, his patience was frayed.

Judge Terry apparently had been unsuccessful in changing Sarah's mind about the ink sample. He told the court they would not allow the mutilation of the documents. Judge Sawyer, who had been more than indulgent up to this time, reluctantly announced that he had no choice but to order Sarah to jail. He sentenced her to twenty-four hours for contempt.

"I am willing to go to jail and stay there," she said calmly, "to protect my rights and protect my papers. The jail has no terror for me, and I will go there."[229]

The trip to the county jail on April 7 took a long, circuitous route. Followed by a group of reporters, the party first went to Sarah's home where she changed her clothes and packed an overnight bag. Then she said she was hungry, so the party went to a restaurant for dinner. They stopped by Judge Terry's place to pick up the companion Judge Sawyer had allowed for Sarah, Mrs. Burkett. After that, "the hack drove directly to the Broadway jail, the guardians of which were in a state of flutter over the anticipated arrival of probably the most notorious guest that the jail has ever contained."[230] Judge Terry had a chat with the warden, arranging for Sarah to be housed in the comfortable apartment of the matron, Mrs. Belmere, instead of the usual accommodations for prisoners.

"Judge Sawyer has imprisoned Mrs. Sharon for twenty-four hours for contempt of Court," Terry said to a *Chronicle* reporter. "On the same basis he ought to send me to jail for six days, for I have at least six times as much contempt for his Court as the defendant has."[231]

Sarah clearly relished the attention being paid to her during her "punishment." "The Courts don't know Mrs. Bill Sharon," she said, "if they think that she will give up her rights on account of a day in jail....Judge Sawyer has no right to order my papers mutilated, and I'll see they are kept intact....I'm going to sue Sawyer for big damages for false imprisonment."[232]

Her companion Mrs. Burkett asked her about her meals, assuming she would not be eating the food given to prisoners. "I don't know but what I'd better," she said. "I'm going to write a book about this thing and deliver some lectures; so I think it would be a good thing for me to have all the experience I can get."[233] She was preparing to cash in on her celebrity, which wasn't a bad plan. She could summon a crowd just by appearing on the street. She was, in that moment, one of the most notorious and renowned women in the country.

She slept until 10 a.m. the next morning, then ate a big breakfast, not a prisoner's meal after all, but one prepared for the guards. She colored in a scrap-book and wrote poetry until Judge Terry came by to visit. Mary Ellen Pleasant sent a huge bouquet of flowers and a basket of gourmet goodies for her supper. An amateurish poem Sarah wrote, addressed to Judge Sawyer, was published in the *Chronicle*, and included the following verse:

> Oh, cursed gold, that would corrupt
> The Judges of the land—
> Give way to honesty and truth
> And let them mighty stand.

When it was almost time for Sarah's release, a carriage decorated with four bouquets of flowers pulled up in front of the jail. A crowd of about five hundred had gathered outside and were impatiently waiting to catch a glimpse of the prisoner. From behind barred windows, she "surveyed the mob in the street, and commented on their belief in her right and purity."[234] She was always certain that the people were with her. Many of them were, but there was more than one man who had offered his services to William Sharon to kill Sarah for hire. She claimed to have had similar offers from supporters anxious to take care of the Sharon problem for her. "And how much worse off would the world really be," asked the *Fresno Republican* of May 23, 1885, "if it should be deprived of Sarah Althea Hill and William Sharon?" But, really, that was a hypocritical statement. The newspapers were buttering their bread with the story.

On her exit from jail, Sarah Althea was in her glory. "As the turnkey swung open the door she stepped out on the balcony and received a cheer from one portion of the mob and howls from another. In response, she shouted to them to follow her example, 'and always, in litigation with a rich man, stand up for your rights. Be brave like me,' she concluded, and the crowd yelled again, and she entered the hack....and was driven rapidly down Kearny street, with her head out of the window."[235]

25. DEAD AND RELUCTANT WITNESSES

In June, 1885, the perjury trial of Martha Wilson finally came to court, hampered by not having access to the marriage contract. Sarah Althea was called to the stand and asked to turn it over. She said she didn't know where it was. She had given it to Judge Terry and he had sent it out of state. "I would trust Judge Terry with anything I had in the world," she added.[236]

Ultimately, Martha Wilson, whose lawyers were paid for by William Sharon, was acquitted.

Also during this time, the Supreme Court said it would hear the Sharon case and ordered a hold put on all the actions that Judge Sullivan had decreed, meaning the payment of alimony and attorneys' fees. This was a major victory for William Sharon, who was convinced, like most people, that another trial would end with completely different results. As the *Alta* observed, "The plaintiff's case is slowly and surely crumbling to pieces. All of her important witnesses have either confessed that they perjured themselves, or are under grave and serious charges of felony."[237]

Things were not looking good for Sarah at this point. But she was a woman with an unquenchable spirit. Denied alimony and faced with another court battle, she decided she could raise money by lecturing. "I intend to begin my lecturing tour in the San Joaquin valley somewhere and after going through the country I will lecture in this city....I think I can safely appeal to the sympathies of the women of the State."[238]

Now geared into serious retaliation, William Sharon spared no expense in his fight to prove the marriage contract a forgery. He produced dozens of affidavits denouncing Sarah's character prior to the two of them meeting, primarily from the staff at the Baldwin Hotel where she had lived. They contained juicy details about her love affair with Reuben Lloyd and her shameless flirtations with other men, even men on the hotel staff. There seemed to be no shortage of people happy to denounce her. Without even trying, George Tyler had found out unsavory details about Sarah early on. He told Neilson he had spoken to a man who said he "had relations with her, as he described, more times than he had hairs on his head."[239] Neither Tyler nor Neilson named the man.

The incriminating affidavits were not made public, but were reserved for the eyes of the attorneys and judges. In an effort to counter them, Sarah and her lawyers cast about for witnesses to testify that her reputation was unblemished. That turned out to be an uphill battle.

To this end, Sarah herself paid Reuben Lloyd a visit at his office. She asked if he would make a statement saying she was a virtuous woman and that nothing inappropriate had ever happened between them during his visits to her hotel room. Lloyd refused, saying he didn't want to be drawn into the mess. Sarah lost her temper and pulled a revolver on him, putting it under his nose. He slammed the door between them, quickly locking it. She stood in the hallway pounding on the door with the butt of the revolver and screaming curses at him.

After her appeal to Lloyd failed, Sarah wrote a letter to the Masons asking them to intervene and persuade Lloyd, as a Mason, to do his duty and testify on her behalf to disprove the "affidavits of bell-boys, porters and chambermaids of the Baldwin Hotel, reflecting on my virtue and morality." Her request was ignored.[240]

Lloyd could not have done any differently. Sarah wanted him to swear in court that she was virtuous and chaste. Sarah lied so effortlessly and with such conviction that she seemed not to understand that others could not easily do the same. The relationship between Lloyd and Sarah was almost certainly sexual. If he had told the truth, he would have done exactly the opposite of what she wanted. Not to mention his professional allegiance to William Sharon and his son-in-law Newlands. Lloyd's position would seem to define the saying, "between a rock and a hard place."

George Tyler had been working his own angles to find new witnesses, especially since the ones Sarah had bought had fallen by the wayside. One of those he found would erupt into a huge scandal that would send two people to prison. For once, Sarah Althea had nothing to do with it. Mary Ellen Pleasant, who had already produced most of the witnesses for the plaintiff, helped to find this one as well. Sarah always considered her a brilliant planner, but if plans are judged by their ultimate success, those associated with the Sharon divorce were titanic failures. The lies simply could not stand up to intense scrutiny.

The affidavit that got several people into hot water was from Isabella Clark, a black fortune-teller, previously known as Madam Salome. She was willing to swear, Mary Ellen told Tyler, that Sharon had introduced Sarah as his wife. By this time, 1884, Isabella Clark was no longer telling fortunes and was living in the almshouse. Of course, Tyler was anxious to have a statement, so Mary Ellen sent her good friend, Notary James E. Brown, and one of her best buddies, Eleanor Weile, out to take a deposition from Clark. Recall that Weile was one of the women who had testified that Sarah Althea was in the Bell mansion when she was actually at the Masonic graveyard (yet another spectacular failure of Mary Ellen's).

The affidavit Brown and Weile obtained said that Madam Salome "had been approached by Senator Sharon, who desired to procure some love tokens and lucky charms; that on the occasion of one of these visits, Mr. Sharon was accompanied by Sarah Althea, whom he introduced as his wife."[241]

After seeing the affidavit, Tyler took Isabella Clark out of the almshouse and gave her a place to live where she was cleaned up and properly nourished to prepare her for testifying in court. A month later, she was returned to the almshouse after Tyler decided she couldn't be used as a witness after all. Her affidavit, however, was still on file as evidence.

Every affidavit filed by Tyler was followed up on by Sharon's lawyers, this one included. They visited Isabella Clark in the almshouse, finding a woman who was completely demented. She could not even recognize people she saw every day and could tell nothing about her life. Nor could she sign her name. Both Brown and Weile were charged with falsifying testimony, a felony.

The trial of James E. Brown and Eleanor Weile came up in August, 1885. Numerous witnesses, including doctors and nurses, testified that Isabella Clark, who died while this trial was ongoing of "softening of the brain," had been far too insane in 1884 to make a statement regarding the Sharon case. The defense of Brown and Weile consisted of both of them insisting that when they met with Clark and took her statement, she was sane. Both Judge Tyler and Mary Ellen Pleasant testified to the same thing, that on the single occasion they had spoken to Clark, she seemed perfectly coherent and competent. They had no idea there was anything wrong with her.

Brown and Weile were convicted and sentenced to five years in San Quentin. As usual, Mary Ellen remained just outside the circle of guilt. But the bogus affidavit of Isabella Clark was not forgotten. It would resurface again to take a swing at Judge Tyler.

26. A STACKED DECK

During the summer of 1885, the case of Sharon vs. Hill to declare the marriage contract invalid continued in Judge Lorenzo Sawyer's court. Recall that Sawyer was the judge who sent Sarah to jail for contempt. He was already unpopular with her team, but the deck was about to be stacked even more heavily against her.

Serving a summer stint in the California circuit, Stephen J. Field, associate justice of the United States Supreme Court, came on the scene to share the bench with Sawyer. Justice Field, like the other prominent men in this story, had come to California during the Gold Rush days. He and David Terry, personally and professionally, went way back. Coincidentally, he had succeeded Terry as chief justice of the California Supreme Court in 1859. Ultimately, he had gone on to be a justice on the U.S. Supreme Court, appointed in 1863 by Abraham Lincoln.

In 1884, Field sought the nomination of the Democratic Party as a presidential candidate. Knowing that Judge Terry had substantial influence at the Democratic Convention in Stockton, Field asked Terry for his help. Terry actively opposed him instead and put Grover Cleveland forward as California's choice. Because California was Field's home state, the move was seen as a huge vote of no confidence. If his own state did not support him, what chance did he have with the rest of the country?

Terry believed Field held a grudge against him for his lack of support in 1884. In opposing the nomination of Field, Terry wrote, "I could not give him the California delegation; and if I could I would not, as his judicial record would absolutely prevent my giving him my support; that no place in the records of his decisions could it be found that he had ever given a judgment for a poor man against a rich one, no matter what the evidence."[242]

Added to this bias, Field was an old friend of William Sharon's and had ruled in his favor in the past. Field's influence in helping Sharon in the federal courts cannot be disregarded, as the two were tight. When Field was in San Francisco, Sharon let him stay at the Palace Hotel for free. Though a Republican himself, Sharon worked unofficially to promote Field for the presidential nomination. "He is considered one of the most able jurists in the country," Sharon remarked, "and his general record on the Supreme Bench is viewed as without reproach."[243] Sharon's son-in-law, Frank Newlands, now acting as one of Sharon's lawyers, had also campaigned for Field. Additionally, Field had been friends with Senator David Broderick, the man David Terry mortally wounded in the 1859 duel. If you were David Terry, Stephen J. Field would have been the last man you would want sitting on your case.

Justice Stephen J. Field (Courtesy of the Library of Congress)

In addition to the less than friendly bench, Sarah Althea was causing more than her usual share of trouble. It was during this trial that she lost all sense of decorum, swearing, yelling and making threats in court. It seemed a change had come over her. Whereas during the first trial, she had let herself be guided by people like Tyler, Terry, Neilson and Mary Ellen, now she was constantly in an uproar. Perhaps it was simply that things were not going well for her. So many people had deserted her, and the organized, well-financed attack against her was deadly. She was like a cornered cat.

When Sarah made her deposition during this trial, she had become younger than she had been before. When she came to California, said her statement, "she was a little girl in short dresses and her hair hanging down her back."[244] She also said she was twenty-five when the marriage contract was signed in 1880, despite having put down twenty-seven at the time, and despite her actual age of thirty. It's no wonder that her true age at the time of her death was anybody's guess.

On August 3, depositions were being taken in court by the Master in Chancery, Stephen Houghton. The judges were not present, nor was David Terry. Oliver Evans and William Stewart were there for the defense. Sarah sat beside William Tyler, her junior counsel, in a state of high anxiety, insulting Sharon and members of his family loudly enough for everyone to hear. As R. U. Piper, the handwriting expert, was being examined on the stand, Sarah was more interested in reading the deposition of Susan Smith, the woman she had called after poisoning herself over Reuben Lloyd. As she read, she became more and more agitated, aiming her venom primarily at William Stewart, the attorney who had taken Smith's deposition.

"When I see this testimony," she said, ignoring the repeated requests of Houghton to stop interrupting, "I feel like taking that man Stewart out and cowhiding him. I will shoot him yet; that very man sitting there. To think he would put up a woman to come here and deliberately lie about me like that. I will shoot him. They know when I say I will do it, that I will do it. I shall shoot him as sure as you live; the man that is sitting right there; and I shall have that woman, Mrs. Smith, arrested for this, and make her prove it."[245]

Houghton asked Tyler to make her stop talking, but Tyler was hopelessly ineffective. Houghton finally took the pages away from her, saying that if they were so upsetting, she should read them later. Still she made defiant remarks.

"I have at all times been disposed to be as tolerant and lenient with you as possible," Houghton said to Sarah, "but toleration should have a limit, and the limit has been reached. Early in the proceedings the court suggested that I ought to be very lenient with you, and, in conformity to that suggestion as well as from my own inclination, I have treated you with the greatest consideration and forbearance....Since the commencement of the examination in this case your offensive conduct has frequently disturbed the orderly course of the proceedings, and I have tried in every way which my imagination could suggest to check you— by considerate treatment, by ignoring your misbehavior, by courteous protest and persuasion, by rebuke, by appeal to your counsel, by threatening to report your conduct to the court. But, instead of abating, the evil is constantly growing worse. Now this thing must stop."[246]

The statement, "the court suggested that I ought to be very lenient with you" is extremely interesting. Why was she being allowed to behave so badly? That isn't clear, but it may simply have been that Sarah was so disruptive in the past that the men in charge had grown weary of trying to make her conform to courtroom decorum. After all, they couldn't stop the proceedings every day to deal with her outbursts. Although she may have felt unfairly persecuted by Sharon's counsel, they too were passing over innumerable opportunities to harass her. They never asked that she be charged with contempt, for instance, though they faced numerous opportunities.

While the next witness was being questioned, Sarah pulled her pistol from her bag and set it on the table in front of her, pointing the barrel at Evans. "The nervous fingers of one of Sarah's hands were toying about the lock and trigger, and for a moment it seemed as though her crazy threats were about to be carried into execution. Evans asked: 'I beg pardon, Madame, but may I inquire what you propose doing with that thing? Is it your intention to kill me?'"[247]

"I am not going to shoot you just now," she replied, "unless you want to be shot, and think you deserve it."[248]

Houghton took the pistol from her and court was adjourned. The incident was reported to Judge Sawyer and Justice Field.

This wasn't the first time Sarah had waved her pistol in the courtroom and threatened to shoot somebody. Sharon's attorneys, Evans and Stewart, who had every right to seek retribution against her, held back. "They have not asked the court to proceed to punish defendant for the contempt committed. They only ask, and it is certainly a very moderate and reasonable request, that they shall not be required to practice their profession in the circuit court of the United States at the muzzle of their opponent's pistols."[249]

Justice Field was outraged at Sarah's behavior and forbade firearms in the courtroom altogether. During the discussion, he also said that any member of the bar who comes into the court armed should be disbarred. William Tyler took exception to this, saying that a man had a right to defend himself. If you recall, he had pulled his gun in court during

Sharon vs. Sharon. Field told him that the proper way to deal with armed witnesses was to report them to the court. "That will not stop a bullet," Tyler objected.[250] Field would not relent, saying that the early days of California when everybody was armed were over and that the law was supreme. The carrying of arms in court, he said, would not be tolerated.

This was only the beginning of Justice Field's crusade against the old style of California justice. Civilized men of law behaved in a certain way, and it had nothing to do with firearms, duels or other obsolete and barbaric means of obtaining personal satisfaction. The law was supreme to him, as he said. It had to be obeyed and it had to be respected, and those who would not work within the law had no business in the legal profession.

27. THE KING IS DEAD

In October, 1885, William Sharon became seriously ill. Toward the end of the month, he appeared to be improving, but by early November, he was on his death bed, suffering from heart disease and unable to eat solid food.

Concurrent with Sharon's illness, Sarah announced that she was making her stage debut. She had been offered the coveted role of Portia in *The Merchant of Venice,* to be performed at the Grand Opera House. How apt that Sarah should play Portia, the beautiful, intelligent heiress who proves her wit and worth in a courtroom. She would appear under the name "Mrs. William Sharon." The *Alta*, with its usual cheek, greeted the news with, "It is a long jump from farce to tragedy."[251]

The acting debut was to take place the weekend of November 13, and she would perform six nights a week and lecture on Sundays. After her Shakespearean role, Sarah would star in a new play, a "comic drama" written by journalist Oscar T. Schuck and based on the events of Sharon vs. Sharon. The play was titled "Wife or Mistress; or Althea's Dream." After her theater engagements, she planned to travel around the country, living in a specially-outfitted train car, lecturing. After the East Coast, she would carry her show to Europe.

A New Zealand gossip columnist in San Francisco, commenting on this plan, said, "[She] will probably visit Australia, just as if anyone cared one dot about Sharon v. Sharon outside of America." And, yet, he knew his New Zealand readers would be interested. Sarah Althea was a world-wide phenomenon. "I shall follow Sarah's course carefully," he wrote, "and transmit the facts as they are developed."[252]

A few days before the play was to open, it was "indefinitely postponed." There was no explanation, but we can imagine several. Perhaps Sarah wasn't much of an actress or she was too disruptive, or both. There is also a high probability that William Sharon or his toadies had something to do with the cancellation of Sarah's performance. Her appearance on a San Francisco stage under the name "Mrs. William Sharon" would have been an outrage to him and made him an even greater laughing stock than he already was. Most citizens only knew Sarah Althea from newspaper articles. If they saw her on stage, she could command an even larger following. Sharon knew how enchanting Sarah could be. Even if her stage career made no reflection on him at all, he was bitter enough toward her by now that he might have jumped at the chance to dash her dreams any way he could. It is safe to say that if William Sharon didn't want Sarah performing in San Francisco, she wouldn't perform. Her much-anticipated acting career was over before it began.

During his illness, Senator Sharon deeded all his property to his heirs, and included in the deed a statement about his nemesis, repeating his claim that he had never married her or promised to marry her, that all the evidence she had produced were forgeries and lies. He empowered and directed his heirs to "vigorously contest in every Court where a contest can be made the false claim and pretension of the said Sarah Althea Hill."[253]

A few days before he died, Sharon sent for Fred Davis, a detective who had been with him throughout the ordeal with Sarah. "I want you to stay by those wretches, Fred," he said. "They have driven the knife into me, and they deserve punishment. Stay with them till they get it."[254]

William Sharon, the King of the Comstock, died on November 13, 1885, coincidentally the day Sarah Althea was to have begun her acting career. His funeral was held in the lobby of the Palace Hotel.

It is tempting to hearken back to the charm Sarah placed in the Masonic cemetery grave, intoned with the spell that Sharon should either marry her or die.

He left large sums of money to charity, including $50,000 to Golden Gate Park. The original plan for the money was to build a marble gate at the Stanyan Street entrance, but that turned out to be an unpopular idea with the public. Eventually, the Sharon Building was built in the park to serve as the center of the Children's Quarter. The building sustained considerable damage in the 1906 earthquake and had to be closed for a while. In the 1960s, it became an art studio. The Sharon Art Studio still stands in the park near the children's playground and operates under the stewardship of San Francisco Parks and Recreation Department.

By the conclusion of the case of Sharon vs. Hill on December 26, 1885, too late for Sharon to witness, Justice Field had returned to Washington, so was not involved in the judgment. Judge Deady and Judge Sawyer rendered the decision against Sarah Althea. She was ordered to surrender the marriage contract for cancellation, as it was deemed a forgery.

The decision was based in part on the character of the litigants. William Sharon was described by Deady as "a person of long standing and commanding position in this community, of large fortune and manifold business and social relations, and is therefore so far, and by all that these imply, specially bound to speak the truth."[255] Of Sarah Althea, he said, "On the other hand, the defendant is a comparatively obscure and unimportant person, without property or position in the world. Although apparently of respectable birth and lineage, she has deliberately separated herself from her people, and selected as her intimates and confidants doubtful persons from the lower walks of life." Furthermore, he said of her testimony, "It is full of reckless, improbable, and in some instances undoubtedly false statements."[256]

If Sarah had not perjured herself so frequently and thoroughly, bribing witnesses, lying about things that didn't matter, and forging supporting documents, the outcome might have been different. "And while it is possible that," Deady conceded, "the alleged declaration may be genuine, it must be conceded that neither that fact, nor any circumstance tending to prove the same, can be established by her uncorroborated oath."[257] In other words, if she weren't such a bald-faced liar about everything else, we might have believed her about the secret marriage.

What was next for Sarah's suit? Sharon had urged his heirs on his deathbed to fight her to the end. His death wouldn't relax his offense against her. If anything, it would become more resolved in the hands of Frank Newlands. Newlands had nothing but contempt for Sarah. The lingering warmth that William Sharon had allowed to soften his assault against her would be absent in Newlands.

With the overwhelming information now made public that none of her evidence would stand up to the light of day, it seems Sarah would have given up her fight to be recognized as William Sharon's legitimate wife. But that was not the case. Her first legal move after Sharon died was to contest his will. That case was quickly decided against her.

An interesting side note to the Sharon divorce trial was that the name "Sarah Althea" became quite popular, maybe not among women naming their offspring, but certainly among men naming race horses and sailboats.

28. MRS. TERRY

What had been a laughable joke made by General Barnes sixteen months earlier became a reality on January 7, 1886, when Sarah Althea Hill and David Smith Terry got married in St. Mary's Catholic Church in Stockton. The beautiful Gothic building on Washington Street still stands as one of the city's most distinctive downtown landmarks. Father W. B. O'Connor presided over a quiet, private ceremony in which State Treasurer Denis J. Oullahan was best man. There were no bridesmaids, no family members, and reporters were not admitted. Terry was sixty-two and Sarah, despite the age of thirty-two on the marriage license, was thirty-five.

St. Mary's Church

On the morning of her wedding, Sarah took a boat to Stockton. "Judge Terry's fiancée was aboard the steamer to arrive at daylight, and in expectation of seeing the bride a number of persons gathered on Stockton slough, near where the steamer *T. C. Walker*, with Miss Hill aboard, arrived from San Francisco about 3 o'clock. Their curiosity was ungratified, because the programme provided that Miss Hill should remain aboard until within a few minutes of the time set for the wedding ceremony."[258]

Both bride and groom were dressed in plain, dark clothing. The event was intentionally subdued. Since nothing Sarah ever did was subdued, the mood of the day must have been Terry's idea, in respect to his first wife and the general feeling of disapproval that hung over the union. His son Clinton, though he was in the neighborhood, did not attend the ceremony, making his feelings clear. At the time of the wedding, Clinton and his young family occupied the Terry's Stockton house. His father bought him a ranch in Fresno County, and Clinton moved out on his father's wedding day, making way for the newlyweds.

Judge Terry's House - Fremont Street

The Terry home was at Center and Fremont Streets and faced McLeod Lake among a cluster of early dwellings that included the home of Charles Weber, founder of Stockton. The Terry house was torn down in the 1930s.

Clinton Terry was not the only one who objected to this marriage. Many of Terry's friends were shocked and disheartened. Some of them would go as far as to withdraw from his life. It is safe to say that most people who knew him thought the marriage was a huge mistake. A newspaper editorial that appeared a few years later said that Terry's many and good friends had felt "that his marriage with Miss Hill was an insult to them and to the memory of the mother of his children, and a menace to society."[259]

Some people speculated that this wedding was the latest ploy in the Sharon case to gain some legal advantage for Sarah, maybe because it was so low-key, so much so that Judge Terry went into his office later that same day. But the two of them seemed genuinely happy together. He admired her willfulness, intelligence, and determination, and even though her crusade against William Sharon was misguided, she exhibited a ferocious bravery in defending herself. One of Terry's most bitter insults toward anyone was an accusation of cowardice. His appreciation for Sarah was genuine. But what about her? What did she want from him? A reporter for the *Daily Democrat* of Stockton pegged it when he wrote, "...Sarah Althea at last decided to let her head rest upon the bosom of her stalwart legal friend and defender and to be henceforth protected by him. Judge Terry has stood by her nobly in all her troubles since he became acquainted with her and the lady should be well satisfied with the kind fate that has landed her in such a safe harbor."

We have to wonder what would have happened to Sarah at this point in her life had Judge Terry not married her. When she came to San Francisco, she was beautiful, popular, surrounded by family, and had enough money to live comfortably. She was respectable and had wonderful prospects for marriage. But a few years later, she had nothing. She had lost her money through bad investments. She had been socially ruined by her notorious affair with William Sharon. To many people, she was no better than a prostitute. Though she had aspirations for a career on stage, her one attempt to break into acting had fallen flat. A lecture tour might have worked out, if she could have maintained the discipline for it, but that would not have lasted for long. Her claim to fame would soon have become yesterday's news. It is not much of a stretch to see David Terry as her savior.

They had spent months together already and Terry never seemed angry or exasperated with Sarah. He had been patient, solicitous and indulgent with her. She was fond, trusting and even obedient. She was Kate to his Petruchio. So far, he was the only man who could tame her. Not that he would take all the fight out of her. He didn't want to. Together, the two of them could be a ferocious pair of wild cats, as time would tell. Some people said that his first wife had a steadying influence on him, inhibiting his wild nature. Perhaps so, for once paired with Sarah, he seemed to become infected with her stormy temperament.

Although Judge Terry did suffer some loss of respect as a result of his association and then his marriage to Sarah, he still had considerable influence in Stockton and San Joaquin County. He played a leading role, for example, in the 1886 Democratic Convention there.

Though successful, Terry wasn't rich. He owned acreage in Fresno County, interest in a cattle ranch, a house and two lots in Stockton and a house in Fresno, but most of his property was heavily mortgaged. Nevertheless, Sarah's life was comfortable and respectable. She was the wife of a famous judge, a highly successful lawyer, a man with influence and many friends. In San Joaquin County, he was a celebrity of long standing and may as well have been Prince of the County. Just as Sarah had preferred the pet name "Sen" or "Senator" for William Sharon, even in private, she frequently called her husband "Judge." Sarah's yearning for a position of importance in society was satisfied at last. She slipped quietly out of the news. She gave parties and traveled around the state with her husband, but she caused no controversy. Married life suited her.

Meanwhile, the fallout from the Sharon case continued to fall, though Sarah was not directly involved during 1886. Eleanor Weile and James E. Brown were serving time in San Quentin because of the phony Isabella Clark affidavit. Recall that Isabella Clark was the demented woman in the almshouse who supposedly remembered William Sharon introducing Sarah Althea as "Mrs. Sharon," though she was so mentally enfeebled she could not even sign her own name or answer the simplest of questions about her life.

Brown and Weile were not serving their time quietly. They were both applying to General Barnes for interviews, saying they had important information about fraud in the Sharon case. Sharon's team promised to help Weile and Brown beat their felony convictions in new trials if they could give any information that would help put George Tyler in prison.

Weile took the bait and admitted to lying in her earlier testimony. She told Barnes that the story about Sharon fathering the Bertha Bornstein baby had been made up by Mary Ellen Pleasant. She went on to confess that she had been mistaken about the evidence she gave putting Sarah Althea in the Bell mansion the day of the graveyard incident. She had not seen her there that day after all. Weile also admitted that the Isabella Clark affidavit was a deliberate fraud, but she stopped short of implicating Mary Ellen Pleasant in that. General Barnes knew that if anybody had the inside scoop regarding Mary Ellen, it was Eleanor Weile, and like all of us, Barnes wanted to know once and for all who was responsible for authoring the marriage contract. He asked Weile about it, "but she said she could not say anything without consulting Mrs. Pleasance."[260] Her statement implied that she knew something and that Mary Ellen also knew something about the contract. Time and time again, there were implications that the marriage contract, and thus the entire scheme, had been masterminded by Mary Ellen, but proof was always just out of reach.

James E. Brown, the notary and long-time friend of Mary Ellen, was interviewed by District Attorney Wilson. Brown told Wilson that he "could produce the person who drew up the original marriage contract, and could also connect Tyler with the affidavit and other crimes."[261]

George W. Tyler was put on trial in the summer of 1886 for manufacturing fraudulent evidence in the Sharon case. William Tyler and David Terry were his lawyers, with Mrs. Terry on hand to observe, "richly dressed and apparently in the best of health and spirits."[262]

General Barnes and the District Attorney were confident that Brown and Weile, to save themselves, would deliver Tyler up on a plate, blaming the Isabella Clark debacle on him. It was never completely clear when and what Tyler had known about Isabella Clark's state of mind. Because he removed her from the almshouse with the goal of having her testify, he must have thought her capable of testifying. But then he sent her back, presumably realizing she was an unfit witness. If anyone on Sarah's team had known that from the beginning, it had to be the person who suggested Isabella Clark in the first place: Mary Ellen Pleasant. But the Sharon team was not going after Mary Ellen. She had no official capacity in the suit. As Sarah Althea's attorney, George Tyler was the big fish. Also, the attitudes of those carrying on the torch for William Sharon were colored by his own attitude, and he had always seen his primary enemies as William Neilson and George Tyler.

At his trial, Tyler repeated the testimony he had given earlier, that the one time he had spoken to Isabella Clark in 1884, she seemed perfectly intelligent and coherent. Mary Ellen Pleasant testified in a similar vein to support him.

Then James E. Brown was called to testify, but the spirit of his testimony was not what Barnes and company expected. He said he was visited in prison by Sharon emissaries who told him they could help him if he would put the blame for the Clark affidavit on Tyler himself.[263]

Both Brown and Weile gave testimony to the effect that Sharon's people attempted to bribe them to falsely blame Judge Tyler for the phony Clark affidavit. They did not implicate Tyler in any criminal activity, nor did they name the author of the marriage contract.

Brown and Weile may have faltered briefly in their loyalty to Mary Ellen while they were in prison, asking for a deal from Barnes, but by the time Tyler came to trial, they were back on track. They had clearly been coached by Mary Ellen to turn the tables on Barnes and D. A. Wilson.

When Mary Ellen herself returned to the stand, she had a marvelous new story to tell about how she had received a visit from Henry Williams, who had come on behalf of Barnes and Newlands, to make her an offer "to reimburse her for what money she had advanced plaintiff in the Sharon divorce case, and also to raise a mortgage on some of her property if she would testify that Tyler had procured the Clark affidavit fraudulently. She put Williams off, she said, and had him call again, when she had secreted two witnesses in an adjoining room, who heard the offer repeated. Her testimony was corroborated by those two witnesses. One was her coachman, J.W. Allen, and the other Hugh Mauldin, a clerk in a jewelry store in this city."[264]

Henry Williams said that this never happened; he made no such offer to Mary Ellen Pleasant. This testimony of Mary Ellen and her supporters is reminiscent of the original trial where she put up five witnesses to swear that Sarah was at the Bell house the day she was at the cemetery. One is tempted to believe Henry Williams. Thus the defense of Tyler, which appeared to be engineered mainly by Mary Ellen, was to prove there was a Sharon conspiracy against him to railroad an innocent man into a prison sentence.

The end result was a hung jury.

Meanwhile, David Terry obtained pardons for Brown and Weile from the governor on the grounds that they had no criminal intent in committing the fraud.

29. THE TIGER WAKES

Though Sarah was living quietly and presumably contentedly in Stockton as "Mrs. Judge Terry," her court battles were not over.

In November, 1887, David Terry appealed the case of William Sharon vs. Sarah Althea Hill to the U. S. Supreme Court. Recall that this was the case where Judge Sawyer had declared the marriage contract null and void. He had ordered it surrendered to be destroyed, but the Terrys had no intention of obeying that order.

William Sharon's appeal to the California Supreme Court was also still pending. It finally came up in August, 1887, and was concluded at the end of January, 1888. Sarah was again victorious. The court upheld Judge Sullivan's decision granting her a divorce. The original judgment was for $2500 a month alimony and $55,000 for counsel fees. The Supreme Court reduced the amount of alimony to $500 a month and granted nothing for counsel fees. The decision was four to three. They didn't take up the question of the validity of the marriage contract itself, but only if such a contract constituted a legal marriage. They felt the alimony of $2,500 was excessive, especially since Senator Sharon had been supporting Sarah on $500 a month during their "marriage." The three dissenting judges believed that there had been no marriage in a legal sense. This case rested almost entirely on whether a marriage can be legal if it occurs secretly.

Public opinion on the latest victory for Sarah was described by the *Los Angeles Herald* as follows: "This outcome of the plucky fight made by Miss Hill against the millionaire (now deceased) was generally received with satisfaction; for the American public is always in sympathy with the weak when fighting the strong. In this case there is a wide-spread belief that money had been lavishly used by the defendant in order to crush the woman who stood so bravely up against him to vindicate her honor and assert her rights."[265] Sarah could not have summed it up better herself.

The fact that the marriage contract was ruled a forgery and voided by a federal court may seem at odds with this new court decision, but the contract, valid or not, was not the entire proof of marriage. Now that her rights as a wife were reaffirmed by the court, Sarah was again in a position to receive half of the community property acquired during her marriage to Sharon. Her counsel estimated his worth at the time they were married at five million, and his wealth at the time of divorce at ten million, putting her rightful settlement at a cool five million. Today that figure would be close to 130 million.

Following this decision, Fred Sharon and Frank Newlands filed a bill of revivor to have the circuit court enforce its earlier decision (William Sharon vs. Sarah Althea Hill, December 26, 1885) to force Sarah to surrender the marriage contract and have it nullified. Since the contract had never been given up and the plaintiff had died before the decision was rendered, the court order had not been enforced. So the case was back in court in 1888 and, fatefully, two of the three judges presiding over it (George Sabin, Stephen Field, Lorenzo Sawyer) were already considered unsympathetic to the Terrys. Judge Sawyer was the one who had previously declared the marriage contract a forgery. Who needs three guesses to figure out how he would vote this time around?

This was not good news for Sarah. That dirty, crumpled document was her most prized possession. Judge Sawyer had almost gotten it away from her once. Now he was back. She considered him her enemy and she had done nothing in the time since he sentenced her to jail to endear herself to him. In August, 1888, she chanced to be on the same train with him and took the opportunity to express her resentment. With a great deal of self-satisfaction, she described the incident: "...I went up and caught him by the hair and pulled it until he cried for mercy."[266]

According to Judge Van Dyke of Los Angeles, who was traveling in the same car, the Terrys came on board at Fresno. Mrs. Terry passed Judge Sawyer and glared at him. When she passed him the next time, she reached over and pulled his hair sharply. Another witness said, "...after Mrs. Terry made the attack she joined her husband...and related what had occurred with a great deal of glee, at which Judge Terry laughed, then said that the only fit thing to do with Judge Sawyer would be to take him out in the bay and drown him."[267] A short time later Sarah got up and sat behind Judge Sawyer, making him extremely uncomfortable and nervously handling her parasol with what witnesses described as a menacing manner, as if she were going to hit him over the head with it. Before she could do it, her husband came and sat beside her and talked her down, then the two of them moved to another seat.

These incidents seem childish and not particularly ominous. Though Sarah carried a pistol with her always and brandished it on occasion, making threats to kill anybody and everybody who crossed her, she had never fired a single shot at anyone. She had kicked, hit and pulled hair like a child. David Terry, however, had a history of serious violence. His animosity and threatening words were to be taken more seriously. And they were. On the day the court was to announce its decision in the revivor suit, September 3, 1888, Marshal J. C. Franks was in the courtroom with a full complement of deputies and police officers.

Sarah sat beside her husband and their friend R. Porter Ashe. Ashe was a lawyer and race horse owner whose forebears gave their name to Asheville, North Carolina. He had married the flamboyant heiress, Aimée Crocker, in 1887, then struggled through a messy divorce and custody battle over their daughter. Ashe's father, Richard Ashe, who was deceased, had been an intimate friend of Terry's from his earliest days in California, and Ashe, Jr. was to remain an important person in this story for several years to come.

As Justice Field read his decision, it appeared, not surprisingly, that the court would decide in favor of Sharon's heirs, sustaining the previous decision of Judge Sawyer. Unable to contain herself, Sarah stood up and asked, "Justice Field, are you going to order me to give up that marriage contract, which is the evidence of my rights, to be canceled?"[268]

Field told Sarah to sit down, but she became agitated and accused him of having been bought off. She went on, "It appears no one can get justice in this court unless he has a sack. We want to know what you have been paid by the Sharon people."[269]

Field ordered the marshal to remove Sarah from the courtroom, and as he made his move to do so, mayhem ensued.

The events that occurred that day are well documented, though some of the details vary, as they will whenever so much happens so fast. The testimony of the Marshal Franks provides the flavor of the incident. His statement of the events of September 3, which coincides generally with others, follows:

> Judge Field had read for a few minutes when Mrs. Terry stood up, interrupting the court, and said, among other things, "You have been paid for this decision." Judge Field then ordered her to keep her seat, but she continued, saying, "How much did Newlands pay you?" Then Judge Field, looking towards me, said, "Mr. Marshal, remove that woman from the court-room." Mrs. Terry said, in a very defiant manner, "You cannot take me from the court." I immediately stepped to my left to execute the order, passing Judge Terry to where Mrs. Terry was standing. Mrs. Terry immediately sprang at me, striking me in my face with both her hands, saying, "You dirty scrub, you dare not remove me from this court-room." Mrs. Terry made this assault upon me before I had touched her. I

immediately moved to take hold of her when Judge Terry threw himself in my way, getting in front of me, and, unbuttoning his coat, said, in the most defiant and threatening manner, "No man shall touch my wife; get a written order," or words to that effect. I put out my hands towards him, saying, "Judge, stand back; no written order is required"; and just as I was taking hold of Mrs. Terry's arm, Judge Terry assaulted me, striking me a hard blow in the mouth with the right fist, breaking one of my teeth, and I immediately let his wife go and pushed him back. He then put his right hand in his bosom, while at the same time Deputy Farish, Detective Finnegass, and other citizens, caught him by the arms and pulled him down in his chair. I caught hold of Mrs. Terry again, Mr. N. R. Harris, one of my deputies, coming to my assistance, and we took her out of the court-room into my office, she resisting, scratching, and striking me all the time, using violent language, denouncing and threatening the judges and myself, claiming that I had stolen her diamonds and bracelets from her wrists, and calling several times to Porter Ashe to give her her satchel. I, during the whole time, using no more force than was necessary, considering the resistance made by her, addressing her as politely as possible. When we got her into the inner room of my office, I left her in charge of Mr. Harris, went into the main office, saw a body of men scuffling at the door, heard Deputy Marshall Taggart say, "If you attempt to come in here with that knife, I will blow your brains out." I said, "What, has he a knife?" Deputy Farish answered and said, "He had a knife, but we took it away." I then took hold of Judge Terry, and with the assistance of others, pulled him in the main office and shut the door. I had him and his wife placed in my private office in charge of Deputy Marshals Harris, Donnelly, and Taggart. I then went into the court-room, and when I had been there but a short time, Mr. Farish came in and said, "Mrs. Terry wants her satchel, which Porter Ashe has." I went into the corridor and found Mr. Ashe with the satchel. I requested him to hand it to me; at first, he refused, saying that it was Mrs. Terry's private property, and he was going to deliver it to her. I told him she was my prisoner, and her effects should be in my custody, and if he did not give the satchel up I would place him under arrest. He then gave it to me, and I told him to come with me into my office, and I would open it in his presence. He did so, and I opened it and took a pistol therefrom, a self-cocking 41-caliber Colt's pistol, with five chambers loaded, the sixth being empty—after which I delivered the satchel to Mrs. Terry. Mr. Ashe then said he did not intend to give the satchel to her with the pistol in it.[270]

The same general account was given by Deputy Marshal Henry Finnegass, who added, "Terry's conduct throughout this affair was most violent. He acted like a demon."[271]

It is only fair to give equal time to Terry himself, whose version of events was published in the Stockton *Mail*, as follows:

> I made no resistance to any order, and the record is a lie. I was sitting down when my wife interrupted Judge Field, and when he said, "Marshal, remove that woman from the court room," I rose to take her out. As the marshal came towards me I said, "Don't touch her. I will take her out of the court room." Marshal Franks yelled out, "I know my business," and grabbing me by the lapels of the coat tried to force me back into a chair. Two others seized me by the shoulders and forced me down. Again I said, "I will take her out." The men who were bending me back hurt me, and I wrenched myself free and struck at Franks, the blow hitting him in the mouth.
>
> I struck at him because he assaulted me without any right or order of court. By that time they had dragged Mrs. Terry out of the court room. Then their duty ended. They had obeyed the order brutally. The order was to take her out of the court room, and she had been taken out. But that was not enough. They dragged her to a room and shut the door. I heard her scream and went to her. I was a free man and she legally a free woman, and I had a right to be by her side. They had no order to lock her up or keep me from her. But they barred the door, and to scare them away I drew my knife. I told them I did not want to hurt any of them, but they pulled their pistols. I could have killed half a dozen of them if I had wanted to. Two of them had pistols pointed at me. Someone said, "Let him in if he will give up his knife." I said, "Certainly," and gave up my knife. They did not take it from me....The fact is, the court was frightened of something, and had the room full of deputies and fighters of all kinds who wanted a chance to make a showing of bravery, and after it was all over Judge Field lied in the record. I want to get him on the witness stand to repeat his story, and then we will see if there is any law against perjury.[272]

Marshal Finnegass had described Terry as a "demon" during the disruption while he characterized himself as self-controlled and rational. But a close friend of Terry's, Judge Creed Haymond, was forced to question Terry's sanity after this event. He was in the midst of the action that day and had this to say: "It was not the Terry of a few years back who caused that disgraceful scene...in the United States Circuit Court. I witnessed that remarkable defiance of the judiciary. I tried to calm him in his fury. When he thrust his hand into his bosom beneath his vest I caught his arm with my hands. With his great strength he threw me off as if I were a child. Several weeks later a friend of mine told Terry my experience with him. He was surprised, hardly believing it. With some emotion he said that he hadn't the least recollection of my actions. If United States Marshal Franks had not been remarkably courageous that day Terry would have been killed. A timid man would have shot him."[273]

It is important for our story to note that Deputy Marshal David Neagle, so critical in future events, was present in the courtroom that day. This was the incident that formed his opinion of the hot-blooded Terrys. Judge Terry's ferocious anger, his powerful blow to Marshal Franks' face and, most of all, the nine-inch Bowie knife with the five-inch blade, must all have created a vivid image that Neagle would carry into the future.

During this entire episode and afterwards as well, Judge Field never lost his composed demeanor. As soon as the excitement had abated, he continued to calmly read his decision, the conclusion of which was to grant the revivor and reinstate the decree of the earlier court, to again render the marriage contract null and void. That was the expected decision, but it is clear from Sarah's outburst and Judge Terry's later statements that both of them believed the decision had been bought.

While Justice Field finished reading, David Terry was retained in the marshal's office, where he angrily cursed the judges loudly enough to be heard in the courtroom. He called Sawyer a "corrupt son-of-a-bitch," and Field "a bald-headed old son-of-a-bitch."

David Terry was sentenced to six months in jail for contempt. Sarah Althea was also charged with contempt and sentenced to one month. Both of them were taken away to the Alameda County jail. Both Terrys vowed to get revenge against the judges, and Sarah threatened to kill both Field and Sawyer. The Terrys were put in the private apartment of the jailer during their incarceration.

The Terrys had moved from Stockton to Fresno in 1888, where Terry had been a large landowner and a popular figure for many years. Several prominent citizens of Fresno gathered in a show of sympathy and support for the Terrys, making an official statement that included "...we regard Judge Terry's act in protecting his wife to be a chivalrous impulse which will not fail to appeal to the best sentiments of American manhood."[274] The *Fresno Republican* then felt obliged to run an article to say, "We hope that no one will be misled by the resolution adopted by a few of the personal friends of Judge Terry to suppose that the people of Fresno county approve of the violent acts of that gentleman or his wife in resisting the law."[275]

Terry's friend Judge Heydenfeldt offered to petition Field to see if he could reverse the charge of contempt, asking for assurance that Terry wouldn't cause trouble if he were released. Terry answered him in a letter that read, in part, "I do not expect a favorable decision from any application to the Circuit Court....Field probably wishes to pay me for my refusal to aid his Presidential aspirations four years ago....You may say as emphatically as you wish that I will not commit a breach of the peace; that so far from seeking, I will avoid meeting any of the parties concerned. But I will not promise that I will refrain from denouncing the decision and its authors. I believe the decision was purchased and paid for with the coin of the Sharon estate, and I would stay here ten years before I would say what I did not believe."[276] Heydenfeldt petitioned the court for leniency and was denied.

David Terry, like his wife, did not simmer down easily. After two days in jail, he was threatening to have Judges Sawyer and Field impeached when he got out. In some ways, the husband and wife were similar in temperament. Neither of them knew when to back away from a conflict. By now it was obvious to anyone and everyone that the endless litigation in the Sharon case had long ceased to be profitable or even favorable to the Hill-Terry side. This latest episode in court was seriously damaging to Judge Terry's reputation. It might have been forgiven and forgotten if he had simply apologized and waited his imprisonment out quietly. But he didn't stand down.

The six months' sentence was unprecedented. Terry's explanation for the severity of Field's punishment: "He is a monstrous coward, and he safely measures the time he will be detained on this coast holding court. He meant that I should remain in prison until he had returned East, knowing that he deserved punishment, and fearing that I would mete out the punishment he deserved."[277]

One visitor to the jail, J. H. O'Brien, reported that Terry said, "When I get out of jail I will horsewhip Justice Field. He won't dare to come back to California, but the earth is not big enough to hide him from me...If he resents it, I will kill him." Sarah, who was also there, said, "No, don't kill him, Judge; only horsewhip him."[278]

Although Terry had many visitors while in jail, there were many more of his friends and admirers who were afraid to openly support him, men with political aspirations and those employed with large corporations or in federal employ. Field was said to be a tool of the railroads and had tremendous influence in federal government and large corporations, and he was not above using it.

One of the first things Terry did after going to jail was to file a complaint against Marshal J. C. Franks, requesting damages of $10,000 for holding him for three hours without probable cause. He then sued the *Post* Publishing Company for $5,000 damages for libel for an article they ran about what had happened in the courtroom on that auspicious day.

Meanwhile, the Grand Jury issued indictments for crimes committed in the Circuit Court by the Terrys, four indictments against David and two for Sarah.

At the end of Sarah's sentence, she remained in jail with her husband, as she was reportedly too ill to leave.

Porter Ashe, acting as Terry's lawyer, and Thomas Williams, friend to all parties, went to Washington to seek a pardon for David Terry from the President, Grover Cleveland. If you remember, Justice Field had attempted to run for president in 1884, but Grover Cleveland beat him out of the Democratic ticket, largely because California, headed by the Democratic convention at Stockton, did not support Field. Terry, as always, had been a vocal participant in that decision, so might have expected Cleveland to do him a favor. Cleveland met with Ashe on October 7 to hear his appeal. He said he would pass the matter on to the Attorney-General, but by Oct. 17 that hadn't happened. Ashe withdrew the petition, as it appeared Cleveland was not going to act.

When Sarah got out of jail, she was immediately arrested on charges of assault against Marshal Franks. She pled not guilty and introduced a new wrinkle into the case. She said she had merely been defending herself against the marshal's assault. "Marshal Franks kicked me and I will make him suffer for it."[279] She was released on bail. A couple of months later she sued Marshal Franks for $50,000 in damages. At the time of the courtroom scuffle, she said, she had been pregnant. Marshal Franks pushed her against a table in his office. As a result of Franks' rough handling, she had lost the baby while in jail, and the miscarriage had been why she was too ill to leave at the end of her sentence. Her pregnancy was the reason, she said, that her husband had been so determined to defend her against being manhandled.[280]

This suit against the marshal sat untouched for two years, then was dismissed in January, 1891, after Sarah said she no longer wanted to prosecute.

Though she moved about freely while her husband was in jail, Sarah stayed there at night to be with him.

When Terry had served five months, Sheriff Hale was ready to release him, awarding him the usual time off for good behavior, but the sheriff was called into court where Judge Sawyer decided that good behavior did not apply in this case, as it was not a criminal offense. Hale was ordered to hold Terry for the entire sentence.

From his makeshift law office at the county jail, Terry tried every legal trick he knew to get out early, his last appeal a writ of habeas corpus to the Supreme Court, which was dismissed. Nothing worked. No judge and no court came to his aid, and he served his entire six months. The punishment had been severe and had given Terry ample time to stew over what he felt was unfair and vindictive treatment, creating a deep resentment for the judges in the case.

Terry was released from jail on March 3, 1889 and arrested on the four criminal charges outstanding against him. He was released on bail, arraigned, and pled not guilty on all counts.

Two months later the Terrys were back in court on one of the Sharon appeals. They were ordered to produce the marriage contract and Judge Terry announced that the document had been destroyed in a fire that burned his Fresno law office on August 11, 1888. "For a few moments the silence in the court was oppressive, even the justices evincing their evident surprise. Mrs. Terry looked immensely pleased at the result of her coup, and beamed upon the court for a full minute, as she tapped the long table with a pencil."[281] At last Sarah was able to withhold the document without getting into trouble.

Less than a month after his release, Terry got into an argument with druggist L. H. Thompson in Fresno, disputing the druggist's bill of $2.50. Cursing at Thompson, he said his wife had already paid it. Thompson, his ire up, said she hadn't. "The Judge…advanced on Thompson with flushed face, glaring eyes and the movements of an enraged tiger. When within a short distance of Thompson, Terry aimed a terrific blow at the druggist. Thompson stepped aside and, before Terry could strike him a second time, he struck the Judge over the right eye, drawing a stream of blood."[282] A crowd had gathered by now and a few of the onlookers pulled the men apart. While being held by three men, Terry attempted a vicious kick at Thompson's employee, but lost his balance and fell on his back.

Apparently, Terry's adversarial personality wasn't dampened by his time in jail. In fact, he seemed to be losing control.

He was advised by a friend to forget the business with Justice Field and not to seek revenge. "I do not intend to injure Field bodily," he replied. "but if the opportunity presents itself, while I shall not seek it, I shall slap him in the face or horsewhip him. I have made up my mind to that and nothing can alter my determination."[283]

30. LOCKED AND LOADED

Justice Stephen Field, on a year hiatus from his Circuit Court duties, had planned to vacation in Europe in the summer of 1889. But he kept hearing reports of Judge Terry boasting that he didn't dare set foot in California again for fear of his life. It was too much for his ego to endure. He swapped with another justice and took the summer tour of California, much to the dismay of his friends. An entire year away would have given the Terrys a chance to cool off, but Field refused to be intimidated by David Terry's bluster.

Having decided to go, he was urged to arm himself, but refused. "I do not and will not carry arms," he said, "because when it is known that the Judges of the Courts are compelled to arm themselves for defense from an assault offered in consequence of their judicial action, it will be time to dissolve the courts, consider government a failure, and let society lapse into barbarism."[284]

Understanding the potential for violence, U. S. Attorney-General William H. H. Miller wrote to Marshal Franks in San Francisco, instructing him to provide protection for Justice Field during his stay in California. Franks assigned Deputy Marshal David Neagle to act as Field's bodyguard. Neagle had earned a reputation for bravery going back to Arizona mining camps where he was cool and quick with a gun. Neagle had been deputy sheriff in Tombstone, Arizona, where he claimed he stood down the Earp family and chased Wyatt Earp out of town. Earp disputed the claim, saying that Neagle was ordered to disarm him and chickened out when Earp told him the only way he was getting his guns off him was to shoot them off.[285]

Later on, in 1896, when Neagle was getting himself into a lot of mischief in San Francisco, Wyatt Earp came to town and spoke about the Tombstone incident. "I don't like to court notoriety by speaking of the matter," Earp told a reporter. "It is past history, but it was very displeasing to me at the time." Since then, he had told David Neagle that whenever he was in San Francisco, Neagle had better be somewhere else.[286] Though Neagle had apparently never stood down an Earp, he had done his share of killing. A man who knew him well from Arizona, said, "He is one of those fellows that when he appears anywhere men who know him say, 'Who's got to be killed?'"[287]

As soon as Field was back in town, rumors spread that Judge Terry would do him physical harm, though Terry was making no public statements during this time about Field and made no attempt to seek him out.

Near the end of June, a reporter visited the Terrys at their Fresno home and tried to get an interview. He got the brush off from Judge Terry, but Sarah did offer him a glimpse into her frame of mind. "Mrs. Terry, with a glitter in her eyes like cold steel, remarked, 'I only regret that these are not the days of challenges. If they were, Justice Field might have a chance to try his shot against mine.'"[288] In the same article, it was reported that a few days earlier she had been target shooting with her revolver and hit the center three times out of five at thirty paces. It is probable that Judge Terry too longed for the dueling days. Defending his honor in the courts wasn't working out so well for him.

Aside from the humiliation he still felt over his imprisonment, his professional life was going well. He was at the top of his career, being the lawyer of choice for all important cases in San Joaquin County. But on a personal level, he had suffered some significant losses. He was estranged from his son and only grandchild. Some of his old friends had withdrawn in disapproval when he married Sarah Althea, and many of the society women actively rebuffed her. Other friends had permanently severed ties to avoid being implicated in the dangerous enmity between Terry and men of tremendous power: Sharon and Field. Terry was painfully aware of his social ostracism and loss of honor. To a man like David Terry, honor was much more than a noble word or pretty concept. It was a code to live by. He felt it was essential to defend it. Not much had changed for him, philosophically, since he had resigned his position as Chief Justice of the Supreme Court to answer the insult of David Broderick. He believed that Justice Field had dishonored him with an unwarranted punishment. He was incapable of letting it go without a response.

It seems a bit prophetic that the *Sacramento Daily Union*, in their column "30 Years Ago," was at that time reviewing the events that surrounded the duel of 1859 between Judge Terry and Senator David Broderick. Terry had a well-entrenched reputation as a hot-tempered, violent man, and that reputation was largely derived from this thirty year old event. In the intervening years, he had conducted himself honorably, honestly and professionally, and his reputation as a litigator was irreproachable. But still the stigma of his dueling days hounded him, and coupled with his recent behavior, the image of David Terry as a dangerous, antagonistic man was reignited in the public consciousness.

But more important than the public view of Terry was the private view of the man assigned to protect Justice Field. He knew that Terry was capable of violence and always traveled armed, usually with a Bowie knife. Neagle had been hired to protect a man from a highly specific danger, namely Judge and Mrs. Terry. He would have been quite focused on that threat and have no need to second guess the Terrys' intentions should they strike.

Sarah signed a deal to give a series of lectures along the Pacific Coast during July, 1889. She was to get all expenses and seventy-five percent of the take. Her first two lectures were scheduled for San Diego and Los Angeles. A few days before her appearance, her agent, Charles McGeachy, telegrammed to say that he was cancelling her engagements because he was ill and couldn't travel. Sarah assumed McGeachy had been bought off by Sharon's people, who obviously wouldn't want her speaking in public about the Sharon case. She decided to defy them and go on with the show. She went outside of Sharon's influence to procure C. F. Riggs of the Riggs' Theater in Fresno as her replacement manager, but the schedule was delayed as a result of the changes.

In July, the California Supreme Court ruled on an appeal by the heirs of Sharon on Judge Sullivan's earlier decision that Sarah and Sharon were legally married. The court said no, that a secret marriage is not a legal marriage, and allowed for an entirely new trial on that basis. In effect, this decision reversed the earlier Supreme Court ruling that declared a secret marriage by contract valid. An astonished Judge Terry told a friend, "The Supreme Court has reversed its own decision in the Sharon case, and made my wife out to be a strumpet."[289]

Judge Terry seemed ready to start over with a new trial. The marriage contract, the main and nearly sole piece of evidence that Sarah had a claim on Sharon's estate, had been declared a forgery by two courts. Now the marriage itself had been declared invalid by the California Supreme Court. Why did the Terrys keep fighting? It seemed that money had quit being the motive a long time ago. In fact, Terry often told his friend Porter Ashe that no matter how many millions they won from Sharon, he would never touch a cent of it. Terry certainly knew that his wife was never married to William Sharon. What was driving these two? Principle? Honor? Notoriety? Revenge? Terry's sense of justice must have convinced him that even if Sharon had never married Sarah, he *should* have married her. Some people believed Terry married her, at least partly, as a direct comment on William Sharon's unethical behavior, to make a point about gentlemanly decency. Sharon had insulted her honor. Such an insult, we have already established, had to be avenged.

Since Terry's release from jail, he had been shadowed by a private detective named Henry Felton, hired out of the Finnegass detective agency in San Francisco by an unknown party. Felton told John Barker, the Chief of Police in Fresno, that there was money to be made in this business, implying there was a price on Terry's head. The Chief was Terry's friend and said he wanted no part of it. He warned the detective that if Terry found out what he was up to, he'd beat him to a pulp. Felton wasn't worried. "Whenever I am in Judge Terry's presence," he said, "I have my hand on my gun. All of us are fixed for him, and if he ever makes a break we will take no chances."[290] It seems there were armed men around every corner just waiting for a chance to gun down David Terry.

31. THE FALLEN KNIGHT

On August 14, 1889, the Terrys left their Fresno home at O and Tuolumne Streets to take the Southern Pacific overland train to San Francisco for a court date. Before they boarded, a friend of Terry's, J. F. Grady, handed him a pistol, saying, "Take this, Judge, you may need it." Terry replied that he had no use for the gun, that he never carried one, but Grady insisted, so he took the pistol and handed it to his wife.[291] They then boarded the train.

They were unaware that Justice Field was on the same train, traveling from Los Angeles to San Francisco. In fact, Sarah later said that they had delayed their trip one day to avoid being on the same train as Field, but had miscalculated his schedule. David Neagle knew the Terrys were on board and advised Field to remain in his car. He offered to bring his breakfast to him there. But when the train stopped at the Lathrop station just south of Stockton for a twenty-minute layover, Field, apparently determined to aggravate the Terrys, disembarked to have breakfast at the railway dining room. His actions, both insisting on coming to California and making himself prominently visible to his enemies, were acts of defiance, perhaps even taunts. Either he did not take the threat seriously or he was simply obstinate beyond reason, putting not only himself needlessly in danger, but endangering the lives of his bodyguard and others in proximity. He knew that Sarah Althea carried a gun and was anxious to use it, yet he went into a crowded public restaurant, inviting a confrontation.

Neagle sat with him in the restaurant. He was not wearing a uniform and the Terrys had not been told that Field was protected by an armed guard.

When the Terrys came into the restaurant, Sarah saw Field immediately, said she was going back to the car for her purse, and rushed away. The proprietor of the restaurant, Stackpole, approached Judge Terry and asked him if there was going to be trouble. When Terry asked why, Stackpole told him Field was in the restaurant and pointed him out. Alarmed, and realizing Sarah had gone to get the pistol, Terry said there might be trouble, yes, and to keep his wife out of the restaurant. Stackpole posted two men at the door to intercept her.

Terry then walked coolly up to the seventy-three year old judge where he sat and slapped him on the face, knocking off his glasses. Neagle drew his pistol as Terry lifted his hand again, apparently preparing for another blow. Without rising from his chair, Neagle shot twice and Terry fell dead, one bullet having pierced his heart.

R. B. Purvis, the sheriff of Stanislaus County, ran into the room at the sound of gunfire. "Upon the floor lay the body of Judge Terry, just as if he had lain down to sleep. His eyes were wide open, and his features wore an expression that bespoke no anger nor perturbation of spirit. I stooped down over him and watched his lifeblood ebb away, saw his last gasps for breath, and then closed his eyes, which were staring placidly up at the ceiling."[292]

Sarah ran back into the room. She was stopped and disarmed, most likely preventing more bloodshed. She dashed to her husband's body and threw herself over it, distraught and calling for the crowd to apprehend her husband's murderers.

Some of the many witnesses said that Terry had slapped Field's face twice before he was shot, the second blow being harder than the first. Some said he had slapped once and was in the process of raising his hand to strike again when he was shot. Sheriff Purvis, who entered Field's train car soon after the event, said that Justice Field had no mark on his face, so he could not have been hit very hard. There was little support for Neagle's subsequent position that he thought Terry was reaching inside his clothing for his knife. Perhaps Neagle believed that or perhaps he decided to say so during his trial to more strongly justify his actions. Everyone did agree that the entire incident took place quickly, that there was no hesitation on the part of Neagle. He fired two shots in rapid succession as soon as he was able to draw his gun. Like the detective Henry Felton, he had been thoroughly ready for such an occasion. According to most witnesses, including Sheriff Purvis, Neagle never identified himself to Terry and didn't say a word before killing him. Terry had no idea he had been shot by an officer.

Neagle and Field got back on the train and took their seats, anxious to get away from Sarah Althea's calls for vengeance. Constable Walker of Lathrop arrested Neagle. They got off the train at Tracy and took a buggy to the Stockton jail, while Field continued on to San Francisco.

Field, who had watched the last flicker of life go out in Terry's eyes, said afterward, "I must say here that, dreadful as it is to take life, it was only a question of seconds whether my life or Judge Terry's life should be taken. I am firmly convinced that, had the marshal delayed two seconds, both he and myself would have been the victims of Terry."[293]

Neagle's recounting of the incident became more graphic and detailed with each telling. About ten days afterward, he spoke to a reporter and described the scene: "His eyes were filled with hate and defiance, and as he drew back I noticed that his teeth were set, and he seemed to growl and draw in his breath like an infuriated beast. I saw his hand brought back as if he was about to draw something from his breast, and I knew then that I must either kill him or be cut to pieces."[294] To further support his position, Neagle claimed that Mrs. Terry threw herself on the body of her husband, fumbled with his vest and removed his knife, concealing it on her person.

Afterwards, she demanded that her husband's body be searched to prove that he was unarmed. "I made him put away his weapons before he went out of the train," she said. "I thought it was only going to be a fisticuffs affair."[295]

Terry's body was brought to Stockton, and Sarah stayed with it on the trip to the morgue. No weapon of any kind was found on Terry. The autopsy showed that the first bullet had pierced his heart and the second had clipped his left ear as he fell.

People flooded into Stockton from the countryside to pay homage to their dead hero and voice their outrage over his murder. With a mob in town, there was concern that Neagle was in danger. No one was allowed near the jail, which was guarded by six officers. Citizens were overheard discussing storming the jail and lynching Neagle.

"This morning the situation is ominous. No loud professions of a programme are made by the Terry men, but they are holding whispered conferences at street corners, and evidently intend to carry out some desperate plot at the funeral this afternoon. There is great alarm in all the country around Stockton, and citizens have ordered the women and children to remain indoors till the threatened trouble is over."[296] But there was no violence and no attempt was made to take Neagle from the jail.

The character that had served Terry well in his wild youth, the treacherous frontier of early Texas, and the lawless Gold Rush days of California, was ill adapted to the more civilized culture that emerged at the end of the nineteenth century. Ironically, Terry himself was partly responsible for those changes, intentionally and unintentionally. His duel with Broderick resulted in legislation against dueling. His work as judge, attorney and citizen was directly responsible for increasing law and order in California cities. At the core, however, he resisted the changing climate and always fell back on his gut impulses. There was an inherent irony in the person of David Smith Terry. He was a man of law who attained the highest position possible in the state of California, yet he was unwilling to be governed by the law.

The dining room at the Lathrop train station became a tourist attraction for some years after this incident. Anybody coming into Lathrop felt obliged to go take a look for himself. "Everybody does it," said one Lathrop citizen, "and the habit has taken root to such an extent that many people who live at Lathrop go up to the depot every day to look at the spot where the killing occurred and point out the bullet-holes."[297]

To what extent, if any, did the thirty year old killing of David Broderick have to do with the enmity between Justice Field and Judge Terry? Judging by the number of times the name "Broderick" popped up in discussions of Terry's death, the old tragedy was on the minds of nearly everybody else. It was mentioned in terms of "retribution" and "justice." If Broderick had won the duel, he would have become the villain who had killed a respected, accomplished Supreme Court Justice. David Terry's legacy would have been magnificently different. As it was, however, even Governor Waterman said his death was a blessing to the state.

In the minds of many, he had become a bully and a brute, and he had done his standing no favor by marrying Sarah Althea Hill. In fact, his biographer, A. E. Wagstaff, took it one step further, claiming that his association with Sarah was the reason his legacy was ruined. "While his death was untimely, he did not die too soon. Rather, he did not die soon enough. Had he passed away two years before, when the wife of his earlier life departed, he would have been remembered as the just and upright judge, the great counselor, the incorruptible lawmaker and citizen, the tender and loving husband and father...and the man of acknowledged ability and sterling integrity."[298]

Interestingly, Justice Field himself had been challenged to a duel by fellow judge William Barbour in 1858, and had accepted, but neither of them fired a shot. There were few men in the west in those days who hadn't been involved in some type of gun-related violence. Terry was made out to be a barbarian by men such as Field, but it was mere happenstance that his own slice of dueling history had been uneventful.

Newspapers across the country were filled with opinions about what had happened and whether or not the killing was justified. They reflected the two polar extremes of the reaction to Terry's death.

Of Neagle's actions, the *Los Angeles Herald* (August 15) said, "It was his duty to at once arrest Terry and place him beyond the power of doing harm. But for a Marshal to take the law into his own hand and to execute extreme punishment because an assault is committed in his presence, would require very strained reasoning to justify. In ordinary cases this kind of killing would be murder."

The *Daily Alta California* (August 15): "Terry was a man of gigantic stature, and, though aged, in possession of a giant's strength; and there is no one who was acquainted with him, or has had opportunity to learn his past history, who does not know that he was a desperate man, willing to take desperate chances, and to resort to desperate means when giving way to his impulses of passion, and that any person who should at such a moment attempt to stay his hand would do so at the risk of his life."

The *Stockton Mail* (August 20), satirically: "Terry had a Bowie knife all the way from a foot to eighteen inches long, with the blood of his last victim still upon the blade. He stood picking his teeth with it when Rev. Mr. Neagle, a distinguished prelate from Arizona, entered the room upon the arm of Stephen J. Field, a sacred personage descended from Heaven to execute the will of God upon earth."

As usual, the *Sacramento Daily Union* (August 15) had no sympathy for Judge Terry. "With the tragic taking off of Judge Terry there disappears from this State the last remnant of the bullying chivalry which has sought to terrorize decency in California and overawe authority, and has crimsoned the eventful annals of the Commonwealth with the blood of some of its best and bravest citizens." It sounds like the *Union* was still looking to avenge the death of Senator Broderick.

The *Los Angeles Herald* (August 16) continued to take a different view. Two days after the killing, it read, "The more we examine the facts connected with the killing of Judge Terry, the clearer does it appear to us that Justice Field's bodyguard committed a crime unjustified by the circumstances of the occasion....There is a great deal of wild talk about Terry having made repeated threats to take Justice Field's life. These lack authentication. Terry was indisputably a brave man, and brave men do not go around making threats."

From the *New York Sun* (August 16): "Terry was one of the most reckless and desperate survivals of the early days of California development. His slaying of Broderick embittered his life, exasperated and defeated him at all points and made him lawless, irresponsible and a menace to society. He is well out of the way."

The *New York Evening Post* (August 24): "Somebody ought to have killed Terry a quarter century ago—if not the public executioner, some friend of civilization....He had force of character, great courage, and doubtless some knowledge of the law...but a person as much out of place in our modern industrial and busy communities as a tiger in a barn yard."

The *Portland Oregonian* (August 15): "The moment the news of Terry's killing flashed through the city the name of David C. Broderick, whom he killed in a duel in 1859, was uttered by many tongues, and many old Californians now living here said: 'Served him right; it is just retribution.'"

The *New York Herald* (August 15): "Has the last act in the eventful drama been reached? Sarah Althea Hill, the leading actress, still lives." Indeed!

32. FAME AND INFAMY

David Terry's funeral was held Friday, August 16, 1889 at St. John's Episcopal Church on El Dorado Street in Stockton. The magnificent old church still stands at that location and is still in service as St. John's Anglican Church.

Clinton Terry, the judge's son, was interviewed on his way to the funeral. "I am a very quiet person," he said. "I have, too, since my father's marriage to this woman, been rather estranged from him. Soon after his marriage…to which I was bitterly opposed, my father gave me a ranch in Fresno county, but I couldn't make it pay, so I went to San Francisco, where I hold a position in the Mint. I never had any personal difficulty with this woman only when my father was in jail in Alameda county. I went to see him one day and she wouldn't permit them to let me in."[299] About his father's death, he said, "I was not much surprised to hear of my father being shot, as I knew there was considerable feeling and he was quick tempered. I wouldn't say much about it if Judge Field had himself killed him. Then it would have been man for man, but I don't think it was right for this man Neagle to shoot him."[300]

Clinging to the body of her dead husband prior to the funeral, Sarah sobbed and spoke excitedly. "Oh, if I could be in your place, my love! Oh, if I could lie here in your place! If it was only I instead of you, who have so many to love you! He was such a good, kind husband; nobody ever had a better; nobody ever had a more loving husband. Oh, how can I give him up! My love, oh, my love!"[301]

Significantly, Sarah's brother Morgan, along with his friend Thomas Williams, came to Stockton for the funeral. He spent some emotional moments with his sister beside the bier the day before. He then escorted her into the church for the ceremony.

During the course of the afternoon, Sarah several times went up to the casket and draped herself over it in sorrow. After the service, she stood by for one last look at her husband. "Tom Williams stood on her left and her brother, Morgan Hill, at her right. She was permitted to lay her head on the glass over the face of the dead, and again she cried out.

In her grief she threw her arms over the casket, and, with her face over that of the dead, she moaned till her escorts led her from the casket. A minute later she was led from the church by Tom Williams and a lady friend of this city. Her face was exposed to the curious gaze of a large crowd until Tom Williams drew her veil over it."[302]

At the graveside in Stockton Rural Cemetery, Sarah had to be supported after she sank to her knees beside the grave. When she saw that David Terry was to be buried between his first wife and son Samuel, she objected, saying she wanted room left so she could be buried beside her husband. The grave had been dug at the order of Clinton Terry, leaving no place for his father's second wife. Morgan attempted to quiet her and Sarah relented, deciding that Sam Terry could be moved later to make way for her.[303]

David S. Terry – His Fame, His best epitaph

On the day of the funeral, Judge James Crittenden of the California Supreme Court, an old friend of Terry's, asked that the Court adjourn for the day in honor of Judge Terry, since he was once Chief Justice of the court. Chief Justice Beatty decided against the adjournment, saying, "The circumstances of Judge Terry's death are notorious, and under those circumstances this Court has determined that it would be better to pass this matter in silence...."[304] The Superior Court of San Joaquin County in Stockton, however, did adjourn in respect to Terry's memory.

The members of the bar in Stockton got together to draw up a resolution. In it, they praised Terry unreservedly. "He stood intellectually in the front rank of the distinguished men who have, by their services, rendered the history of the Western slope illustrious....His intellect was imperious, and submitted to but few limitations that hedge the ordinary mind, and that under any conditions, and in any country, he would have been by reason of his many great qualities, a leader of men."[305] They praised him as a judge, a lawyer, a friend, and a citizen.

Sarah Althea demanded that Justice Field be arrested, saying that he had hired an assassin. On the basis of Sarah's complaint, Sheriff Thomas Cunningham of Stockton went to San Francisco to arrest Field as an accessory to murder. There was a debate in the courtroom about whether or not the judge should endorse the warrant, as many of the attorneys felt it was misguided. The most vocal opponent of the warrant was Davis Louderback, who said, "It is an outrage that this bad and wicked woman should have the Justice arrested."[306] The judge decided to endorse the warrant, and Cunningham made timid motions toward arresting Field, but Field had already applied for a writ of habeas corpus from his good buddy Judge Sawyer. Field was released on his own recognizance, avoiding a trip to the Stockton jail.

Louderback was not the only one outraged at the arrest of Field. This action, initiated by Sarah, brought wide condemnation on her from the legal community and the press. The *New York World* of August 18 spared no punches, calling Sheriff Cunningham "a donkey" and Mrs. Terry "the demented widow of the dead desperado."

In a controversial move, Judge Sawyer then ordered a secret transfer of David Neagle from Stockton into federal custody. He was taken to San Francisco on a special train ordered just for this purpose and put in the county jail there. The move was designed to take his prosecution off of Terry's home turf and away from State control. Accompanying Neagle were Sheriff Cunningham and District Attorney Avery White of Stockton. When the Circuit Court opened that morning, White lodged a protest about the transfer of the prisoner, calling it illegal. Neagle had been arrested by the State for a crime committed against the laws of the state, and the federal authorities had no jurisdiction in the matter. Judge Sawyer justified his action by saying that the incident had occurred while Neagle was employed as a federal agent; therefore, the feds did have jurisdiction. This debate would become the focus of the Neagle case, the ultimate decision setting precedent into the far-reaching future.

When D. A. White returned to Stockton, he met with Sarah at her hotel and no doubt explained the implications of Neagle being removed from the custody of the state. She was extremely upset by the turn of events. "What can I do? I was waiting for the examination next Wednesday. It will never take place. They will release him in San Francisco, and this county will not have a say in Judge Terry's murder....Neagle was taken away for the best cause in the world. Had the examination and trial been held in this county it would have implicated Justice Field beyond doubt."[307]

Many prominent citizens, lawyers and newspapers condemned the transfer of Neagle's case to the federal courts.

Neagle seemed in good spirits and had no regrets about his actions. He didn't express any sympathy for Terry and his wife, nor did he second guess himself. An old miner who knew him back in Arizona and Nevada in the shoot-em-up days, told the *San Francisco Call*, "Here's Dave Neagle, whom we all knew so well as a shotgun miner up in Nevada, posing now as a hero, because he shot down a man." He then proceeded to tell several old stories about Neagle's easy way of putting a bullet in a man.[308]

Justice Field was now crying "foul" and threatening to bring charges against the Stockton authorities for charging him with murder without evidence. At the request of Governor Waterman, Attorney-General Johnson ordered the Stockton D. A. to drop the charges against Field. Sarah wrote to the Attorney-General saying that he didn't have sufficient knowledge of the evidence to make such a request. She said the evidence against Field hadn't yet been made public. "Let him in justice to the people of this State stand trial, and if innocent let him go free; if guilty, as charged, let him receive the punishment which the law lays down for such crimes....There is no law to say that Field shall employ assassins, and...induce the Governor of this State to order him released without examination."[309] But D. A. White was suitably intimidated by the state brass and dismissed the charges against Field.

Both lawyers who had originally stepped up to prosecute Neagle for the State withdrew from the case because of the unorthodox way it was being handled. By now it was clear that Neagle had impressive and intimidating power behind him. Field had rounded up a team of six high-profile attorneys to represent him. Attorney-General Johnson said that since nobody else would take it, he would prosecute himself. It was clear from his letters that he had already made up his mind that Neagle had done no wrong. Also, he did not intend to participate in the day-to-day proceedings.

When the Neagle case came up on September 3 in the San Francisco Circuit Court, there was no one there to represent the people. Furthermore, the case was presided over by Judges Sawyer and Sabin, the very judges who had sat on the previous case where the Terrys had been jailed for contempt, the very judges who had had their lives threatened along with Field. The circumstances of this case were reminiscent of the mockery of a trial that Terry himself had faced over the killing of Broderick. Sarah took no part in the proceedings, not even as an observer.

The defense called their witnesses, who testified without cross-examination, then stepped down. When Justice Field took the stand, he described the incident much as everyone else had. About his relationship with Judge Terry, Field said that "he had never had any difficulty with Terry of any nature, whatever, prior to the rendering of judgment in the Sharon case a year ago. In fact they had always been on most friendly terms. Terry had often tried cases before him and on entering court had always spoken to him pleasantly. During the last year or two, however, he seemed entirely changed and to have lost the respect which he formerly had for the courts."[310] This was clearly a shot at Sarah Althea and the implied negative influence she exerted over Terry.

The trial was a rehash of the Sharon vs. Hill case and the events leading to the Terrys' jail sentences. Everyone who had ever heard Mr. or Mrs. Terry make threats against Justice Field was called to repeat it, and all were asked what they thought about Judge Terry's capacity and inclination for violence. They were almost all unanimous in saying that he had been a formidable, fearless and dangerous man.

Neagle's defense was able to produce a witness who said he positively saw Mrs. Terry remove a Bowie knife from her husband's body and hide it in her clothing. The thought that a woman who had just learned that her husband had been shot dead would be thinking about evidence at some not yet conceived of trial was incredible. By all other accounts, she was hysterical in those moments. She had to have been in shock. How is it imaginable that she saw her husband's dead body for the first time and immediately thought that it would be better in the long run if he was thought to have been unarmed? It doesn't seem possible that this witness saw what he said he saw. Nobody else saw it. And most importantly, no sheath was found on Terry's body. If he had been carrying a knife, he would have worn it in a strapped-on sheath. Sarah wouldn't have been able to remove that from his lifeless, prone body without a significant struggle, and not without being detected.

There was no prosecutor to argue the point or to call refuting witnesses. Sarah Althea was not called to testify.

If there had been any evidence against Neagle, such as his history of killing people in sneaky and cowardly ways, or the exact nature of his instructions from the marshal's office, or various pieces of evidence that there had been a price on Terry's head, there was no one there to bring it. There was nobody to say that he had overreacted, that he had been out for blood, and that he had shown no remorse for killing a man. The trial was a farce. There was hardly any point in going on with it. In the end, Attorney-General Johnson showed up to give a closing argument. He had nothing to say about the validity of Neagle's actions. His main point was that the state court should have jurisdiction to try Neagle rather than the federal court.

Neagle's case boiled down to the issue of state vs. federal jurisdiction, which was argued at length. Judge Terry had always been a proponent for state rights over federal, so it is ironic that final justice for him was denied over this very issue.

On September 16, Neagle was acquitted. Judge Sawyer read the decision, deeming Neagle's action justifiable homicide, and went a step further, calling it "commendable." "In our judgment he acted under the trying circumstances surrounding him in good faith and with consummate courage, judgment and discretion. The homicide was, in our opinion, clearly justifiable in law, and in the forum of sound, practical common sense, commendable."[311]

Justice Field heartily congratulated Neagle and gave him a handsome gold watch inscribed with praise for his brave act in Lathrop. Field may have considered Neagle a hero, but a lot of other people did not, and he had to live with his infamous act just as Terry had done after killing Broderick. Neagle would forever after carry the appellation, "the Arizona gunfighter who shot Judge Terry."

Just as Broderick's friends had never let up in their criticism of Terry, Terry's friends continued to revile Neagle in any way they could. Some, like R. E. Culbreth, editor of the *Argus*, and James H. Barry, editor of the *Star*, had newspapers at their disposal, in which they liberally condemned Neagle. This was true for many years, not just in the immediate aftermath of Terry's death. In 1896, Barry published an article after Neagle roughed up a man on the street, saying, "That infernal miscreant Neagle, who murdered Judge Terry, at Judge Field's instance, and who should long since have dangled on the gallows, is now, it appears, employed as hired villain by the Southern Pacific. That is just where such wretches belong, if they must be outside of a jail or the gallows….Neagle is a dangerous character, who should be shot dead by any man whom he approaches."[312]

Neagle took offense and threatened to kill Barry, then accosted him on the street, spat at him and drew his gun. Barry resisted his first impulse to lunge at Neagle. Instead, he spoke coolly. "You have been making the threat about town that you intended to kill me on sight. You are now trying to provoke me into making an assault upon you in order that you may have some excuse—the same programme that you followed in the Terry case. Here I am; shoot."[313] As there were witnesses, Neagle had no choice but to walk away.

While the press had been brimming over with opinions about the shooting on both sides, some people praising Neagle, some condemning him, Stephen Field was often portrayed negatively by both sides. Even when Terry was being vilified, Field was still seen as a weakling hiding behind a hired gun. But there were a lot worse things being said about him, such as these words from James W. Stevens of the Manhattan Life Insurance Company: "I look upon this affair as a cold-blooded, premeditated murder. Field is openly accused of receiving bribes, and this looks like he was not above conspiring to commit murder."[314]

Stephen M. White, a respected U. S. Senator from California, in writing to a friend, complained of the laudation of Justice Field, saying, "To be candid, it makes me tired to listen to the flunkey talk that is going on at this time about a man who, in my judgment, is one of the most dishonest characters that has ever discharged the function of a judicial office."[315]

He may have escaped getting a broken nose by Neagle's actions, but Field's image was permanently tainted.

Justice Field's bitterness toward Terry seemed to grow as the months went on. He even changed the way he told the story. When interviewed the day after the shooting by the *Chronicle*, he came off as honest and rational. "The Judge never really believed that his life was in danger and said that he thought Terry's intention yesterday was to publicly humiliate him by personal chastisement. Terry had no weapon in his hands so far as Judge Field saw nor did he see any taken from the dead man's person." But Field's attitude had radically changed since that day. Now he routinely referred to Terry as a "murderer," which is nothing if not ironic. There was only one man who had been murdered in the Lathrop train station: David Terry. It wasn't enough for Field to be responsible for the man's death. He sought to assassinate his character as well, going so far as to thwart the career of a man who wrote a tribute to Terry.

Edwin G. Waite, who called Terry "a man of sterling integrity of purpose," was about to be appointed to Register of the Land Office of San Francisco. His praise of Terry enraged Field. He took it as a personal affront and pushed the article in front of state officials with the purpose of discrediting Waite, as if admiring Terry were a crime.

Waite's article, "An Estimate of the Life and Character of David S. Terry," published in *The Overland Monthly*, was not especially flattering to Terry. It was a sober account of his accomplishments and a brief history of his life. It made no accusation against Field and did not try to justify Terry's behavior. There were much more emotionally-charged tributes to the murdered judge making the rounds. But somehow this one article hit a nerve with Field.

Field continued to pontificate in a most self-righteous manner when he explained why he had campaigned against Waite's appointment: "...I do not expect to uphold would-be assassins or those who eulogize them or gloss over their crimes."[316]

President Benjamin Harrison, who had nominated Waite, succumbed to Field's pressure and withdrew his name. Field's behavior was petty and vindictive, damaging his image even further. There was a backlash among the Republican Party in California. Because of Field's smear campaign at the federal level, they nominated Waite for Secretary of State and he was elected.

Even the man responsible for Judge Terry's death, Stephen Field, came away from the tragedy diminished. But no one would suffer more from the loss than Sarah Althea, who was now adrift like an abandoned ship on a stormy sea.

33. THE WIDOW

Not long after Judge Terry's funeral, Sarah went to the county offices in downtown Stockton to demand her pistol back. It had been confiscated the day her husband was killed. She argued with Deputy D. A. Gibson, who tried to explain that it was being held because it might be needed as evidence in Neagle's trial. Then he qualified his statement by telling her they didn't trust her with a gun.

Everybody expected Sarah to go after Field to avenge her husband. She would not have had a chance to get near him if she had tried. She was still being watched by detectives, and all law enforcement officials in the San Joaquin Valley and in San Francisco were wary of her.

But instead of responding with violence, Sarah attempted to raise money in Stockton to fight for the conviction of Neagle and Field. Her friends did not want to support what they saw as a futile fight. They advised her to give it up. She felt betrayed.

The San Joaquin County society that Sarah had inherited upon her marriage to Terry would soon dissipate. They had been his friends to begin with and had accepted her uneasily as his wife, but they had already begun to withdraw from her. Her manner, always difficult, especially in desperation, would drive them away even faster. With the loss of her husband, Sarah's foundation had been blown apart. Terry had kept her steady and focused like nobody else could. Now she was unsettled again.

The press began speculating immediately that Clinton Terry would remove his stepmother from the Terry property and break all ties with her. Sure enough, he made a move in that direction when, a couple of months after the judge's death, he took a thug with him to forcibly throw Sarah's Cousin Rodney out of the Fresno land where he had been installed as caretaker. They tossed Rodney and his possessions out into the road. But what Clinton didn't know was that Judge Terry had deeded a large portion of his property to Sarah, so she was the legal owner. She sued and won, reinstalling Rodney to the property.

Sarah Althea Terry circa 1889 (Courtesy of the Bancroft Library)

Judge Terry's death provided only a brief respite from court for Sarah. She still had to face the criminal charges for her disruptive behavior the day she and her husband were charged with contempt. Though her lawyer had moved to dismiss the assault charges against her shortly after Terry's death, the court persisted in prosecuting. There was no sympathy to be had for Sarah, though she made a determined plea for it when she appeared on August 29 in Judge Hoffman's courtroom. It had been only two weeks since David Terry had been killed. Sarah was "dressed in deep mourning and heavily veiled. She uttered not a word during the entire proceedings, but kept up a continual wail" of mourning.[317] Her trial was set for November 5.

Sarah would find it hard to get sympathy from lawyers, judges, and others who had witnessed the soap opera of the last few years. She had so often been acting, playing upon the emotions of her audience. Many had caught on. There were plenty of people who believed her overwrought displays of grief were insincere. Like the boy who cried wolf, she could no longer summon help. Though she may have been performing misery for the audience, the pain was real enough. She simply did not know the value of dignified understatement.

Terry's estate was valued at $132,456. Sarah was given $300 a month for maintenance while waiting for the settlement of the estate.

Clinton Terry was clearly a bitter man, perhaps justifiably so. If not for "that woman," as he called Sarah, his father would still be alive, and father and son wouldn't have been on the outs. After making sure there was no place in the family plot for Sarah and attempting to throw her cousin off the Terry property, he tried unsuccessfully to have Sarah removed as administrator of David Terry's estate, claiming she was incompetent. Then, when he heard there was a $5,000 life insurance policy on his father, he filed a suit claiming the money for himself instead of Sarah. Apparently no beneficiary was declared and, almost unbelievably for a lawyer, Terry died without a will. The insurance money was eventually divided equally between Clinton, Sarah and Joseph C. Campbell, Terry's former law partner.

In January, 1890, the Terry estate was sued for $7,000 owed on the mortgage of the Terry's primary residence in Fresno, the house in which Sarah was living. In February, another creditor began foreclosure on a Terry ranch east of Madera, and so began the erosion of Sarah's financial resources.

February 20, 1890, Sarah finally went on trial for contempt of court. The previous October, Judge Matthew Deady, who would be hearing the case, had denounced her character in the press. "Yes, I sat in the Sharon-Hill case," Deady told a *Washington Post* reporter. "The fact is, that woman was merely his mistress. He gave her $500 a month, furnished magnificent quarters for her, and spent money on her lavishly. Her influence on Judge Terry was undoubtedly bad. She urged him to acts beyond even his own inclination. In November she will be tried before me for resisting the authorities. Very likely she may, at some favorable opportunity attempt the lives of Justice Field, Judge Sawyer or myself. I predict she will die a violent death."[318]

The *Los Angeles Herald* of October 23, responded: "There is an intensity of bitterness in the denunciation of Mrs. Terry by Judge Deady, in a reported interview with a Washington reporter, which clearly shows that lady need expect no nice consideration in her litigation before the Federal Courts."

There were three charges against Sarah: boisterous conduct in court, assaulting and wounding United States Marshal Franks, and insulting Justice Stephen J. Field.

Both attorneys in the case gave emotional opening arguments, dragging in the characters of both Terrys, Justice Field, the U. S. marshals and their deputies. When Davis Louderback extolled the lengthy list of Field's virtues, the judge stopped him, saying Field's character was not on trial and Field's merits had no bearing on Mrs. Terry's alleged crime. But it was clear that there was so much more going on than whether or not Sarah had kicked Marshal Franks.

Porter Ashe testified on Sarah's behalf, saying he had not seen her kick Franks. He was asked how Marshal Franks took hold of Sarah to remove her from the courtroom. "The Marshal took hold of her, I think, in a particularly cowardly and brutal manner,"[319] replied Ashe, glowering at Marshal Franks. Ashe was a true friend to Sarah, standing up for her for no other reason than friendship. His previous loyalty and affection for David Terry had extended to her, and he was one of the few of her husband's friends who maintained warm feelings for her.

In closing arguments, the prosecuting attorney, Louderback, called Sarah a "lewd, indecent woman." Nobody would have spoken that way if David Terry had been in the courtroom. He would not have sat idly by during such a slander. But Sarah no longer had a champion.

On the charge of resisting arrest and assaulting Marshal Franks, the jury was hung, eight for acquittal and four for conviction. Sarah had always said that before a jury, she would be victorious.

34. THE CALDWELL AFFAIR

At the age of forty, Sarah Althea was still alluring enough to turn the heads of men who, being aware of her history, should have known better. By this time, she had acquired a reputation as a destroyer of men. But that did not deter Nathaniel C. Caldwell, a Fresno attorney with a wife and four kids. Caldwell was a partner in the firm of Sayle and Caldwell, the law office administering the estate of David Terry. He was "known as a fierce, bluffing fellow" with "a long, flowing, sandy moustache."[320] Sarah portrayed him as a violent drunk, saying he had once knocked Cousin Rodney down the stairs of her home and another time kicked a door in. In Caldwell, Sarah had finally met someone as combative and violent as herself.

Their affair was going strong in the spring of 1890 with Caldwell hanging around her house in Fresno, turning up in San Francisco when she was there, and writing her silly love letters whenever they were not together. Sarah complained that his wife would come around watching for him. "She would come almost every night and peep in the windows and sit on the porch and watch for him to come in or go out. One night the whole top of the back stoop was burned to a char. Oil had been poured on and set fire, but it did not burn long. I can't think of anybody else who would do it but her."[321]

Though Caldwell often refused to be interviewed by reporters, saying he wasn't one to kiss and tell, others, like his wife, did talk. After the affair went sour, she said that Sarah stalked her husband, coming out to the house at night. One night she crouched under a window and listened to them talking. Caldwell went out and found her coachman there and slapped him in the face. On another occasion, Mrs. Caldwell met her outside and Sarah repeated one of her favorite phrases when she said, "He is my only friend on earth, and I want him all my own." When Mrs. Caldwell objected, saying he was her husband, Sarah said, "Yes, but you can keep the children."[322]

"It is a filthy mess," Caldwell said to a reporter, "and I regret that I have been made a figure in one of the many ridiculous situations brought about by the vagaries of this absurd woman."[323] Sarah denied that she was stalking him or wanted anything to do with him, claiming he was hounding her with his love-sick attentions.

In April, 1890, the relationship hit the papers when a scene took place in the offices of Sayle and Caldwell. Sarah made a visit to Sayle's office to ask for money, as she had not had her allowance for two months. He said there was none available, but there were some law books that could be sold. Dissatisfied with Sayle's answer, she went next door to Caldwell's office. Witnesses in the building were soon treated to a loud and violent fracas in which Caldwell tried to throw Sarah out of his office. The brawl culminated with the glass in the door being shattered. Sayle, who witnessed the whole thing, said he overheard Sarah scream, "I have a marriage contract with you, and I will see you abide by its terms."[324]

She then burst into the corridor, "her mourning veil streaming behind her like a meteor in the breeze. She was white with passion. After she recovered her balance, which had become sadly deranged by the suddenness of her exit, she turned suddenly, assuming a striking attitude, and with outstretched hand, held in front of Mr. Caldwell's face, exclaimed in tones that vibrated with anger or fear: 'Stop, Mr. Caldwell; if you continue to abuse me thus I will be forced to kill you; I shall have to blow your brains out!'"[325]

Shortly after the incident, a local reporter asked her about the trouble with Caldwell, focusing on the question of the marriage contract. "I don't want to say anything about the contract," she replied. He told her everybody was talking about it around town. "I don't care about that," she said, "they have talked about me for the last twelve years."[326] The reporter repeatedly tried to get her to admit or deny the existence of a marriage contract with Caldwell, but she refused to address it either way.

An Associated Press reporter came to Fresno to interview the lover combatants. Caldwell declined to talk. The AP reporter visited Sarah at her house and wrote, "She seemed greatly worried over the turn affairs have taken and kept repeating: 'I don't know. I don't know. I can't tell.' She said: 'Whether it is a scheme planned by the Sharons, or the administrators of the estate of Judge Terry, its object evidently is to compromise me and somebody will profit by it.'" When asked about the marriage contract with Caldwell, she replied, "I said nothing of the kind," and accused Judge Sayle of deliberately lying.[327]

The reporter thought she appeared a little unhinged: distracted, worried and unsure of the facts. Sadly, at the end of the interview, she said, "What can I do? I am a woman, alone and almost friendless, and this will leave me with less friends. He is a man, and such things don't hurt men. He has a wife and children. I am here alone. I often almost wish I were dead. I wish I could get so far out of sight that nobody would ever hear of me again."[328]

How prophetic!

By the summer of 1890, Sarah was living month to month and was unable to pay her $378.75 bill at the Lick House in San Francisco where she stayed when attending court. She was also still accruing legal expenses, as the litigation resulting from the Sharon case continued.

In November, another incident occurred involving Caldwell. He appeared in court to confirm sales of Terry real estate to which Sarah objected, saying it was being sold too cheaply. During his argument in court, he made a comment that offended Sarah, to the effect that Judge Terry's association with her had dragged down a once honored name. She met him outside in the corridor and slapped him. He cursed at her and threatened to toss her over the balustrade. Afterward, she had him arrested for disturbing the peace. "This man," she said, "has harassed me a great deal, and seems to take a delight in attacking me in one way or another at every opportunity." She threatened to read his love letters in public to prove that he was hounding her. "I used to be flooded with them when I was in San Francisco last spring. I have been away from home considerable and such silly letters I received from him."[329]

Caldwell's trial took place a few days later. The first order of business was to disarm the defendant of a .45 caliber pistol he had brought along for protection. Sarah was searched, but, for a change, was unarmed. Tempers on both sides were high. Caldwell especially seemed bitter and exasperated. "My name has been coupled with this woman until I am covered with infamy. I am tired of hearing it." He confirmed that he had written her love letters, but Sarah was not allowed to enter the letters in evidence.

As always, Sarah's presence in court brought in a crowd of gawkers. She was up to the audience, "dressed in black silk, wearing a black Gainsboro hat," and, in the opinion of a reporter, looking "ten years younger than she did a year ago, having recovered much of the color and vigor that were so admired in the early days of the Sharon trial. Her hair is a shade darker. She was cold as an icicle and calm as an unruffled sea."[330]

In an impromptu speech to the courtroom assembly, Sarah said, "'This man is persecuting me....He goes into saloons and the lowest places here and makes false statements for the purpose of ruining my good name. I fought for eight years for nothing else but to be an honorable woman and an honored wife. At the end of the fight my attorney, David S. Terry,...showed his faith in me by making me his wife, and giving me his name and I don't propose that any such man as this fellow Caldwell shall degrade it....I think the people of this city should take him and ride him on a rail for his insults to me.' Mrs. Terry stood by the chair which she had occupied. Her face was flushed with anger, and her eyes, which rained tears the moment before, snapped like balls of fire."[331]

Sarah's fury had its equal in Caldwell. He gave a speech at the end of the trial in which he literally hissed out the words as he glared at his erstwhile paramour. "'This woman,' he said, 'is entitled to no protection. She is not entitled to it. She has defiled her widowhood and disgraced the womanhood of the world.' By this time Caldwell looked more like a maniac than anything else. All color had faded from his face. His eyes glittered and every muscle trembled. Articulation failed him and he ceased his tirade and rushed out of the room into the air."[332]

These two seemed to be cut of the same cloth except that Caldwell was truly livid and Sarah was almost certainly performing, as she frequently did when defending her honor in public.

The next day, Caldwell was found guilty of disturbing the peace. He reacted by saying, "I want to say that the very next time I am called upon to disturb the peace of that woman I will disturb her peace with a bludgeon instead of my tongue...."[333]

Sarah was not in the courtroom, but she had already had her say. Having been denied the opportunity to show off Caldwell's love letters in court, she had turned them over to the *San Francisco Examiner* to be published. The content and sentiment of the letters are all similar, Caldwell expressing his love and wishing for Sarah to come home. They were written between January and April.

"It is night again," he wrote, "and at last a letter. Every doubt is forgotten, and every fear removed. Is this folly? It may be so, but it is something more, and you will know what it is....I know how troubled you are. I know that you are lonely and weary, and it makes my heart ache, and when I think that maybe you are not lonely it makes me grieve again....God only knows how you are missed. There is not a footfall in the hall of this building that does not stir the hope that you may enter the door." In another letter, he wrote, "Please come home soon, so I may say what you will not let me write. I love you now and will love you always."[334]

After the charge of disturbing the peace, Caldwell said he wanted nothing more to do with Sarah Althea. But he was still one of the lawyers handling her deceased husband's estate. So she went to see him on business, accompanied by a friend, in January, 1891. As soon as she entered his office, he flew into a rage and hit her, knocked her down, and then kicked her in the back. Her face was badly swollen from the punch and she was black and blue in several places. Caldwell was arrested on a charge of assault and battery. Sarah said that she hadn't uttered a word and the attack was completely unprovoked. For once, her version of the story seemed undistorted. When asked why he did it, Caldwell explained, "I told Mrs. Terry to stay away from me; told her repeatedly to do so....I'll kick her again if she comes to my office."[335]

This case came to court March 5 with both Sarah and Caldwell serving as counsel for themselves. "Mrs. Terry showed considerable skill and much venom," said a Fresno reporter. "She would make a first-class lawyer, and should adopt it as her profession."[336]

Caldwell was acquitted.

While all of this drama was going on back home, Sarah was frequently in San Francisco continuing her business with the many legal actions related to the Sharon case. In June, 1890, the Supreme Court ruled that the U. S. Circuit Court, which had found the marriage contract to be a forgery and declared it null and void, had in effect overturned the earlier ruling in Sharon vs. Sharon by Judge Sullivan that had awarded Sarah alimony and costs. Prior to this decision, the marriage contract had been nullified, but the alimony and costs had still been granted. The Supreme Court argued that if the marriage contract was invalid, then the marriage never existed; there could be no divorce, hence no alimony.

Also in the summer of 1890, Sarah's request to appeal the Sharon vs. Hill case (where the marriage contract was declared a forgery) was denied. The end of legal action in the Sharon divorce trial was now in sight.

You may recall that the Sharon heirs petitioned for a retrial and it was granted. The new trial began in July, 1890, in Superior Court before Judge James Shafter. General Barnes represented Sharon, and William Baggett was Sarah's lawyer. By now, she had lost every gain she had made through numerous court cases. There was nothing left to take from her. By pursuing a new trial, Sharon's heirs could only have been after a moral victory. Or revenge.

Since the main piece of evidence from the original trial, the marriage contract, was no longer allowed because it had been nullified, Baggett tried to build a case around an oral agreement between Sharon and Sarah Althea. He understood that an oral agreement would be just as binding as the written contract had been. But Judge Shafter was reluctant to allow any new evidence to the burgeoning file he already had from the first trial. Because no new evidence was admitted, the case proceeded quickly, mainly involving Shafter reviewing the records already extant.

On August 1, 1890, Shafter announced his decision for the defendant, declaring that Sarah Althea Terry was not entitled to any portion of the Sharon estate, as there never was a marriage. Sarah was ordered to pay costs, and Fred Sharon submitted his bill for $2667.85.[337]

Unbelievably, Sarah was not finished with William Sharon. She appealed Judge Shafter's decision to the Supreme Court. She was unable to get an attorney, as she had no money, so she initiated the action herself in the fall of 1891.

A bit of good news came Sarah's way in October of that same year. District Attorney Carey decided not to prosecute the two outstanding criminal charges against her.

Sarah was unable to follow through with her appeal to the Supreme Court, so it was dismissed in 1892. This brought the legal action resulting from Sharon vs. Sharon to a final close after more than eight years. Sarah never received a penny of Sharon's estate. But she kept fighting as long as she was able, against all sense, for what she unwaveringly referred to as "my rights."

The fallout from the case was monumental. Some said that Senator Sharon died before his time due to the stress of the case. Certainly Judge Terry died as a direct result of the animosity caused by it. Judge Tyler, Sarah's lawyer, was disbarred for actions in an unrelated case. The charge   against him during Sharon vs. Sharon for manufacturing evidence certainly contributed to his diminished reputation. General Barnes, Sharon's leading counsel, lost his practice through neglect because of the many years spent in litigation on this case. Judge Sullivan, who ruled in Sarah's favor against all bets, failed twice for his bid to get a position on the Supreme Court, and there were those who blamed the still powerful forces of Sharon's influence for impeding his career. As for Sarah Althea, her decision to sue William Sharon had cost her everything but her life, but her losses were not yet over.

35. THE MADWOMAN

Tis the last rose of summer, left blooming alone;
All her lovely companions are faded and gone.
—Thomas Moore, 1805

By 1891, Sarah was in severe financial trouble. She had not gotten an allowance from the Terry estate since the spring of 1890. Her home was heavily mortgaged. There was furniture, a law library, jewelry, household goods and works of art that were valuable, but Sarah had never had a head for business, and now she was suffering from debilitating grief and growing disorientation. She lived mainly off the generosity of her friends Porter Ashe and Mary Ellen Pleasant. "Her brother refused her assistance to buy the necessaries of life," said Ashe. "I have mailed letters written by her to him at my solicitation and have read his churlish refusal."[338] In return for Ashe's generosity, Sarah sold a block of Fresno property to Ashe for $5 in December 1891. He later said he tried to refuse the gift, but Sarah insisted. The property was eventually returned to the Terry estate.

Sarah wasted a great deal of money consulting mediums for help contacting her dead husband, her already impressionable mind made even more receptive to quackery by tremendous neediness.

During the last half of the nineteenth century and the beginning of the twentieth, spiritualism surged in popularity, becoming a serious occupation for some and a recreational dalliance for others. It started with a pair of sisters who could crack the joints of their toes, creating rapping noises that were attributed to spirits. The Fox sisters were hired by P. T. Barnum in the 1850s, and the spiritualism fad swept the nation. At the heart of spiritualism was the belief that living people could communicate with the dead through mediums. Often, a group of people would come together for a séance in which a medium would go into a hypnotic state and bring messages to the participants from their departed loved ones.

Sarah became completely absorbed by spiritualism. Considering how popular it was and what a hole Judge Terry's death left in her life, it is no wonder.

Rumors began to circulate that she was going mad. Her belief that she could talk to her dead husband was only part of it. When in San Francisco, she would aimlessly wander the streets for hours, often looking for her friend Porter Ashe, with whom she was becoming obsessed.

In October, 1891, while living at 418 Sutter Street, she reported that someone had broken into her rooms and stolen some silk material, dresses and patterns from a trunk. Sarah believed someone in the building was responsible, so all the rooms were searched, but nothing was turned up. The press treated this incident as a delusion, another piece of evidence that Sarah was losing her mind.

She moved back to her house in Fresno for a time and trained to become a medium, having no money to hire them. She told people that she could read minds and could command magnetic influences that allowed her to master singing and painting. In her more optimistic moments, she revisited her dreams of becoming a professional entertainer.

Whatever else was going on with her, Sarah Althea never let herself be defeated, and everything she did, she did with passion. During this time, she briefly tried her hand at a profession with which she had long been intimate: law.

Her first client was Bianco Alfonzio, an Italian charged with assault with a knife. When Sarah announced her intention to defend him, excitement and bewilderment rippled through the town. "Mrs. Terry is not only reading up on the law," reported the *Republican*, "but is hunting up evidence, having become deeply interested in the poor fellow's case. And may the Lord have mercy on the prisoner's soul."[339] By the time his case came up, Alfonzio had found himself another lawyer and politely told Sarah her services would not be needed.

Next, she came to the rescue of Hong Ah Kee, her former cook, who had been arrested for vagrancy. She went to court to demand a trial for him, as he had been languishing in jail for three days. He was released on his own recognizance.

Sarah's sojourns into the legal profession were treated with derision and amusement, as well as indulgence by Judge Prince who presided in the Fresno court. He was no doubt relieved when this phase was over.

During her time dabbling in spiritualism and law, Sarah also became obsessed with electricity. At the conclusion of the nineteenth century, electricity was a novelty, not yet installed in people's homes. From our point of view, most of us having lived with electric lights all our lives, it is hard to imagine why anyone would find them objectionable. In 1882, as the city of Los Angeles contracted to have electric lights installed on the streets, a reporter for the *Los Angeles Herald* enumerated the demerits of electric light.

> In the first place, the light is a glaring and dazzling white light, so intense in its brilliancy that the eye can scarcely stand looking at it....Then again every species of winged insect collects around the illuminating centre [sic], attracted by its bright rays, and it is usual to see thousands of bugs, of every description peculiar to the locality, dead or dying around the foot of the light....Everything is bathed in a ghostly whiteness under electric light, the soft tints of color in the complexion are effaced and a deadly pallor takes the place of the roses and the lilies of those who are blessed with the adjuncts of feminine beauty.[340]

In addition to the oddness of the light itself, people didn't understand the science of electricity. It seemed mysterious, even magical, a powerful force invisibly carried by wires to light up the darkness. Electricity, it was commonly believed, could alternately kill the living and revive the dead, not like resuscitating a heart attack victim with a jolt from a defibrillator, but as portrayed in *Frankenstein*.

Electricity and spiritualism were already bound together in popular consciousness. The first practical use of electricity was the telegraph, a technology that could send a message almost instantaneously around the world on a wire. The telephone followed, allowing an individual to talk in real time to anyone on the planet. If you believed in an afterlife, it was not much of a stretch to suppose that a telegraph or telephone might be able to communicate via electricity and wires with the spirit world.

Though Sarah Althea was an educated, intelligent woman, she was incredibly superstitious. The mystery of electricity inflamed her fantasies, and she was both attracted and repelled by it. Her definition of "electrician" was someone who could control or command electricity, like a magician with magic, and she believed she was such a person. And just like magic, electricity could be used for both good and evil.

Spiritualism became linked in her mind to still other popular beliefs. Spas were places where people went to soak in mineral baths, the purpose being to purge their bodies of toxins. Mineral baths and other forms of body purging are still popular today, but in Sarah's time, some of the baths included powerful magnets and/or mild electrical shocks to stimulate the release of bad juju from the body. There were various versions of the "water cure," as it was known, and hydropathic retreats that claimed to be able to cure almost any malady sprang up around the country.

There was yet one more aspect of spiritualism that Sarah believed in, and that was hypnotism, a method of mind control that was newly on the scene. That people could be made to say and do things unknowingly through suggestion was both fascinating and frightening to her.

As will be apparent in the description of Sarah's behavior in early 1892, her troubled mind took parts of all of these new concepts and wove them together into a confused matrix of nonsense.

Once Sarah's sanity was called into question, people started looking back over her behavior of the past several years, her many violent outbursts, her lack of self-restraint and her eccentric conduct in general, and began to wonder if her mind hadn't been "softening" for a long time. But even as a girl she was described as hot-tempered, willful and emotionally turbulent. She was true to this character all along, and her mercurial personality may have had nothing to do with mental illness. Now, however, there was something new. She appeared to be experiencing delusions and hearing voices. Because of her involvement with spiritualism, she believed the voices were from the spirit world.

The people of Fresno reported that they had seen signs of a weakening mind for about a year. But it was only within the last six weeks that they had begun to think Sarah was actually insane. She neglected her affairs and her appearance and often wandered around town aimlessly, acting disoriented and talking to herself.

In February, 1892, she took a steamer to San Francisco and was observed on the way talking continuously to an invisible companion. She went to stay with friends, the Culbreths of 417 McAllister Street. Robert E. Culbreth had been an old friend of Judge Terry, and the Culbreths and Terrys had visited each other on many occasions. While there, she exhibited episodes of violent behavior and spoke constantly to the voices in her head. She did not sleep, but paced the floor of her room all night. The Culbreths called in a doctor.

Dr. Gilmore gave the following statement to a *San Francisco Call* reporter:

> I am treating Mrs. Judge Terry for monomania. Her delirium is confined to one object. She is pursued day and night by the same ideas and affections, to which she gives profound ardor and devotion. The character of her delusions is the continual presence of spirits, to whom she talks and from whom she receives messages. At times she is extremely violent, even without apparent cause flying into a passion or fury. If she is dangerous to any one, I should say it is herself. Previous to her excitement she has a burning head, with pulsation within her skull, which she allays by pouring cold water on her head by the tumblerful, every half minute for hours at a time. She talks incessantly to spirits, running rapidly from one subject to another, sometimes in the most boisterous manner. Then she will suddenly lower her tone. She can stand the action of cold in a high degree without suffering and seems to be tormented with great thirst. At night she is most turbulent and is better at the break of day...I am treating her with bromides, chlorides and Indian hemp to quiet her and produce sleep. While conversation is carried on with the unfortunate woman she continuously holds a picture of her deceased husband to her right ear. When alone she imagines that she is studying clairvoyancy and mutters continuously. She will not obey me or any one else unless the spirits command her to. [341]

In an effort to find a relative to take responsibility for Sarah's care, Dr. Gilmore contacted an uncle, Dr. Milburn Hill Logan, who said he wanted nothing to do with her.[342] Dr. Logan, a highly successful medical doctor, taught at the California Medical College and coincidentally had just been extolled in the press for his accomplishments. "Dr. Logan's sociability at home and in the fraternal organizations to which he belongs, and his sympathy for his patients are proverbial."[343] But his sympathy for a suffering relative was apparently nowhere to be found.

Understanding that Sarah had no use for reporters, a *Call* reporter, by posing as an emissary from a doctor, was able to gain access to her room at the Culbreth's.

Suspicious of her visitor, Sarah said she would find out if he was an imposter, then she held a photo of her husband to her ear and appeared to be having a conversation. The end result of her appeal to the spirit world was to conclude that the visitor was a friend and his offer of help genuine. "You can do nothing for me, for I need no assistance from any one on this earth," she said, then dismissed him.[344]

The *San Francisco Call* ran the headline, "Hopelessly Unbalanced," and went on to say, "Beaten at every turn since Judge Sullivan rendered the famous decision granting her a divorce from William Sharon, Sarah Althea Hill-Sharon Terry has at last been stricken by the most cruel blow of her life. In short, she is seriously, perhaps hopelessly insane on the subject of spiritualism. Night and day she sits alone in a room on the top floor of a pretty McAllister-street residence continuously conversing with friends in the spirit land. Her method of communicating with departed friends is by a peculiar imaginary telephone of her own invention. As a transmitter she uses a photograph of her late husband, ex-Judge David S. Terry...."[345]

Another account of Sarah's particular brand of madness appeared in newspapers across the country:

> Her mania is of a violent type, with occasional intervals of lucidity. Saturday she sat in her room and held a handkerchief to her ear. She said it was a spiritual telephone and that she was receiving communications from the other world. On the bed lay a photograph of Judge Terry, her dead husband. She said she had received messages from him. Saturday night she eluded her nurse and was found on the front steps clad only in a sealskin sacque. Then she climbed on a bureau and sat crouching there for four hours, talking to the spirits all the while....She is suffering from incipient pneumonia, contracted through her insane freak of pouring cold water on her head, saturating her clothes.[346]

In the evenings, Sarah became loud and violent, alternately demanding and begging her nurse and the spirits to send her Porter Ashe, with whom she claimed to be madly in love. During her nightly ordeals, she regularly called out for the three men she felt closest to: David Terry, Porter Ashe, and Morgan Hill. Her brother Morgan was in California during this time, but he and his wife would soon leave for Paris. Not that he would have intervened on behalf of his sister anyway. The Culbreths let her stay, not knowing what else to do.

On February 14 Sarah "escaped" from the Culbreth house. She had not been locked in, but was being watched. Mr. Culbreth reported that nobody in the house had gotten any sleep the night before because of Sarah's ravings. She had spent the night in the bathroom pouring cold water over her head and exhorting the evil spirits to depart. The Culbreth's reported her disappearance to the police, and friends and authorities were out looking for her in San Francisco, Oakland, Stockton and Fresno.

A couple of days later she was tracked to the home of Mary Ellen Pleasant, now aged seventy-seven, at the Bell residence, 1661 Octavia Street. When a reporter deduced that she might have sought refuge with Mary Ellen, he showed up to ask questions, eventually getting an admission that Sarah was with her. "We have been out car-riding to-day," she said breezily. "Mrs. Terry is just as sound in her mind as you or me."[347]

A *Chronicle* reporter also caught up with them that evening as they came out of the gate of the Bell home. He was well-acquainted with Sarah and chatted with her for a while about her recent days in the city as they took a walk. She felt nauseated and sat on the steps of a house to continue the conversation. The reporter was struck with a stab of melancholy, writing, "there in the pale light of the gas lamp on the corner sat the woman whose name at one time was familiar to the whole civilized world and who has had more sensational experiences in the short space of about eight years than perhaps any other woman alive."[348]

She sounded perfectly sane, he reported, and spoke rapidly "in her peculiar nervous style" that he was long familiar with, but there was nothing odd about her discourse until she began to describe her reason for leaving the Culbreth's. She had not been feeling well and wondered if something had been put in her tea. "Then she went on in a rambling fashion to say that Mrs. Culbreth was a spiritualist and a medium and apparently was trying to gain notoriety by mesmerizing the well-known Mrs. Terry. Why, they had even the rooms charged with electricity, she said, and big holes were in the wall which poured out volumes of magnetism."[349]

The following day when again confronted by a *Call* reporter, Mary Ellen said, "Mrs. Terry is not crazy, but you cannot say she is quite right in her mind."[350]

During this widespread discussion in the press on Sarah Althea's sanity, the Los Angeles *Herald* (February 16) weighed in on the subject with a compassionate perspective, and one that paralleled that of the public at large who had no direct involvement with her or the powerful men who figured so tragically in her life. These neutral bystanders could easily reduce the whole affair to a relatively simple account of a rich and powerful man preying on a young, blameless woman.

There seems to be no doubt that Mrs. Sarah Althea Terry has gone insane. This is a sad ending to a career that was once most bright and promising. As a young lady, Miss Hill (that was her maiden name) broke upon San Francisco society with all the charms and allurements of fascinating beauty and intellectual distinction. She was of a good family, possessed moderate wealth, and was welcomed warmly into the best circles. In an evil hour a roué millionaire laid his toils to make her a victim to his lust, and accomplishing his purpose signed a contract of marriage which she believed to be a legal one. We all know how Miss Hill fought to vindicate her honor and to compel the old reprobate to do her justice. One of her counsel, Judge Terry, a man of singular integrity of character, was so convinced of the justice of her cause that he made her his wife when the suit terminated against her. When Judge Terry was killed by Deputy Marshal Neagle, the cup of Mrs. Terry's bitterness was full. She has shown signs of mental unbalance ever since, and it is no wonder, that after all the trials and troubles this lady has gone through in the past eight years her mind should have succumbed to the terrible pressure to which it had been subjected. Who can say in his inner consciousness, with a knowledge of the terrible experiences through which she passed, that this demented woman was not more sinned against than sinning? For our part, we can only look upon her as a beautiful and fascinating woman in the flower of youth, wrecked by an aged libertine, whose immense wealth gave him every advantage in a contest with his brave but unfortunate victim.

Of course, reporters were now watching Sarah's every move. A report from February 22 described her conducting a business transaction to get her watch out of hock, as she frequently pawned her trinkets for ready cash. "She talked in a rational manner and appeared perfectly sane,"[351] observed the reporter on the scene. Sarah announced that as soon as she could get her affairs in order in Fresno, she would be moving back to San Francisco permanently.

On February 28, a serious and coherent article appeared in *The San Francisco Examiner*, written, or at least signed, by Sarah and summing up the general events of the past few years. It was a three-column story that described how she was dazzled by the senator's wealth and consented to be his wife like any other woman in her position would have done. The article went on to praise Mammy Pleasant as the only true, incorruptible friend she had left. The conclusion of the article is quoted here, beginning with a description of David Terry, followed by a paraphrased version of his death.

> He was as brave as a lion and gentle as a woman. It is untrue that he ever made threats against Judge Field. He never made threats against anybody. It was not his way. Once, when asked what he would do if Field challenged him to duel, he only laughed and said: "The coward will never challenge anybody, but I would let my right arm be torn out by its roots if he would challenge me." He knew perfectly well that he was to be killed, just as an apostate Mormon knows that the Danites are on the track to avenge his blood. His fate had been marked out for him months before, and he knew it was but a question of time, and he lived as a man always ready to die, and I always felt that each week might be the last that we would enjoy each other's love, and so I was always at his side, and the only token I have left now is the remembrance of his grand qualities, and the fact that he died in my arms where I could kiss his smiling lips as his last breath fluttered out.
>
> He met his death without flinching, and smiled lovingly in my face as he passed away, the victim of as cold-blooded an assassination as ever was recorded in the United States. After he was in his grave, Judge Field denounced me over his signature in the newspapers in terms I will not repeat here. What cowardice! He waited until my husband and protector was in his coffin before he dared insult me. Were Judge Terry alive he would never have dared, even for a million dollars, to do such a thing, and he has never had the respect of the community since. Today I am destitute, for the estate has been divided up, and my friends tell me I have been swindled. But, destitute and homeless, I leave the men who conspired to bring about my present hapless condition, and who betrayed my

cause for Sharon's gold, to the miserable companionship of their own consciences.

For a moment, it looked as if Sarah, under the care of Mary Ellen, might be emerging from her psychosis.

But just a week later she was seen wandering through the streets in a distracted state. A *Chronicle* reporter found her in Union Square sitting on a bench. He had a chat with her, noting that she did not look well. Her hair was disarrayed and her clothes neglected. She had an eighteen inch strip of wood that she sometimes put to her ear before muttering something unintelligible that the reporter assumed to be an incantation. She claimed that various newspaper men were trying to hypnotize her. "Her mind constantly reverted to the sciences of mesmerism, hypnotism, etc., and she seemed to especially dread the electricians, who, she declared, had filled her body with wires and magnets, and controlled her thereby."[352] She referred to the Culbreth house and said her pursuers had "electrized" the bathroom there with the goal of taking nude photos of her. She had had to tear the walls apart to remove the wires.

Sarah next went to Dr. Loryea's luxurious and reknowned spa for a Turkish bath. Things did not go well. She was stricken with an episode of madness in which she refused to leave and stayed on a marble slab for four hours, claiming that the spirits were in command and that the tub was full of electrical wires and the water charged with electricity. She eventually went home and told Mammy Pleasant all about it.

This was apparently the last straw for Mary Ellen.

36. PORTIA'S LAST CASE

At the request of Mary Ellen, Porter Ashe went to the County Clerk's office to ask about the proper procedure for having an insane person committed. At this sad point in Sarah's life, it is safe to say that there were only two people alive who truly cared about her, Porter Ashe and Mary Ellen Pleasant. Previous friends, like the Culbreths, wanted nothing more than to be rid of the turmoil of her presence. One can hardly blame them. Sarah had never been easy to deal with, and now she was impossible. So impossible that Mammy Pleasant, the loyal rock of Sarah's life, turned to the only recourse left. In a statement to the press on March 9, 1892, she said that she no longer had any doubts about Sarah's insanity, and "in the absence of any near relatives to act in the matter, she has decided tomorrow to take the necessary steps to commit her to an asylum where she can be properly cared for."[353]

Mary Ellen's biographer, Helen Holdredge, implied that she was acting out of selfish motives, that she wanted to get rid of Sarah once and for all. Although Mary Ellen might have been anxious to be free of the trouble and expense of Sarah's care, it would be hard to make a case that she was a sane woman being unfairly institutionalized by unscrupulous people. Her behavior at the Culbreths, for instance, stands in evidence, not to mention Mary Ellen's initial denials to the press that Sarah was insane. She made a genuine effort to shelter and protect her one last time. Though there are many suspicious dealings connected with Mary Ellen, she demonstrated over and over again intense loyalty and generosity toward the younger women generally termed her protégés.

The only person who could have saved Sarah at this point was her brother, if he had stepped forward to act as her guardian. It seems unlikely that he could have done much for her, even so, since the manifestations of her affliction were so violent. What he might have done, however, is take charge, as her closest living relative, and provided for her care financially. But even after he returned from Paris and found his sister locked away, he did nothing.

For an unknown reason and with an unknown female accomplice, Sarah left the Bell house in the middle of the night on March 8 and had her companion book a room at the Nucleus Hotel while Sarah stayed in the background, veiled and unidentified. The companion left the hotel sometime after getting Sarah settled there. Maybe Mary Ellen had told Sarah she was going to have her locked up. Something drove her to leave.

If it was Sarah's intention to keep her identity secret at the hotel, she quickly forgot. When morning arrived, "She began by ringing the bell violently and claiming that some noisy working people were disturbing her slumbers." When she was told that she would have to leave the room for the workers to continue, she said, "I am Mrs. Judge Terry, and I do not intend to be ordered out of my room until I get ready to leave it." Once the staff realized who they had on their hands, they called the manager.

"Landlord Ford called her attention to the fact that he had let no room to her, that another person had engaged the room, and he added parenthetically that if he had known who was with her she certainly should not have been admitted. Mr. Ford afterward explained to a *Chronicle* reporter that he could not take such a risk as to let a room to Mrs. Terry. 'I should be afraid to do so,' said he. 'She is liable to set the house on fire or to leave the water running. I certainly would not dare to take her as a guest.'"[354]

By now, everybody in town had heard that Mrs. Terry was a raving lunatic.

"When the clerk went up to turn her room over to the carpenters she refused to vacate, and finally when the door was forced open she pummeled the clerk with everything within her reach."[355] The manager called the police, but they did nothing. "She paced up and down the hallway for hour after hour during the day, bewailing her fate and threatening vengeance on her enemies. Suddenly she disappeared from view. It is supposed that she finally gave up the contest and removed her base of operations to some other field."[356]

She was arrested later that same day on the warrant initiated by Mary Ellen Pleasant.

"As she appeared in the courtroom she was the picture of woe. Her raiment was in a wretchedly dilapidated condition, her hair unkempt and her eyes glassy and glaring....Her conversation was rambling and disconnected at all times, but the prevailing strain seemed to be a fancy that she was under electrical and spiritual influence."[357]

Mrs. Terry Addresses the Court.

Courtesy of the *San Francisco Call*

Sarah demanded that she have her lawyers, Knight and Heggerty, present for the hearing. Feeling betrayed by Mary Ellen, she said she wouldn't return to her house. She asked to be put under the care of Dr. Livingston, but she was taken instead to the Home for the Care of the Inebriate, violently resisting all the way.[358]

The Home for the Inebriate was established in 1859 as a humanitarian way of dealing with alcoholics. It was an alternative to the drunk tank, providing shelter, food and medical care, often only until the resident sobered up. As is shown by this example, it was also used as temporary housing for people with other types of conditions.

At the home, Sarah set out immediately to pull things apart looking for electric wires. The staff put a pair of leather mittens on her to prevent her from destroying everything. When Dr. Jewell, the resident doctor, interviewed her, she was calmer and he allowed the mittens to be removed. After that, she had a good meal and slept through the night.

Meanwhile, Mary Ellen had applied for a guardian to be appointed to Sarah. Porter Ashe was assigned the task.

The presiding judge for the insanity hearing was Walter Levy, one of Sarah's lawyers from her original team in Sharon vs. Sharon. He allowed the proceedings to be public, moving the case to a larger courtroom to accommodate the anticipated crowd. Spectators packed in by the hundreds to witness the last chapter of the story that had occupied their imaginations for over eight years. Among these was General Barnes, a contemplative observer, here to see that his work was truly finished.

Despite Sarah's feeling of betrayal from the previous day, she walked into the courtroom on the arm of Mary Ellen, wearing a new outfit provided by her friend, looking, if not beautiful, then at least tidy and clean.

"Mrs. Terry carried a small satchel, a lead pencil and a huge canvas-covered ledger, in which she probably intended to jot down the proceedings as the case wore along. She wore a long black cloak and a small bead-trimmed bonnet with a bunch of red artificial flowers at the top. Her light blonde hair, which harmonized with her pallid face, was coiled into a hard knot at the back of her head. She looked haggard and careworn, and the heavy eyes and drooping mouth gave the face an expression of extreme weariness. As she took her seat at the lawyer's table and deposited her book thereon she nodded and smiled to a few friends that greeted her, but a moment later she buried her face in her hands and burst into tears."[359]

She asked for her attorney, Heggerty. He said that he had not been engaged on her behalf, but came to court and sat by her side out of sympathy. Though she wanted him there, she said she would represent herself.

The first witness called was Mary Ellen Pleasant, who testified in hushed and reluctant tones that Sarah believed she could speak to spirits and that she communicated with Judge Terry. She told of an instance where Sarah had thrown a spool of thread out of an upper story window to use as a telephone line to the spirit world. Other witnesses spoke of a bundle of wire that Sarah carried around, claiming it had some special power.

Dr. Jewell, after his one night with Sarah, optimistically testified that he thought she suffered from a temporary mania, that he saw evidence that she was unbalanced on only one subject, that of electricity, and that he was used to seeing drunks who were afraid of wires. Sarah, he understood, did not drink. In her case, he believed her trouble was due to malnourishment and that once she was given a healthy diet for sixty to ninety days, she would be cured.

At this time in history, it was not only the drunk tanks, but also the mental asylums of the country that were filled with people who were terrified of electricity.

Most of the witnesses Sarah had asked for did not show up. Porter Ashe was not present. Witnesses were hardly necessary, as it happened. As Sarah questioned the few witnesses of the morning and spoke on her own behalf, she gave the court a clear view into her tormented mind.

When Mary Ellen explained that the reason she was pursuing this course was that Sarah talked to spirits, Sarah countered, "I don't believe so much in spirits now as I do in electricity. I'm full of wires and can transmit myself to people in another world and get answers."[360] This was her way of denying the supernatural explanation and adopting a more reasonable, scientific one.

She told the judge that several people had tried to hypnotize her. Her discourse was rambling and sometimes incoherent. Several times she broke into laughter described as "hysterical" and "chilling." Mary Ellen at one point was seen to be openly weeping. The hearing was an evident strain on her emotions. There are those who would say she was putting it on because she was renowned as one of the coolest and most unemotional people to ever live. But Sarah had been special to her for many years and it must have been tough to see her in this condition.

After about an hour, when Sarah appeared to be getting over-excited and nearly fainted, Heggerty suggested she might need a break. The judge adjourned the court until two o' clock.

Outside, Sarah encountered a crowd of gawkers. "More than a thousand people had assembled to see Mrs. Terry leave, and she rather enjoyed the notoriety, declaring that the crowd had always been with her."[361]

She was put on a carriage and, accompanied by Mary Ellen, was driven back to the Home for the Inebriate. She expected to return to court for an afternoon session, but the Commissioners had heard enough. Immediately after her departure from the courtroom, they judged her insane and ordered her to be sent to the asylum in Stockton.

"Mrs. Pleasant has never lost interest in Mrs. Terry," reported the *Chronicle*, "and to-day is her one stanch true firm friend. It was at her request that Mrs. Terry's insanity has been tested, and she at first desired that she should be sent to Napa where she might often see her, as she has a ranch nearby. On reflection, however, she decided that Stockton would be preferable as most of Mrs. Terry's and Judge Terry's old friends live in that vicinity, unselfishly relinquishing her own preferences. Mrs. Pleasant accompanied Mrs. Terry to the Home for Inebriates, has clothed her, and will to-day accompany her on the way to the asylum. Damon was not truer to Pythias than Mrs. Pleasant has been to her poor child, as she lovingly calls Mrs. Terry."[362]

The following day, March 11, no one was permitted to see Sarah except Dr. Jewell and those in charge of transporting her to Stockton. Though he had known her only a few days, Jewell made a remark that seemed straight to the heart of her when he said, "If there is one thing more than another that she likes, it is to make her believe you think that all her past actions were proper and right."[363]

Accompanied by Mammy Pleasant, Deputy Sheriff Fidder of San Francisco and a matron of the sheriff's office, Mrs. Winkler, Sarah was taken in a carriage to the ferry dock. She had been suspicious and reluctant to go, but had been told she was being taken to Judge Levy's courtroom where he was waiting for her. A crowd watched her enter the carriage outside the Home for the Inebriate. A similar crowd waited for her arrival at the docks. She was by then frantic to escape, as she realized she had been lied to and was being taken across the bay. She threatened to cut Mrs. Winkler's throat and tried desperately to get out of the carriage.

When she saw the crowd, she yelled out to them for help. "'I am being abducted. These people are carrying me away to lock me up somewhere. They have no warrant to do so; there is no commitment and I appeal to you to release me.' These words were spoken through the partly open back window through which Mrs. Terry peered wildly as she was making her appeal. 'I am not crazy; I have a better mind than my enemies and this is an outrage,' she added"[364]

"Sarah Althea's appeals and struggles were pitiable and many men turned away with tears in their eyes."[365]

She saw a man she knew and called to him to protect her from being locked up. Then she asked him if he was an electrician. He seemed unsure how to respond. "I am," she said. "I am not a mind reader, but I am an electrician. This woman, pointing to Mrs. Winkler, is a hypnotizer. I feel the electric influence now. I feel it in my legs as it is coming away from her."[366]

The carriage drove onto the ferry and the crowd followed. Sarah proclaimed that it was Mammy Pleasant who was responsible for her predicament. "'She caused my arrest because I had detectives watching her house one night,' she repeated over and over again….'There was something wrong up there and I got on to it. I'll tell it to you some day. It will come out. To keep me from revealing it, she is going to have me locked up.' Then Mrs. Terry lapsed into silence for a minute during which she was apparently holding conversation with some persons at a distance."[367]

The trip across the bay to Oakland was accompanied by Sarah's non-stop talking as she jumped from topic to topic, and then a renewed bout of struggling at the other side when she was driven to the train. She refused to get on the car. "I am not going to Stockton," she declared.

"The officers, of whom three had gathered, finding that persuasion would not do, were compelled to resort to force….Mrs. Terry was lifted bodily to the first step of the car by a burly deputy, having his strong arms clasped about her waist holding her up while the other two were lifting her or attempting to do so. When on the first step, she grasped the iron railing of the car and held her own against the three officials for five minutes. Indeed, her fingers had to be released by great force and some damage before the top of the platform was reached. There she gained a new hold on the guard rail and another desperate struggle ensued. 'Oh, I am strong,' she yelled as the struggle was in progress. 'That's my electric power. Give me a chance and six men cannot move me. Why do you not help me?' addressing herself to the bystanders. Don't you see the outrage they are perpetrating? They have no commitment. I am not crazy. Won't you help me?' At last she was safely seated in the car, and after again attacking Mrs. Winkler became quite calm."[368] Then she amused herself by boasting about her strength and challenging any of the men assembled to test it. Her mood swung rapidly from wrath to elation to docility and back around again several times during the train trip. During one episode, she complained that she had been falsely imprisoned in the "drunkard's asylum," and to prove it, took a small piece of linen from her purse that contained the monogram "Home for the Inebriate." She then took the head of a bird from her pocket and said the ladies of the Home had presented it to her.

When the train arrived in Stockton, she mistakenly thought they had stopped at Lathrop where her husband had been killed. She was unaware that the Lathrop station had burned down a few weeks earlier. She stood on the train platform, leaning on the railing, and addressed the crowd that had assembled to see her. "Gentlemen, three years ago my husband was shot here." She went on to explain how she had arrived in her current predicament. "This is a job of Mammie Pleasant."[369]

In that moment, she believed that her dearest friend had betrayed her. Certainly, there was nobody left to come to her rescue. And in the years after her internment, Mary Ellen Pleasant never visited her, nor did she write.

Sarah had to be pried off the railing by two policemen and was put into a carriage, along with the matron, Mrs. Winkler. She lashed out at Mrs. Winkler on the short trip to the asylum, hitting her, kicking her and sticking a pin in her. She gave her one last kick as she was removed from the carriage.

The asylum matron and a dozen female attendants waited at the door to watch Sarah brought forcibly into the building. Once they had her through the doorway, she turned to face the onlookers and said, "I suppose you are satisfied now that you have got me in the asylum."[370]

"The unfortunate woman presented a sad picture," wrote the *Chronicle* reporter who had been along through the entire ordeal. "Her face was pinched and flushed and her hair was disheveled, the hat being far back on her head. Her dress was mussed and the long dragging train was dirty, giving the poor woman the appearance of one who was entirely careless of her look."[371]

The Stockton asylum was the first public mental health hospital in California, completed in 1853, and was considered quite progressive for its time. The project arose from the large numbers of people suffering from mental health issues related to the Gold Rush. In an ironic twist, David Terry had been appointed one of three trustees for the asylum in 1852, so oversaw the construction of the institution where his widow would live out the rest of her life.

Women's Wing, Stockton State Hospital (Courtesy of Alex Wellerstein)

Once inside the asylum, Sarah made one last attempt to save herself by resisting being taken to the receiving ward. She demanded to see Sheriff Cunningham, a potential ally. Cunningham was the sheriff who had issued the warrant for the arrest of Justice Field at her insistence. But this day her demands were ignored.

The initial evaluation of Sarah's condition was conducted by Dr. Lilienthal, who wrote the following report:

> Evidence of Insanity: Very talkative and rambles much in conversation. Is quite delusional about electricity and hypnotism and believes she is endowed with superhuman strength. Has great self-esteem and courts notoriety. Is very unreasonable and exacting.
>
> Physical condition: Rather thin and haggard and has coated tongue.
>
> Diagnosis: Acute Mania[372]

On the commitment register, her age was listed as thirty-five. In two weeks, she would actually be forty-two.

The elegant four-story building surrounded by sprawling grounds and a high fence was to be Sarah Althea's home for the next forty-five years.

37. THE INMATE

By now, with Sarah cutting such a pathetic, defeated figure, most of public opinion was sympathetic, revising the past by making William Sharon, the cause of all her trouble, into a heartless monster.

Although Sarah was out of the picture, the drama was not yet over. On March 15, under the authority of Porter Ashe, now the administrator of Sarah's estate, the house in Fresno was searched for papers and valuables. A safe was blown open. Inside, a letter was found from someone who claimed to have been a former sheriff of a California county who had been offered $25,000 and immunity from the law to kill Judge Terry about two months before he was shot by Neagle. The letter writer turned down the murderous job and left California to keep himself safe, as those offering the job threatened him with murder if he said anything or remained in California. He had written to offer Mrs. Terry proof of this conspiracy if she would come to Dubuque, Iowa to meet with him.[373] Apparently she never did.

Details began to emerge that there had indeed been a conspiracy afoot during the Sharon vs. Sharon trial, plans to abduct Sarah and kill Judge Terry. Judge W. F. Fitzgerald, for instance, admitted that he had been approached and offered $50,000 if he would help the case, understanding that what the Sharon people really meant by "help" was to kill Judge Terry. Fitzgerald's answer to the unnamed men who made the offer was, "Gentlemen, you are mistaken in your man. It is true that in the course of my life I may have killed a man or two, but I had to do it in self defense....I know Judge Terry well, and I respect and esteem him for his manly and upright character, and I will therefore take no part in the case."[374]

Judge Terry himself had discovered evidence that Judge Sullivan had been offered a blank check from Sharon to find in his favor in the original trial. He did not name his source and Sullivan declined to comment, but even Terry's enemies did not believe he would make up such a story. If it had actually happened, Sullivan clearly did not take the bribe.[375]

A new biography of Terry's life was about to come out. His biographer, Alexander E. Wagstaff, confirmed that he had found evidence during his research that there had been a conspiracy to kill Terry and he was sure that Neagle had been handsomely paid for being the one to accomplish the task.[376]

Ashe gave the job of organizing the contents of the Fresno house to Mrs. Whitney. The house had been sitting vacant for about two months, and was as Sarah had left it. Whitney oversaw the packing of her belongings, to be shipped to San Francisco and put in storage, awaiting her recovery. Among the surprises in the house was a fortune hidden under the carpets: gold coins, paper money, diamonds, set and unset, and gold jewelry. The jewelry was the same that Sarah had reported stolen to the San Francisco police a few months before. She had apparently hidden these valuables under the carpets and then forgotten. In total, an enormous amount of jewelry, furs and clothing was found, estimated to be worth more than $10,000. Meanwhile, Sarah had gone wandering through San Francisco, unable to pay her bills and relying on handouts from her friends.

Also found in the house were two partially completed lectures on the subject of the Sharon case. Sarah had never given a single lecture of her planned tour.

Sarah's personal possessions were given to Mary Ellen Pleasant for safe-keeping, and were stored in an upstairs room at the Bell mansion.

After Sarah's confinement to the asylum, there are a few sporadic glimpses into her life, and these became fewer and further apart as time passed.

On March 22, shortly after her confinement, she was put in a straightjacket because of her violent ravings. It was reported that she was still getting her directions from spirits.

The following update was from May 31, 1892: "Mrs. Sarah Althea Terry is said by the asylum doctors to be improving physically, but is growing worse mentally. She was moved a few days ago to a ward in the rear of the asylum building, on account of her nervousness. She spends most of her time talking about spiritual communications and sings a great deal. She is careless about her personal appearance; her hair is usually disheveled and her clothes disarranged."[377]

In September, the *Fresno Republican Weekly* received a letter from a Stockton informant who said that Sarah Althea had become somewhat "fleshy," but her mind was more enfeebled than ever.

In January, 1893, a reporter from the *San Francisco Call* went to Stockton to see for himself if certain rumors were true about Sarah's condition. It was being said that she had recovered her reason some time ago, but was being kept a prisoner in the asylum by the influence of her enemies.

The *Call* reporter met with Dr. Young, who believed Sarah was insane long before she came to the asylum, and he had no hope of curing her. Dr. Young also made it clear that the staff had instructions to say as little as possible to the press, and that Sarah was not allowed to have visitors.

The reporter then appealed to Dr. Phillips, who apparently had not gotten the memo about keeping quiet around journalists.

"On the books Mrs. Terry's malady is called acute mania," he said. "This unfortunate patient is not demented; her reason is perverted, only. She remembers occurrences, dates, faces and everything else she has ever known, and quite frequently when addressing any one she will commence her talk quite rationally, but before she has uttered a whole sentence the conversation becomes hopelessly tangled up and is utterly without sense.

"Then, again, she suffers from hallucinations, and constantly imagines things have occurred or are occurring which never existed at all except in her imagination.

"She will hear voices and feel electric currents or complain of having been insulted by some fellow-patient without the slightest foundation for such talk.

"There is also a trait of viciousness in her disease and she quite frequently becomes so spiteful toward the other patients in her ward that she has to be temporarily confined to her room.

"Dr. Phillips then said that one of Mrs. Terry's favorite occupations is to make drawings on pieces of paper which resemble the crude pictures one sees at spiritualistic séances, and are known as spirit drawings.

"When she is so occupied she claims to be working under orders from spiritland. The confined life she must necessarily lead is very irksome to Mrs. Terry, and she constantly wants to be discharged, thinking that she was sent to the asylum only for a short time and that her term has expired.[378]

Dr. Phillips agreed with Dr. Young that Sarah was incurable. He said she was being given no treatment other than to avoid exciting her unnecessarily.

It's no surprise that Sarah thought she would be going to the asylum temporarily. More than one person expressed that idea at her insanity hearing, and it is reasonable to suppose that she was told so directly by any number of people trying to calm her fears and/or assuage their own guilt. But from the description given by Dr. Phillips, nothing much had changed with Sarah after nine months.

The diagnosis of acute mania was later changed to "dementia praecox," an early term for schizophrenia.

The *Call* reporter did not see Sarah's condition for himself and the rumors about her mistreatment continued to the point that she was said to be dying from abuse and neglect. The rumors were no doubt encouraged by the policy not to allow her visitors. So when a reporter from the *Stockton Mail* came for a look late in February, 1893, Dr. Asa Clark, the hospital superintendent, decided to escort the reporter himself, giving the public a rare and chilling tour into Sarah Althea's hell. The reason she was denied visitors became apparent as soon as she had one.

The reporter was led through a labyrinth of corridors to Ward H on the third story. The barred door was opened to a high-walled room with cells on either side.

A width of hallway carpet extended the length of the room, and here and there on each side stood benches, upon which sat patients whose strange eyes were riveted on the visitors. Other patients paced up and down with bowed heads, muttering and mumbling to themselves. Loud talking could be heard in a cell on the left and half way down the ward. It was the cell occupied by Mrs. Terry. The door was shut, but through its white wooden bars the visitors, as they came up, could see a number of women within. They proved to be patients who, being for the time lucid, had been placed as watch over Mrs. Terry to prevent her doing any damage....The footfalls of the visitors caught her ear, and peering around one of the women, she caught sight of Dr. Clark just as the matron opened the door.

"There he is! There he is!" Mrs. Terry shrieked, springing to her feet in a fury.

The patients seized her. The two attendants of the ward, who were at the door when it was swung open, entered and caught hold of the maniac.

"Oh, God, let me loose," screamed the poor, demented woman, struggling to free herself. "I'll kill him! I'll kill him!"

As she said this she pointed to Dr. Clark with an outstretched arm. She was making fierce lunges toward him and seemed to be dragging those who had hold of her....She gave vicious swings with her head, trying to butt her captors in the face. To one she would say, "You ——, you murdered my aunt;" to another, "You ——, you're Mr. ——'s daughter." These were the least vile of the expressions she used.

Mrs. Terry had by this time struggled her way out into the ward....She spat at Dr. Clark four or five times, and every time her marksmanship was good....There was considerable excitement in the ward while this scene was going on. Patients ran to and fro, some of them shrieking and others wringing their hands and crying hysterically.

Sarah recognized her visitor and showed him how her feet were strapped together with straps slack enough to allow her to take short steps. This was to prevent her from kicking. The reporter described most of what she said as "raving." In order to prevent general hysteria in the ward, the attendants carried her back into her cell as she screamed and spat at them. Once she was locked in, she howled and howled, creating pandemonium among the other patients.

"One patient, a little old woman with lips aquiver and hands trembling, ran up to the matron and begged her not to let Mrs. Terry escape into the ward. She showed, at the same time, where a tooth was missing from her jaw, and said Mrs. Terry had knocked it out with her head."[379]

The reporter noted that Sarah wore clean clothes and new slippers, not the rags that had been rumored. Dr. Clark told him that a wealthy San Joaquin County friend of the Hill family had offered to supply any special luxuries she asked for, and the reporter concluded that the patient was being treated as well as could be expected, considering her conduct.

In some ways, Sarah was luckier than similarly afflicted inmates of the hospital who came later. The primary goal of the staff at these institutions was to keep the patients calm and orderly, a challenging task considering the nature of their ailments. Sedatives were routinely used throughout the history of the asylums. After Sarah's time, two other treatments became popular. First, electric shock therapy arrived in the 1940s. Given Sarah's fear of electricity, imagine the terror such an ordeal would have instilled in her. In 1947, lobotomies began to be performed at the Stockton facility. These continued into the 1950s. Over 200 of these procedures, many of which resulted in death, were performed for the purpose of quieting the more disruptive patients. Sarah would obviously have been a prime candidate for the surgery.

By July, 1894, Dr. Clark reported that Sarah, their best known patient, was no longer violent. "...she is very docile, and gives no trouble to any one, and while still unbalanced, has been improving wonderfully of late."[380] Such periods of quiescence were broken during the years following by renewed periods of violence.

A typical window into Sarah's health was provided by Dr. Henry Lauderson in his daily reports on the female patients in 1895. "Mrs.

Terry is incoherent," he wrote, "occasionally troublesome. Sends messages to everyone." The following month he wrote, "Mrs. Terry: noisy, vulgar and somewhat ugly at times."[381] It seems she was still talking to spirits and being abusive to the staff and fellow inmates.

In December, 1894, nearly three years after Sarah was confined, Thomas H. Williams, an old friend of both Sarah and Morgan Hill, applied to replace Porter Ashe as Sarah's guardian. Backed by Morgan Hill, Williams brought charges against Ashe, saying that he had mismanaged the estate of Mrs. Terry, had sold some of her personal property and spent the money on himself, that he had neglected the needs of his ward and had not provided her with the necessities of life.

Although Ashe was willing to transfer guardianship to someone else, as he felt it was a disagreeable burden, he did step up to defend himself against the charges. He and Williams were both horse racing enthusiasts and had been friends at one time. In fact, Williams accompanied Ashe on his trip to Washington to apply to President Cleveland to intervene when Judge Terry was jailed for contempt of court. However, Williams and Ashe were no longer on friendly terms due to a dispute over Ashe's racehorse Geraldine in the previous year. For that reason, Ashe felt that Williams brought the charges against him out of spite. Ashe rightly pointed out that he had stood by Sarah when neither Williams nor her brother had. "I would go on to the end serving her, did I not think that her best interests would be served by the appointment of Thomas H. Williams as permanent guardian of her estate and person, believing that he is the one man who can do what I confess to have been unable to do—make that wealthy brother support an insane sister during the rest of her natural life and prevent her from going to a dishonored grave a state's charge."[382]

After reviewing the records Ashe presented, the judge ruled that everything was in order and officially appointed Williams as guardian. This was in March, 1895.

In May of that year, Ashe transferred all of Sarah's personal property to Thomas Williams. The inventory, untouched and waiting in the Bell house for Sarah's return, was intact.

"Mrs. Pleasant has guarded the property as something sacred," reported the *Call*. "Many of the articles inventoried and appraised were presents from Mrs. Pleasant to Mrs. Terry, given during the trying days of the Sharon will contest and afterward. Among these presents is a gold ring with three empty spaces that once were filled with three beautiful diamonds and cost $500. The diamonds were lost long before the tragedy that ended the earthly career of Judge Terry. Another is a brooch and eardrops, heavily studded with pearls, presented by Mrs. Pleasant to Mrs. Terry on the occasion of her marriage with Judge Terry.

"In the room where all of Mrs. Terry's personal property was stored were six large trunks. On the tops of these were spread dresses, cloaks, skirts and shawls, that once upon a time set the fashions of San Francisco. But the rats have played sad havoc with many of the things and rich silks, satins, velvets and furs have lost most of their value by the encroachments of time and the moth."[383]

Still in good shape, however, were Judge Terry's law books, numerous household objects made of silver, and gold jewelry.

Soon after Williams' appointment as guardian, he began dispensing of Sarah's property. He sold the Fresno house for a high school building, then he auctioned off the personal property in October, 1895. It appears that nothing to do with Sarah Althea Hill Terry would occur without controversy. Several people were outraged when they found out about the auction, claiming it had not been properly advertised and because of that, the property did not fetch its true worth. Porter Ashe was one of those who objected. He claimed that almost everything was seriously undervalued and none of Judge Terry's friends had been informed of the sale. "When I went to see Mammy Pleasant," he said, "she fairly cried and said that if she had only known she would have sent someone to buy the jewelry."[384]

The entire lot of goods fetched a mere $438.45.

By November, 1895, all of the Terry property was gone and cash on hand after expenses was only $232, which Williams slated for paying the $15 monthly fee for Sarah's residence at the Stockton Asylum. That would have covered only a year and a quarter, but Williams made regular payments to the asylum through at least 1913, over twenty years. The extant patients' pay register, which explicitly lists Thomas H. Williams as the payee, ends in that year with an annotation that the accounts were carried over into a new ledger that has apparently been lost. Where was the money coming from? Was Williams paying it himself? Perhaps. He could easily afford it and he was an old friend of the Hills. But Morgan Hill could also have afforded it. Perhaps he was making the payments through Williams. Thomas Williams died in 1915 and there are no payment ledgers to consult after 1913, so it is unknown if the payments continued.

After several years in the institution, Sarah had made no progress toward sanity. In May, 1896, a short article appeared in the San Francisco *Call* reporting an incident at the asylum.

"Several days ago it became apparent that she was getting worse rapidly, and one day this week she attacked her attendant. During the struggle that ensued she nearly bit the finger off the attendant. Luckily, the laceration was treated immediately and blood poisoning did not ensue. She is guarded now more closely than ever. Mrs. Terry's reason has completely fled, and she only broods over her troubles, but many of her past experiences she does not remember."[385]

On the occasion of Nellie Brackett's wedding in 1898, over a decade after the main events of Sharon vs. Sharon, the *San Francisco Call* reminded readers of that infamous scandal. "It created a great sensation at that time, but now has been almost entirely forgotten."[386]

In December, 1902, Robina Bell, adopted daughter of Teresa and Thomas Bell, gave birth to a son. When Teresa was told she was a grandmother, she said, "According to the oracle of the Bell family, [Mary Ellen Pleasant], it's Sarah Althea at Stockton who is that."[387] If Sarah was Robina's mother, it's unlikely she ever knew she had a grandchild. Teresa Bell was long past feeling anything but spite toward her adopted children or grandchildren. "I hope she will have one a year" Teresa wrote in her diary, "and see how she likes sitting up nights for them. Even then it will not be what I done, giving all that love and devotion to the children of another. 'The mills of the Gods to slowly grind' and we shall see if she gets her desserts."[388]

Robina married a second time to Maurice Hessel. They had a daughter who went on to have children and grandchildren of her own, so perhaps Sarah Althea's progeny lives on today.

That same year, 1903, this report issued from the closed world of the asylum: "A party composed of members of the State Insanity Commission, State Superintendent of Public Schools Kirk and other State officials, visited the Stockton State Asylum last Sunday. After being shown through the grounds and buildings they requested that they be allowed to visit the apartment in which Sarah Althea Terry is confined. The latter, with the cunning of a demented person, learned of their proposed visit and planned to make of it an opportunity to escape. No sooner had the woman attendant opened the door to Sarah Althea's room than the latter sprang on her, broke her glasses, blackened her eye and otherwise battered her. It is said that the men visitors fled. At any rate the attendant, after quite a struggle with the woman, overpowered her and locked the door."[389]

Nearly a decade after her confinement, Sarah was still desperate to escape. But this was the last such report. The years passed and Sarah got older and more resigned to her fate. Like all of us, she aged and mellowed. A nurse at the asylum who had been there 25 years in the early 1930s, told a visiting researcher that Sarah Althea had always been a most agreeable patient, but that she had heard of the difficulties the staff had dealt with in the early days. From that report, we can conclude that around 1910 when Sarah would have been 60 years old, she had finally given up the fight. That visiting researcher was Stella Ingram Brown of San Francisco, working on a book about Mary Ellen Pleasant.

Brown's grandmother had been a friend of Pleasant's, hence her interest. The book was never finished, but Brown's notes remain, including a few handwritten details she made about her visit to the asylum. The notes are undated, but Brown's research partner, Muriel Wright, said she started her quest in 1925. Brown died in 1938 and had given up the project by then. Brown likely visited the asylum around 1930, give or take a few years, when Sarah was about 80.

What she found there was a short old woman with fine, bobbed, snow-white hair. Sarah was heavy, weighing between 160 and 180 pounds. She wore a sapphire blue silk dress. Her eyes were still intensely blue and she was easily amused. She seemed to like the attention of her visitors, but evaded some of their questions, "particularly about her age." She remembered Mammy Pleasant with no hesitation and remembered how she had been of so much help during the Sharon case.[390]

Another journalist, Evelyn Wells, came to interview Sarah in 1936 and reported that the withered face retained the "perfume of desirability" from her youth. Sarah remembered some things clearly, but was also plagued by delusions, recalling, for instance, that she had been married to Abraham Lincoln and Ulysses S. Grant.[391]

From reports from the asylum staff in later years, Sarah regarded herself as a lady of means and the staff as her servants. She called the hospital her estate, wrote 'checks' for large sums, and entertained the nurses with tales of champagne suppers, theater nights, and high society parties in gay old San Francisco. She found a way to cope with her situation by turning her prison into a palace.

What was almost certainly Sarah's last visit from the outside world came in July, 1936, when two authors visited. Carroll D. Hall and Oscar Lewis were researching a book about the Palace Hotel (*Bonanza Inn: America's First Luxury Hotel*). They shared some details from that visit in the book.[392]

"The neat, white-haired little figure sat in a rocking-chair. Her shoulders were stooped and she leaned forward slightly, regarding her visitors with bright, shrewd eyes. She had been unwell, her heart was bad, and some years earlier she had broken her hip, so it was hard for her to get about. A crutch was leaning against her chair; she kept her hand on it while she talked….Small talk fell nimbly from her tongue….She spoke politely, like a dutiful hostess, but she was not much interested."

Throughout the interview, Sarah sounded surprisingly rational after forty-four years in an insane asylum suffering from schizophrenia, and, in some ways, very much like her younger self, as when the subject of the Palace Hotel came up. "That's my hotel, you know," she said. "It was built for me."

When asked about Judge Terry, she said, "He was one of my husbands. He was a big man." About Sharon, she said, "He was a rich man. He owned the Bank of California. Is he dead?"

"Do you know my brother, Morgan Hill?" she asked. "Do you know Fred Sharon, my stepson? He looks like you, only he's bald-headed."

They asked her about Mammy Pleasant. "She was a black lady....Took charge of my trial. She was *smart*....Is she dead?"

When they asked her about the marriage contract, hoping to find out once and for all what the truth of it was, she said she knew of no marriage contract.

"San Francisco was mentioned. She repeated the name, adding a bit wistfully: 'I'd like to go there myself....'"

Sarah did not seem to comprehend how much time had passed, but, then, living as she was, how could she?

She outlasted everybody who had known her, physically, but most of her life was lived imprisoned in mind and body. Her world became tiny. Even in death, she traveled just a couple of blocks to her final resting place at the Stockton Rural Cemetery.

She died of pneumonia following on influenza on Valentine's Day, 1937. Newspapers all over the country ran the news of her death with headlines like "Famous Belle of Early Days Dies in Obscurity," but most of the readers would never have heard of her. She outlived her fame. She had blazed like a comet through 1880s San Francisco, riveting the country. She was a woman who had craved attention and adoration, who had wanted to live in the spotlight. So she did, briefly, and paid dearly for it.

The hospital staff had no knowledge of a living relative and made plans to bury her in the hospital cemetery. Thankfully, that did not happen. The remains of thousands of patients buried there lie in unmarked graves today, as the cemetery has been neglected for decades. When Judge Terry's granddaughter, Cornelia Terry McClure, heard that Sarah had died, she stepped up to offer her a burial in the Terry plot, an action her father Clinton would surely have protested if he had been living.

"'I have had no contact with Mrs. Terry all these years,' Mrs. McClure said at her home in Ukiah. The whole affair was so tragic to our family. But I cannot permit Mrs. Terry to go to a pauper's grave, so I will take charge if we do not find nearer relatives.'"[393] Cornelia Terry McClure died in 1949 and is also buried in the Terry plot.

At Sarah's death, a newspaper from her home state, the *Southwest Missourian*, reported the news of the passing of one of their own. Clearly the reporter had no idea who she was and had been unable to find anyone locally who remembered her or her family. The article recalling a Cape

Girardeau native was limited to the information in the press releases, and concluded as follows: "Back in the 80s the former Girardean was the toast of gay San Francisco, her coach and finery being the talk of the city. She was a woman of marvelous beauty, it was said, and after her commitment to the hospital, it is said she maintained a regal sort of dignity and imagined herself wealthy."[394]

Sarah Althea's greatest ambition was to be fabulously rich. In that, she failed, except in her own mind. She held court in the insane asylum with the staff as her servants, imagining the buildings and grounds as her estate. In that way, she ultimately did achieve her goal and became a great lady.

Sarah Althea's Grave - Stockton Rural Cemetery

AFTERWORD

"When the story of the life of Sarah Althea Hill-Sharon-Terry is written—if it ever should be—it will be the history of a trouble-maker." Chicago Mail, *1889*

While Sarah Althea languished in her tiny room at the Stockton asylum, the cast of characters who had assembled around her for a stormy decade all preceded her in death, meeting their various fates as follows:

George W. Tyler, Sarah's blustery attorney, was disbarred in 1886 on charges of unprofessional conduct unrelated to the Sharon case. He made several attempts to be readmitted to the bar, but was unsuccessful and died in April, 1895.

William McCann Neilson, born in Australia about 1839, the man who brought the original divorce case to the courts, was ill and penniless and reportedly on his death bed in 1894. But a few months later he married Nan McFarland from Vacaville. She was from a prominent and wealthy family, so Neilson seemed to be set for life. But his wife divorced him a few years later on grounds of cruelty. He continued harassing her, so she tried unsuccessfully to have him committed to an insane asylum in 1897. The last record of him is from the 1898 voter registrar of San Francisco.

Stephen Johnson Field, the man responsible for the death of David S. Terry, served on the Supreme Court until December, 1897, long after his usefulness as a judge had expired. He was senile and his colleagues had for some time tried unsuccessfully to persuade him to retire. Since he wouldn't go, they gave him fewer and fewer opinions to decide. He sat at least two years on the bench as an incompetent. He died in 1899.

William Henry Linow Barnes, the celebrated orator and attorney who led the charge in all of William Sharon's battles against Sarah Althea, was born in 1836. He continued a successful career in law once the Sharon case was finally put to rest. He was greatly honored and respected during his life. He died of throat cancer July 21, 1902.

Mary Ellen Pleasant, born about 1814, after spending a fortune on Sarah Althea's various litigations, saw the steady decline of her empire, losing her wealth, her property, and eventually being thrown out of the house on Octavia Street by Teresa Bell. Mary Ellen died January 4, 1904, in severely diminished circumstances. Her legacy lives on, however, in legends and mysteries that were never solved. Some people believed she was responsible for several murders, including the death of Thomas Bell who fell, or was pushed, over the banister of the Octavia Street house. Officially, his death was ruled an accident. Of the many crimes Mary Ellen was rumored to have committed, she escaped prosecution on every count and is regarded by many today as the mother of civil rights in California.

The Mary Ellen Pleasant Memorial Park is located at Octavia and Bush Streets. The massive eucalyptus trees lining Octavia Street today were planted by Mary Ellen.

Her life was filled with controversy, and that controversy continued even after her death. A few days before she died, she wrote a new will and left her entire estate to the couple who had kindly taken her in during her final days. The Bells sued and the litigation continued for twenty years.

Reuben Headley Lloyd, born in 1835, was the one that got away. He was a highly successful, respected and popular attorney with several famous clients. Lloyd was also active in community service and became Park Commissioner in 1907. He never married and he never moved from his family home at 1010 Folsom Street, even after his mother died. He was devoted to business and never smoked or drank. He died in 1909 of prostate cancer. He was seventy-four and left a million dollar estate to his sister Mary Hoadley and niece Aphra West. A crowd of 5,000 stood by to raise their hats to his hearse on its way to Laurel Hill Cemetery. In 1913, a marble bust of Lloyd was erected at Lloyd Lake, Golden Gate Park, as a tribute for the work he had done for the park over the years.

Hiram Morgan Hill died lonely and completely deaf on a cattle ranch near Elko, Nevada, in 1913. He was long separated from his wife, who was living in high society in Europe. While his daughter Diane and her new husband were touring Europe in 1912, Morgan had a stroke. When the news reached Diane, she had a nervous breakdown so severe that she was sent to the St. Pancras sanitarium in London. While there, she threw herself out of a high window and was killed immediately by the impact. Hearing of this tragic event, one can't but wonder about a possible genetic disposition toward mental instability in the Hill family. Morgan was buried in Santa Clara Mission cemetery in Santa Clara, CA.

Helen "Nellie" B. Brackett, born 1864, Sarah's intimate friend and ultimate betrayer, remained single for many years, finally marrying lawyer and widower Robert Beeching on January 12, 1898. Nellie was 34. They lived quietly in Alameda, CA, on Santa Clara Avenue.

According to census records, they had no children and Robert Beeching remarried between 1910 and 1920, apparently having become a widower.

David B. Neagle, born 1847, the deputy marshal who killed David Terry, left the marshal service and went to work for the Southern Pacific Railroad Company. He was vilified in the press for his killing of Terry for years after the incident, but he outlived his infamy. As an agent of the railroad, he ended up working in the mine fields, first as a supervisor, but later as an investor and owner of profitable mines in Tuolumne County.

Frederick William Sharon, born 1857, was William Sharon's only son. He married divorcee Louise Tevis Breckinridge and moved to New York. The couple made frequent social and business trips to San Francisco where Fred Sharon still owned considerable property, including the Palace Hotel, which continued to be managed by his brother-in-law Frank Newlands. The hotel was destroyed in the fires resulting from the 1906 earthquake. It was estimated that it would take five million dollars to rebuild. Fred Sharon died at the new Palace Hotel in 1915.

R. Porter Ashe, one of Sarah's few enduring friends, was elected state senator in 1898 and shortly thereafter became Assistant District Attorney in San Francisco. He represented Mary Ellen Pleasant in her various suits against her creditors and got in the middle of the struggle for ownership of the Beltane Ranch between Mary Ellen and Teresa Bell. He remarried in 1905 and died in 1929.

Frank Allen Rodney, Sarah's cousin, born in Missouri in 1860, married a woman named Maybelle from England in 1893. According to census records, they had no children. The couple moved to Mariposa County in 1895 where Rodney got a job working for Stonewall Jackson Harris at Hogan Ranch, a beautiful stretch of land in the foothills west of Yosemite National Park. Rodney was appointed one of three directors of a new oil drilling enterprise in 1911, the year his wife died suddenly of a heart attack at the age of 44. By 1920, Rodney had moved back to San Francisco on his own. Since he did not appear in the 1930 census, he probably died in the 1920s.

In every case, when one of these people died or made news in some other way, Sarah's name was mentioned in the newspaper articles, as if to say, Oh, you know who he was. He was a judge or a witness or an attorney or a friend of the infamous Sarah Althea Hill. Even Justice Field, though he would have hated it, was dogged with that association for the rest of his life. When his death announcement hit the papers, reporters reminded their readers of the part he played in the famous Sharon case and in Terry's death. These associations even extended to second generations. In a story about George Tyler, Jr. in 1901, the article began, "The story comes from Oakland of an assault on a young woman by George Tyler, a florist of that city, and a son of the late Judge Tyler, who became famous as an attorney for Sarah Althea Hill in her suit against the late Senator Sharon."[395] For people like Nellie Brackett and Frank Rodney, their part in Sarah's story was their only claim to fame.

Sarah may have been, as General Barnes said, "a comparatively obscure and unimportant person, without property or position in the world," but by the time the trials were over, she had hitched her wagon to more than one star and, by doing so, became a luminary in her own right.

ABOUT THE AUTHOR

Robin C. Johnson is the author of several novels and books about California history and natural history, both of which she loves to explore. She was born in Central California where she lives conveniently equidistant between the Pacific Ocean and the Sierra Nevada mountains. Robin is a retired computer software designer devoting her time to travel, writing, theater and any culinary adventure that comes her way.

INDEX

NOTES

[1] W. H. L. Barnes, *Argument for the Defendant, Sarah Althea Sharon vs. William Sharon* (San Francisco: Barry, Baird & Co., 1884), pp. 262-263.

[2] Oscar T. Shuck, ed., *History of the bench and bar of California* (Los Angeles: The Commercial Printing House, 1901), p 174.

[3] "Sharon's 'Alleged' Wife," *Sacramento Daily Union*, 10 October 1883, p. 1.

[4] Barnes, *Argument for the Defendant*, p. 91.

[5] "Social Gossip," *San Francisco Chronicle*, 31 December 1871, p. 8.

[6] "Sarah's Sorcery," *Daily Alta California*, 19 March 1884, p. 1.

[7] Beth Wyman, *Hiram Morgan Hill*, self-published, 1983, p. ix.

[8] "Sarah's Sorcery," *Daily Alta California*, 19 March 1884, p. 1.

[9] "Suicidal Sarah," *Daily Alta California*, 17 April 1884, p. 1.

[10] "Suicidal Sarah," *Daily Alta California*, 17 April 1884, p. 1.

[11] "The Resurrectionists," *Daily Alta California*, 9 April 1884, p. 1.

[12] "Hill-Sharon," *Daily Alta California*, 27 March 1884, p. 1.

[13] Oscar Lewis and Carroll D. Hall, *Bonanza Inn* (New York: Alfred A. Knopf, 1945), p. 15.

[14] *Frank Leslie's Illustrated Newspaper*, Volume XLI, Number 1,045, October 9, 1875.

[15] "Senator Sharon," *Daily Alta California*, 16 June 1884, p. 8.

[16] Barnes, *Argument for the Defendant*, p. 23.

[17] "Althea's Story," *Daily Alta California*, 13 March 1884, p. 1.

[18] "Sharon's Side," *Daily Alta California*, 27 May 1884, p. 1.

[19] "'Sen. on the Stand," Daily Alta California, 28 May 1884, p. 1.

[20] "Sharon's Side," *Daily Alta California*, 27 May 1884, p. 1.

[21] "'Sen.' On the Stand," *Daily Alta California*, 28 May 1884, p. 1.

[22] "Maid or Mated," *Daily Alta California*, 14 March 1884, p. 1.

[23] "Barnes Talks," *Daily Alta California*, 28 August 1884, p. 1.

[24] John D. Lawson, ed., *American State Trials, Volume XV* (St. Louis: Thomas Law Book Co., 1926), p. 548.

[25] "Sarah's Sorcery," *Daily Alta California*, 19 March 1884, p. 1.

[26] "Who is Miss Hill?," *San Francisco Chronicle,* 2 October 1883, p. 8.

[27] "Bay Gossip," *Sacramento Daily Union*, 25 December 1880, p. 6.

[28] "Barnes Talks," *Daily Alta California*, 28 August 1884, p. 1.

[29] "My Dear Wife," *Daily Alta California*, 18 March 1884, p. 2.

[30] "My Dear Wife," *Daily Alta California*, 18 March 1884, p. 2.

[31] "Sarah's Sibyls," *Daily Alta California*, 16 April 1884, p. 1.

[32] "Sarah's Sibyls," *Daily Alta California*, 16 April 1884, p. 1.

[33] "Maid or Mated," *Daily Alta California*, 14 March 1884, p. 1.

[34] "Sharon's Side," *Daily Alta California*, 27 May 1884, p. 1.

[35] "Sarah's Sufferings," *San Francisco Chronicle*, 18 March 1884, p. 8.

[36] "Sharon's Side," *Daily Alta California*, 27 May 1884, p. 1.

[37] "California," *Sacramento Daily Union,* 24 December 1880, p. 1.

[38] "Sarah's Sibyls," *Daily Alta California,* 16 April 1884, p. 1.

[39] "Sharon's Side," *Daily Alta California,* 27 May 1884, p. 1.

[40] "Sarah Bounced," *Daily Alta California,* 24 April 1884, p. 1.

[41] "A Belmont Betrothal," *Daily Alta California,* 28 December 1883, p. 1.

[42] "A Belmont Betrothal," *Daily Alta California,* 28 December 1883, p. 1·

[43] "Barnes' Broadside," *Daily Alta California,* 4 September 1884, p. 1.

[44] "Hill-Sharon," *Daily Alta California,* 26 March 1884, p. 1.

[45] Barnes, *Argument for the Defendant,* p. 161.

[46] "Suicidal Sarah," *Daily Alta California,* 17 April 1884, p. 1.

[47] "Cushman's Contribution," *Daily Alta California,* 19 January 1884, p. 1.

[48] "Hill-Sharon," *Daily Alta California,* 27 March 1884, p. 1.

[49] "Sarah Bounced," *Daily Alta California,* 24 April 1884, p. 1.

[50] "Spying Sarah," *Daily Alta California,* 15 April 1884, p. 1.

[51] "Spying Sarah," *Daily Alta California,* 15 April 1884, p. 1.

[52] "Spying Sarah," *Daily Alta California,* 15 April 1884, p. 1.

[53] "Sarah's Suitors," *Daily Alta California,* 23 April 1884, p. 1.

[54] "Barnes Concludes," *Daily Alta California,* 9 September 1884, p. 1.

[55] "Althea's Admirers," *Daily Alta California,* 25 March 1884, p. 2.

[56] "Althea's Admirers," *Daily Alta California,* 25 March 1884, p. 2.

[57] "Sarah's Sibyls," *Daily Alta California,* 16 April 1884, p. 1.

[58] "Sarah's Sibyls," *Daily Alta California,* 16 April 1884, p. 1.

[59] "Charms for Sharon," *San Francisco Chronicle,* 2 April 1884, p. 2.

[60] "Sarah's Sibyls," *Daily Alta California,* 16 April 1884, p. 1.

[61] "Sarah's Sibyls," *Daily Alta California,* 16 April 1884, p. 1.

[62] "Tyler Jr.'s Trophy," *Daily Alta California,* 4 April 1884, p. 1.

[63] Barnes, *Argument for the Defendant,* p. 258.

[64] "Barnes' Broadside," *Daily Alta California,* 4 September 1884, p. 1.

[65] "Sharon's Side," *Daily Alta California,* 27 May 1884, p. 1.

[66] "Sen. on the Stand," *Daily Alta California,* 28 May 1884, p. 1.

[67] Lawson, *American State Trials,* p. 476.

[68] Lawson, *American State Trials,* p. 505.

[69] Barnes, *Argument for the Defendant,* pp. 264 – 266.

[70] "Sen. on the Stand," *Daily Alta California,* 28 May 1884, p. 1.

[71] "Barnes Concludes," *Daily Alta California,* 9 September 1884, p. 1.

[72] "Senator, Dear Senator," *Daily Alta California,* 12 February 1884, p. 1.

[73] "Sarah's Socery," *Daily Alta California,* 19 March 1884, p. 1.

[74] Barnes, *Argument for the Defendant,* p. 364.

[75] "Senator Sharon," *Daily Alta California,* 16 June 1884, p. 8.

[76] Evelyn Wells, *Champagne Days of San Francisco,* (New York: Doubleday & Company, 1947), pp. 172-173.

[77] Third Interview with William Willmore, Helen Holdredge Collection, San Francisco Public Library.

[78] "Tyler and Gumpel," *Daily Alta California,* 19 February 1885, p. 1.

[79] "Mammy Pleasant the Woman," *San Francisco Call,* 29 December 1901

[80] "The Last Week," *Daily Alta California*, 16 September 1884, p. 2.

[81] "Hill-Sharon," *Daily Alta California*, 1 April 1884, p. 1.

[82] "Barnes' Review," *Daily Alta California*, 5 September 1884, p. 1

[83] "Barnes' Review," *Daily Alta California*, 5 September 1884, p. 1.

[84] "Wholesale Perjury," *Daily Alta California*, 6 June 1885, p. 1.

[85] "Tyler Triumphant," *San Francisco Chronicle*, 15 April 1884, p. 8.

[86] "Voodooing William," *San Francisco Chronicle*, 16 April, 1884, p. 4.

[87] "Daughter Will Seek to Clear Up Name Issue", *San Francisco Chronicle*, 18 August, 1922, p 1.

[88] "Barnes' Review," *Daily Alta California*, 5 September 1884, p. 1.

[89] "Sarah's Suitors," *Daily Alta California,* 23 April 1884, p. 1.

[90] Barnes, *Argument for the Defendant*, pp. 315 – 316.

[91] "Hill-Sharon," *Daily Alta California*, 2 April 1884, p. 1.

[92] Lawson, *American State Trials*, p. 477.

[93] Lawson, *American State Trials*, p. 516.

[94] "A New Hamlet," *Daily Alta California*, 8 April 1884, p. 1.

[95] "A New Hamlet," *Daily Alta California*, 8 April 1884, p. 1.

[96] "Althea's Charms," *Daily Alta California*, 23 March 1884, p. 1.

[97] "Sarah's Sibyls," Daily Alta California, 16 April 1884, p. 1.

[98] Helen Holdredge, *Mammy Pleasant* (New York: G. P. Putnam's Sons, 1953), p. 185.

[99] Lawson, *American State Trials,* p. 505.

[100] "A Full Statement," *Daily Alta California*, 6 August 1884, p. 2.

[101] "The Resurrectionists," *Daily Alta California*, 29 April 1884, p. 1.

[102] "A Full Statement," *Daily Alta California*, 6 August 1884, p. 2.

[103] "'Sen.' on the Stand," *Daily Alta California*, 28 May 1884, p. 1.

[104] "Senator Sharon Under Arrest." *Sacramento Daily Union*, 11 September 1883, p. 1.

[105] "The Sharon Scandal," *Sacramento Daily Union*, 25 September 1883, p. 1.

[106] "Sarah Rests," *Daily Alta California*, 29 July 1884, p. 2.

[107] Teresa Bell's Diaries, Helen Holdredge Collection, San Francisco Public Library, July 20, 1898.

[108] Lawson, *American State Trials*, p. 471.

[109] "Althea's Agony," *Daily Alta California*, 10 November 1883, p. 1.

[110] "Sarah Rests," *Daily Alta California*, 29 July 1884, p. 2.

[111] "A Full Statement," *Daily Alta California*, 6 August 1884, p. 2.

[112] "Hill-Sharon," *Daily Alta California*, 28 March 1884, p. 1.

[113] "Hill-Sharon," *Daily Alta California*, 28 March 1884, p. 1.

[114] "Barnes Concludes," *Daily Alta California*, 9 September 1884, p. 1.

[115] "Barnes Concludes," *Daily Alta California*, 9 September 1884, p. 1.

[116] "Barnes Concludes," *Daily Alta California*, 9 September 1884, p. 1.

[117] Barnes, *Argument for the Defendant*, p. 360.

[118] Barnes, *Argument for the Defendant*, pp. 366 – 367.

[119] Barnes, *Argument for the Defendant*, p. 368.

[120] "Hill-Sharon," *Daily Alta California*, 9 September 1884, p. 1.

[121] Barnes, *Argument for the Defendant*, p. 374.

[122] "Hill-Sharon," *Daily Alta California*, 28 March 1884, p. 1.

[123] "San Francisco Items," *Sacramento Daily Union*, 27 December 1883, p. 2.

[124] "Gov. Reighert's Testimony," *Daily Alta California*, 18 November 1883, p. 1.

[125] "Neilson and Tyler," *Daily Alta California*, 19 December 1884, p. 1.

[126] George H. Tinkham, *A History of Stockton from its Organization to the Present Time* (San Francisco: W. M. Hinton & CO., 1880), p. 133.

[127] George H. Tinkham, *History of San Joaquin County California* (Los Angeles: Historic Record Company, 1923), p. 149.

[128] "Silver Ewer Presented," *San Francisco Chronicle,* 23 February 1920, p. 3.

[129] Tinkman, *A History of Stockton*, pp. 248-249.

[130] "David Smith Terry," *Daily Alta California*, 15 August 1889, p. 4.

[131] "The Lathrop Tragedy," *Los Angeles Herald*, 15 August 1889, p. 4.

[132] "The Lathrop Tragedy," *Los Angeles Herald*, 15 August 1889, p. 4.

[133] Edwin G. Waite, "An Estimate on the Life and Character of David S. Terry," *The Overland Monthly*, October 1889, p. 438.

[134] "Barnes' Review," *Daily Alta California*, 5 September 1884, p. 2.

[135] "Althea's Agent," *Daily Alta California*, 12 March 1884, p. 1.

[136] "Conclusion," *Daily Alta California*, 5 August 1884, p. 1.

[137] "Barnes' Review," *Daily Alta California*, 5 September 1884, p. 2.

[138] "Nellie Brackett's Affidavit," *Daily Alta California*, 13 January 1885, p. 1.

[139] "Sarah Bounced," *Daily Alta California*, 24 April 1884, p. 1.

[140] Lawson, *American State Trials,* p. 506.

[141] "Cushman's Contribution," *Daily Alta California*, 19 January 1884, p. 1.

[142] "Sharon's Side," *Daily Alta California*, 9, 27 May 1884, p. 1.

[143] "Falsehood and Forgery," *Daily Alta California*, 27 December 1885, p. 2.

[144] "Barnes' Review," *Daily Alta California*, 4 September 1884, p. 2.

[145] "Sarah Under Fire," *San Francisco Chronicle*, 20 March 1884, p. 2.

[146] "Afternoon Session," *Daily Alta California*, 12 March 1884, p. 1.

[147] "Barnes' Review," *Daily Alta California*, 5 September 1884, p. 1.

[148] "Althea's Agent," *Daily Alta California*, 12 March 1884, p. 1.

[149] Barnes, *Argument for the Defendant*, p. 283.

[150] Barnes, *Argument for the Defendant*, pp. 287 – 288.

[151] "Barnes' Review," *Daily Alta California*, 5 September 1884, p. 1.

[152] "Afternoon Session," *Daily Alta California*, 12 March 1884, p. 1.

[153] "Flournoy's Flourish," *Daily Alta California*, 27 August 1884, p. 1.

[154] "Althea's Story," *Daily Alta California*, 13 March 1884, p. 1.

[155] "Maid or Mated," *Daily Alta California*, 14 March 1884, p. 1.

[156] "Sharon's Dirty Duds," *San Francisco Chronicle*, 19 March 1884, p. 4.

[157] "Sharon's Dirty Duds," *San Francisco Chronicle*, 19 March 1884, p. 4.

[158] "Sarah's Sorcery," *Daily Alta California*, 19 March 1884, p. 1.

[159] "Sarah's Sorcery," *Daily Alta California,* 19 March 1884, p. 1.

[160] "Reopened," *Daily Alta California*, 1 August 1884, p. 1.

[161] "Barnes' Review," *Daily Alta California*, 5 September 1884, p. 1.

[162] Barnes, *Argument for the Defendant*, p. 335.

[163] "Studies in Distant Lands," *Los Angeles Herald*, 23 May 1884, p. 2.

[164] "Hill-Sharon," *Daily Alta California*, 26 March 1884, p. 1.

[165] "Hill-Sharon," *Daily Alta California*, 28 March 1884, p. 1.

[166] Holdredge, *Mammy Pleasant*, p. 205.

[167] "Tyler Still Talking," *Daily Alta California*, 13 August 1884, p. 1.

[168] "Barnes' Broadside," *Daily Alta California*, 4 September 1884, p. 1.

[169] Interview with Agatha Fay, Helen Holdredge Collection, San Francisco Public Library.

[170] "Barnes' Broadside," *Daily Alta California*, 4 September 1884, p. 1.

[171] Barnes, *Argument for the Defendant*, pp. 87 – 88.

[172] "Althea's Alliance," *Daily Alta California*, 20 March 1884, p. 1.

[173] "Althea's Alliance," *Daily Alta California*, 20 March 1884, p. 1.

[174] "Althea's Alliance," *Daily Alta California*, 20 March 1884, p. 1.

[175] "Where's Brackett?", *Daily Alta California*, 31 March 1884, p. 1.

[176] "The Absent Nellie," *Daily Alta California*, 1 April 1884, p. 1.

[177] "The Absent Nellie," *Daily Alta California*, 1 April 1884, p. 1.

[178] "Hill-Sharon," *Daily Alta California*, 2 April 1884, p. 1.

[179] "Startling Scenes," *Daily Alta California*, 10 April 1884, p.1.

[180] "Startling Scenes," *Daily Alta California*, 10 April 1884, p.1.

[181] "Startling Scenes," *Daily Alta California*, 10 April 1884, p.1.

[182] "A Charming Brackett," *Daily Alta California*, 2 May 1884, p. 1.

[183] "Reopened," *Daily Alta California*, 1 August 1884, p. 1.

[184] "Sock and Shirt," *Daily Alta California*, 29 May 1884, p. 1.

[185] "Sharoniana," *Daily Alta California*, 1 June 1884, p. 1.

[186] "Senator Sharon," *Daily Alta California*, 16 June 1884, p. 8.

[187] "Senator Sharon," *Daily Alta California*, 16 June 1884, p. 8.

[188] "Senator Sharon," *Daily Alta California*, 16 June 1884, p. 8.

[189] "Senator Sharon," *Daily Alta California*, 16 June 1884, p. 8.

[190] "Neilson Retires," *Daily Alta California*, 13 July 1884, p. 1.

[191] "Neilson Withdraws," *San Francisco Chronicle*, 13 July 1884, p. 5.

[192] "A Full Statement," *Daily Alta California*, 6 August 1884, p. 2.

[193] "Neilson's Deposition," *Daily Alta California*, 5 December 1884, p. 1.

[194] "Neilson's Deposition," *Daily Alta California*, 5 December 1884, p. 1.

[195] "Neilson and Tyler," *Daily Alta California*, 19 December 1884, p. 1

[196] "A Full Statement," *Daily Alta California*, 6 August 1884, p. 2.

[197] "Neilson and Tyler," *Daily Alta California*, 19 December 1884, p. 1.

[198] "Neilson's Deposition," *Daily Alta California*, 3 January 1885, p. 1.

[199] "Tyler Still Talking," *Daily Alta California*, 13 August 1884, p. 1.

[200] "Argument Resumed," *Daily Alta California*, 3 September 1884, p. 2.

[201] "A Tilt at Terry," *Daily Alta California*, 29 August 1884, p. 2.

[202] "Nearing the Finish," *Daily Alta California*, 17 September 1884, p. 1.

[203] "The Last Week," *Daily Alta California*,, 16 September 1884, p. 2.

[204] "A Very Important Question," *Los Angeles Herald*, 21 September 1884, p. 2.

[205] "The Sharon Case," *San Francisco Chronicle*, 25 December 1884, p. 3.

[206] "The Sharon Case," *San Francisco Chronicle*, 25 December 1884, p. 3.

[207] "The Sharon Case," *San Francisco Chronicle*, 25 December 1884, p. 3.

[208] "At Last," *Los Angeles Daily Herald*, December 25, 1884, p. 2.

[209] "Some Affidavits," *Daily Alta California*, 10 April 1885, p. 1.

[210] "The Sentiment Aboard," *Daily Alta California*, 26 February 1885, p. 4.

[211] "The Sharon Case," *San Francisco Chronicle*, 25 December 1884, p. 3.

[212] "Neilson to Sharon," *Daily Alta California*, 24 January 1885, p. 8.

[213] "Silent Sarah," *Daily Alta California*, 26 December 1884, p. 1.

[214] "San Francisco Items," *Sacramento Daily Union*, 3 January 1885, p. 1.

[215] "Althea's Reception," *Daily Alta California*, 2 January 1885, p. 1.

[216] "A Parody," *Daily Alta California*, 23 April 1885, p. 4.

[217] "A Parody," *Daily Alta California*, 23 April 1885, p.4.

[218] Lawson, *American State Trials*, p. 499.

[219] "Nellie Brackett's Affidavit," *Daily Alta California*, 13 January 1885, p. 1.

[220] "A Falling Out," *Daily Alta California*, 17 March 1885, p. 1.

[221] "Neilson's Acquittal," *Daily Alta California*, 15 March 1885, p. 1.

[222] "Neilson's Acquittal," *Daily Alta California*, 15 March 1885, p. 1.

[223] "Neilson on Trial," *Daily Alta California*, 11 March 1885, p. 1.

[224] "The Marriage Contract," *Daily Alta California*, 26 February 1885, p. 1.

[225] "The Sharon Case," *Daily Alta California*, 20 March 1885, p. 1.

[226] "A Search for Sarah," *Daily Alta California*, 6 April 1885, p. 1.

[227] "A Search for Sarah," *Daily Alta California*, 6 April 1885, p. 1.

[228] "A Search for Sarah," *Daily Alta California*, 6 April 1885, p. 1.

[229] "In a Prison Cell," *Daily Alta California*, 7 April 1885, p. 1.

[230] "In a Prison Cell," *Daily Alta California*, 7 April 1885, p. 1.

[231] "Sarah at Liberty," *San Francisco Chronicle*, 8 April 1885, p. 4.

[232] "In a Prison Cell," *Daily Alta California*, 7 April 1885, p. 1.

[233] "In a Prison Cell," *Daily Alta California*, 7 April 1885, p. 1.

[234] "Sarah's Release from Jail," *Daily Alta California*, 8 April 1885, p. 1.

[235] "Sarah's Release from Jail," *Daily Alta California*, 8 April 1885, p. 1.

[236] "The Perjury Trial," *Daily Alta California*, 5 June 1885, p. 1.

[237] "The Sharon Case," *Daily Alta California*, 30 June 1885, p. 4.

[238] "Sarah Althea," *Sacramento Daily Union*, 3 August 1885, p. 1.

[239] "Neilson and Tyler," *Daily Alta California*, 19 December 1884, p. 1.

[240] "Sarah Althea's Revolver," *Daily Alta California*, 21 May 1885, p. 1.

[241] "Guilty," *Daily Alta California*, 28 November 1885, p. 2.

[242] Alexander E. Wagstaff, *Life of David S. Terry* (San Francisco: Continental Publishing Company, 1892), p. 397.

[243] "Ex-Senator Sharon," *Daily Alta California*, 11 July 1884, p. 2.

[244] "Sharon Versus Hill," *Daily Alta California*, 9 September 1885, p. 1.

[245] Lawson, *American State Trials*, p. 483.

[246] Lawson, *American State Trials*, p. 484.

[247] "Shooting Sarah," *Daily Alta California*, 4 August 1885, p. 1.

[248] Lawson, *American State Trials*, p. 484.

[249] Lawson, *American State Trials*, p. 489.

[250] Lawson, *American State Trials*, p. 492.

[251] "Amusements," *Daily Alta California*, 1 November 1885, p. 2.

[252] "The Sharon Trial," *New Zealand Herald*, 28 November 1885, p. 1.

[253] "Gradually Sinking," *Daily Alta California*, 7 November 1885, p. 8.

[254] "The Last Good-Byes," *Daily Alta California*, 8 November 1885, p. 8.

[255] Lawson, *American State Trials*, p. 494.

[256] Lawson, *American State Trials*, p. 494.

[257] Lawson, *American State Trials*, p. 496.

[258] "Mrs. Terry," *Daily Alta California*, 8 January 1886, p. 1.

[259] Wagstaff, *Life of David S.Terry*, p. 524.

[260] "Burns' Contempt," *Daily Alta California*, 16 January 1886, p. 8.

[261] "Burns' Contempt," *Daily Alta California*, 16 January 1886, p. 8.

[262] "A Disagreement," *Daily Alta California*, 3 July 1886, p. 1.

[263] "G. W. Tyler's Trial," *Daily Alta California*, 29 June 1886, p. 1.

[264] "The Turf," *Los Angeles Herald*, 1 July 1886, p. 1.

[265] "Spring in Southern California," *Los Angeles Herald*, 2 February 1888, p. 4.

[266] "Pacific Coast," *Los Angeles Herald*, 6 September 1888, p. 4.

[267] "The Neagle Case," *Los Angeles Herald*, 4 September 1889, p. 6.

[268] "A Scene in Court," *Daily Alta California*, 4 September 1888, p. 4.

[269] "A Scene in Court," *Daily Alta California*, 4 September 1888, p. 4.

[270] "Terry's Petition," Daily Alta California, 18 September 1888, p 1.

[271] Lawson, *American State Trials*, p. 584.

[272] Wagstaff, *Life of David S. Terry*, pp. 334-335.

[273] Wagstaff, *Life of David S. Terry*, p. 427.

[274] "Pacific Coast," *Los Angeles Herald*, 4 September 1888, p. 5.

[275] "Contempt of Court," *The Fresno Daily Republican,* 5 September 1888, p. 2.

[276] "Terry's Petition," *Daily Alta California*, 19 September 1888, p. 1.

[277] Wagstaff, *Life of David S. Terry*, p. 337.

[278] "Terry's Threats," *Daily Alta California*, 4 September 1889, p. 1.

[279] "Mrs. Terry Arraigned," *Daily Alta California*, 16 October 1888, p. 8.

[280] "Mrs. Terry's Case," *Oakland Tribune*, 4 January 1889, p. 1.

[281] "A Sensation in Court," *Fresno Daily Republican*, 5 May 1889, p. 3.

[282] "Terry the Terror," *Los Angeles Herald*, 3 April 1889, p. 5.

[283] Wagstaff, *Life of David S. Terry,* p. 399.

[284] "Justice Field's Account," *Daily Alta California*, 15 August 1889, p. 1.

[285] "Two Killers," *Los Angeles Herald*, 8 June 1891, p. 6.

[286] "Earp and Neagle," *San Francisco Call*, 6 August 1896, p. 16.

[287] "Neagle and His Gun," *Los Angeles Herald*, 19 August 1889, p. 4.

[288] "Along the Pacific Coast," *Sacramento Daily Union*, 24 June 1889, p. 4.

[289] Wagstaff, *Life of David S. Terry*, p. 314.

[290] Wagstaff, *Life of David S. Terry*, p. 403.

[291] Lawson, *American State Trials,* p. 606.

[292] Wagstaff, *Life of David S. Terry*, pp. 450-451.

[293] Lawson, *American State Trials*, p. 602.

[294] "Marshal Nagel," *Sacramento Daily Union*, 26 August 1889, p. 1.

[295] "What an Eye-Witness Saw," *Daily Alta California*, 15 August 1889, p. 1.

[296] Wagstaff, *Life of David S. Terry*, p. 418.

[297] "Hoffman's Travels," *Sacramento Daily Union*, 20 June 1891, p. 8.

[298] Wagstaff, *Life of David S. Terry*, p. 431.

[299] "The News Abroad," *Sacramento Daily Union*, 16 August 1889, p. 1.

[300] "The News Abroad," *Sacramento Daily Union*, 16 August 1889, p. 1.

[301] "Her Wild Wail for the Dead," *Los Angeles Herald*, 18 August 1889, p. 8.

[302] "The Funeral," *Daily Alta California*, 17 August 1889, p. 1.

[303] "The Funeral," *Daily Alta California*, 17 August 1889, p. 1.

[304] "The Funeral," *Daily Alta California*, 17 August 1889, p. 1.

[305] "Stockton Bar," *Sacramento Daily Union*, 20 August 1889, p. 1.

[306] "A Warrant," *Oakland Tribune*, 16 August 1889, p. 1.

[307] "Mrs. Terry Speaks," *Sacramento Daily Union*, 18 August 1889, p. 4.

[308] "Pacific Coast," *Los Angeles Herald*, 19 August 1889, p. 4.

[309] "Sarah's Sally," *Sacramento Daily Union*, 26 August 1889, p. 1.

[310] "Neagle-Terry Case," *Los Angeles Herald*, 6 September 1889, p. 4.

[311] "Judge Sawyer's Decision," *Daily Alta California*, 17 September 1889, p. 1.

[312] "Drew a Gun on James H. Barry," *San Francisco Call*, 5 August 1896, p. 16.

[313] "Drew a Gun on James H. Barry," *San Francisco Call*, 5 August 1896, p. 16.

[314] Wagstaff, *Life of David S. Terry*, p. 450.

[315] Carl Brent Swisher, *Stephen J. Field: Craftsman of the Law*, (Washington, D. C.: The Brookings Institution, 1930), p. 351.

[316] "The Waite Case," *San Francisco Call*, 20 May 1890, p. 1.

[317] "Mrs. Terry in Court," *Daily Alta California*, 30 August 1889, p. 1.

[318] "Eastern Dispatches," *Los Angeles Herald*, 23 October 1889, p. 3.

[319] "The Trial of Mrs. Terry," *Daily Alta California*, 7 March 1890.

[320] "An Exciting Trial," *The Fresno Weekly Republican*, November 21, 1890, p. 5.

[321] "In Trouble Again," *San Francisco Call*, 26 April 1890, p. 8.

[322] "In Trouble Again," *San Francisco Call*, 26 April 1890, p. 8.

[323] "The Angry Widow," The Fresno Daily Republican, 26 April 1890, p. 3.

[324] "In Trouble Again," *San Francisco Call*, 26 April 1890, p. 8.

[325] "Mrs. Terry Bounced," *Fresno Daily Republican*, April 26, 1890, p. 3.

[326] "Mrs. Terry Bounced," *Fresno Daily Republican*, April 26, 1890, p. 3.

[327] "In Trouble Again," *San Francisco Call*, 26 April 1890, p. 8.

[328] "In Trouble Again," *San Francisco Call*, 26 April 1890, p. 8.

[329] "Mrs. Terry's Anger," *Fresno Daily Republican*, November 16, 1890, p. 4.

[330] "Caldwell's Letters," *Fresno Daily Republican*, November 21, 1890, p. 3.

[331] "Caldwell's Letters," *Fresno Daily Republican*, November 21, 1890, p. 3.

[332] "Caldwell's Letters," *Fresno Daily Republican*, November 21, 1890, p. 3.

[333] "Caldwell is Guilty," *Fresno Morning Republican*, November 22, 1890, p. 5.

[334] "Caldwell's Letters," *Fresno Daily Republican*, November 21, 1890, p. 3.

[335] "Pacific Coast Items," *San Francisco Bulletin*, 19 January 1891, p. 1.

[336] "Caldwell—Terry," *Fresno Morning Republican*, 5 March 1891, p. 3.

[337] "For Court Expenses Alone," *San Francisco Call*, 10 August 1890, p. 3.

[338] "Always a Friend," *San Francisco Call*, 6 January 1895, p. 1.

[339] "The Man About Town," *Fresno Morning Republican*, January 17, 1892, p. 5.

[340] "Electric Lighting," *Los Angeles Herald*, 22 September 1882, p. 3.

[341] "Hopelessly Unbalanced," *San Francisco Call*, 14 February 1892, p. 8.

[342] "Hopelessly Insane," *San Francisco Chronicle*, 14 February 1892, p. 24.

[343] "Prominent Men," *San Francisco Chronicle*, 1 January 1892, p. 29.

[344] "Hopelessly Unbalanced," *San Francisco Call*, 14 February 1892, p. 8.

[345] "Hopelessly Unbalanced," *San Francisco Call*, 14 February 1892, p. 8.

[346] "Messages From the Spirit World," *The Milwaukee Journal*, 15 February 1892, p. 2.

[347] "Sarah Althea is in Town," *San Francisco Call*, 16 February 1892, p. 1.

[348] "Mrs. Terry is Found," *San Francisco Chronicle*, 16 February 1892, p. 12.

[349] "Mrs. Terry is Found," *San Francisco Chronicle*, 16 February 1892, p. 12.

[350] "Sarah Althea Terry," *San Francisco Call*, 17 February 1892

[351] "Mrs. Terry Redeems Her Watch," *Los Angeles Herald*, 22 February 1892, p. 1.

[352] "Hypnotizing Sarah," *San Francisco Chronicle*, 5 March 1892, p. 10.

[353] "Undoubtedly Insane," *Los Angeles Herald*, 9 March 1892, p. 1.

[354] "Sarah's Freaks," *Los Angeles Herald*, 10 March 1892, p. 6.

[355] "Sarah's Freaks," *Los Angeles Herald*, 10 March 1892, p. 6.

[356] "Sarah's Freaks," *Los Angeles Herald*, 10 March 1892, p. 6.

[357] "Sarah Althea Terry," *San Francisco Call*, 10 March 1892, p. 8.

[358] "Sarah Althea Terry," *San Francisco Call*, 10 March 1892, p. 8.

[359] "Mrs. Terry Committed," *San Francisco Call*, 11 March 1892, p. 7.

[360] "Mrs. Terry Committed," *San Francisco Call*, 11 March 1892, p. 7.

[361] "Declared Insane," *San Francisco Chronicle*, 11 March 1892, p. 12.

[362] "Declared Insane," *San Francisco Chronicle*, 11 March 1892, p. 12.

[363] "Ward of the State," *Los Angeles Herald*, 12 March 1892, p. 1.

[364] "The Asylum at Last," *San Francisco Chronicle*, 12 March 1892, p. 10.

[365] "The Asylum at Last," *San Francisco Chronicle*, 12 March 1892, p. 10.

[366] "The Asylum at Last," *San Francisco Chronicle*, 12 March 1892, p. 10.

[367] "The Asylum at Last," *San Francisco Chronicle*, 12 March 1892, p. 10.

[368] "The Asylum at Last," *San Francisco Chronicle*, 12 March 1892, p. 10.

[369] "Sarah Althea Terry," *Sacramento Daily Union*, 12 March 1892, p. 1.

[370] "Sarah Althea Terry," *Sacramento Daily Union*, 12 March 1892, p. 1.

[371] "The Asylum at Last," *San Francisco Chronicle*, 12 March 1892, p. 10.

[372] Commitment Register, 11 March 1892, Stockton State Hospital Records Collection, California Archives, Sacramento, CA.

[373] "Mrs. Terry's Effects," *Los Angeles Herald*, 16 March 1892, p. 1.

[374] "He Declined," *Los Angeles Herald*, 28 March 1892, p. 6.

[375] "Pacific Coast," *Los Angeles Herald*, 2 October 1887, p. 1.

[376] "He Declined," *Los Angeles Herald*, 28 March 1892, p. 6.

[377] "Sarah Althea Terry," *Los Angeles Herald*, 1 June 1892, p. 1.

[378] "No Light There," *San Francisco Call*, 5 January 1893, p. 5.

[379] "A Raving Maniac," *Fresno Morning Republican*, 1 March 1893, p. 4.

[380] "Great Minds That Failed," *Fresno Morning Republican*, July 25, 1894, p. 3

[381] Daily Medical Report, 1895, Stockton State Hospital Records Collection, California Archives, Sacramento, CA.

[382] "Hot Shot from Porter Ashe," *Los Angeles Herald*, 6 January 1895, p. 7.

[383] "Sarah Althea's Jewels," *San Francisco Call*, 14 May 1895, p. 5.

[384] "The Terry Estate Sold," *San Francisco Call*, 18 October 1895, p. 16.

[385] "Hopelessly Insane," *San Francisco Call*, 2 May 1896, p. 4.

[386] "A Girl Who Acted Nobly," *San Francisco Call*, 21 January 1898, p. 5.

[387] Teresa Bell's Diaries, Helen Holdredge Collection, San Francisco Public Library, December 17, 1903.

[388] Teresa Bell's Diaries, Helen Holdredge Collection, San Francisco Public Library.

[389] "Tries to Escape from Stockton State Asylum," *San Francisco Call*, 23 April 1903, p. 5.

[390] Helen Holdredge Collection, San Francisco Public Library.

[391] Milton S. Gould, *A Cast of Hawks* (La Jolla: Copley Books, 1985), p. 336.

[392] Lewis and Hall, *Bonanza Inn*, pp. 212-214.

[393] "Pauper's Grave Escaped by Sarah Althea Terry," *Oakland Tribune*, 16 February 1937, p. 2.

[394] "'Rose of Sharon'" Who Died in West Thought Native of Girardeau," *Southeast Missourian*, Feb. 20, 1937, p. 3.

[395] "Send Him to Kansas," *The San Jose Evening News*, Jan. 23, 1901, p. 3.